BAPTIZING THE DEVIL
EVOLUTION AND THE SEDUCTION OF CHRISTIANITY

BAPTIZING THE DEVIL
EVOLUTION AND THE SEDUCTION OF CHRISTIANITY

CLIFFORD GOLDSTEIN

Pacific Press®
Publishing Association
Nampa, Idaho | Oshawa, Ontario, Canada
www.pacificpress.com

Cover design by Gerald Lee Monks
Cover design resources from iStock / Bliznetsov
Inside design by Aaron Troia

Additional copies of this book are available by calling toll-free 1-800-765-6955 or by visiting http://www.AdventistBookCenter.com.

Library of Congress Cataloging-in-Publication Data

Names: Goldstein, Clifford, author.
Title: Baptizing the devil : evolution and the seduction of Christianity / Clifford Goldstein.
Description: Nampa : Pacific Press Publishing Association, 2017.
Identifiers: LCCN 2017030128 | ISBN 9780816363094 (hardcover : alk. paper)
Subjects: LCSH: Religion and science. | Truth—Religious
    aspects—Christianity. | Knowledge, Theory of. | Scientism. |
    Science—Philosophy. | Pseudoscience. | Apologetics.
Classification: LCC BL240.3 .G645 2017 | DDC 261.5/5—dc23 LC record available at
    https://lccn.loc.gov/2017030128

August 2017

CONTENTS

"IN MY BEGINNING IS MY END."

CHAPTER 1

NEWTON'S WHOLE CABOODLE

Apollo 13 is Ron Howard's cinematic reenactment of NASA's third mission to the moon. Two days after the April 11, 1970, liftoff, an oxygen tank explodes, crippling the Apollo 13 spacecraft about 200,000 miles from home. Instead of reaching the moon, now the only mission is to get the craft back to earth with the three astronauts still metabolizing protein. Tom Hanks, Kevin Bacon, Ed Harris, and others dramatize those efforts.

A great scene unfolds when Flight Director Gene Kranz (played by Ed Harris in a crew cut) stands before a roomful of NASA scientists and technicians during the early part of the crisis. Behind him is a chalkboard with a crude drawing of the earth and the moon, with the spacecraft between them.

The scientists and engineers discuss two options. One is to immediately turn the craft around, fire the engines, and head it home. Others argue that this "direct abort" would consume too much energy, that the ship (and the men in it) will die in space. The second option, a "free return trajectory," is for the spacecraft to orbit the moon so that when it comes around the other side, the moon's gravity will, Kranz says, "slingshot" the ship to the earth. This excursion behind the moon, along with a boost from the lunar module's engine, would provide the needed oomph.

NASA goes with the second option—using the moon's gravity to catapult the men earthward.

And, guess what?

It works. It works even though the science behind the rescue had been formulated before Wilbur and Orville Wright flew; before doctors washed their hands for surgery; before the fountain pen, the light bulb, and the postage stamp were invented. The science is physics, specifically the law of gravity, which Isaac Newton developed in his *Philosophiæ naturalis principia mathematica* (Mathematical Principles of Natural Philosophy), published in 1687.[1] After the orbit around the moon, Tom Hanks, playing flight commander Jim Lovell, says, "We just put Sir Isaac Newton in the driver's seat." If NASA could have transported Newton to 1970, sat him in a room, and given him a sheet of paper, a pencil, and a few variables, he could have told them what to do based on what he wrote in his *Principia*.

No question about it, Newton's *Principia* has been considered not just one of the greatest *scientific* achievements in human history, but one of the greatest *intellectual* achievements as well. His work has infiltrated almost every other branch of Western thought. History, economics, philosophy, biology, theology, psychology, sociology—all were recalibrated by the implications of Newtonian physics, a recalibration that reaches into the twenty-first century (even if by the early twentieth its influence was lessening as a result of Einstein and quantum physics).

So great was Newton's achievement that poet Alexander Pope penned this epitaph for him: "Nature and Nature's laws lay hid in night: God said, Let Newton be! and all was light."[2]

Newton's whole caboodle

An endeavor as successful as Newton's helps show why many believe that science is the best way, if not the only way, to discover truth, especially if one believes that the world is wholly materialistic. This belief, called "scientism," prevails in our culture today.

"Both in the work of professional philosophers and in popular writings by natural scientists," wrote biologist Austin L. Hughes, "it is frequently claimed that natural science does or soon will constitute the entire domain of truth."[3]

Alex Rosenberg defined scientism as "the conviction that the methods of science are the only reliable ways to secure knowledge of anything."[4]

As savant Bertrand Russell had said in the previous century, "What science cannot tell us, mankind cannot know."[5]

Or, as John Loftus wrote: "The only thing we can and should trust is the sciences. Science alone produces consistently excellent results that cannot be denied, which are continually retested for validity."[6]

The *Principia* was, no doubt, a phenomenal achievement of "natural philosophy" (*philosophia naturalis*), or what since the mid-1800s is called "science." But does the success of Newton's physics prove that science is the best way of finding truth? That conclusion might sound reasonable, especially in light of science's many achievements, but it's not necessarily true—and Newton's formulation of gravity exemplifies why.

For starters, Isaac Newton had no idea what gravity was. He could describe, with amazing accuracy, *how* gravity caused matter to move, but he remained clueless as to *why* gravity moved matter as it did. Concerning gravity itself, he famously wrote, "Hypotheses non fingo" ("I feign no hypotheses").[7] He did not know why every point mass in the universe attracts every other point mass with a force that is directly proportional to the product of their masses and inversely proportional to the square of the distance between them. He knew only that they did, even if he called the idea of gravity acting at a distance across empty space "so great an absurdity that I believe no man who has in philosophical matters any competent faculty of thinking can ever fall into it."[8] This is Newton, reflecting on his own theory.

Second, Newton developed his theory on two false assumptions: absolute space and absolute time. That is, the two premises upon which he worked out his law of gravitational attraction are now believed to be wrong.

Third, Newton's law of gravity works only with slow-moving objects; with objects moving close to the speed of light, his theory falls apart and was therefore replaced by Einstein's theory of general relativity in the twentieth century. "The success of Newton's mechanics," wrote Alexander Bird, "may once have been thought to demonstrate its truth. But it is now known to be false and has been superseded by Einstein's relativistic mechanics."[9]

For hundreds of years Newton's *Principia* has been hailed as the classical account of a great scientific theory and, more important, as proof that science is the best way to learn truth.

Yet Newton had no clue what gravity was. He built his theory on two now-debunked premises. His law of gravity applies only in limited circumstances. And Newton's whole caboodle has been superseded by Einstein.

This is finding truth? All the theory did was make predictions. If that's all you think science can do—which many believe is the case—then, fine. Newton's law of gravity was an example of a smashing scientific success (at least under certain conditions). But if you believe that science reveals truth about the real world, then Newton's theory failed.

Why? After all, Newton created a remarkable mathematical *description* of certain aspects of reality. But description is not explanation. Describing an event is radically different from explaining it. Describing what a man looks like falling to the ground dead is quite different from explaining what happens inside his chest when he has the heart attack that killed him. With the right equipment, theories, and math, scientists can describe much about the natural world—from the motion of galaxies to the pull of the color force on quarks. Even Albert Einstein's famous formula, $e=mc^2$, only describes the relation between matter and energy; it explains nothing about why that relationship exists, just as Newton's formula for gravity explained nothing about why objects seem to attract each other through space.

Description and explanation

The story of Newton and his "discovery" (Is description really discovery?) reveals crucial issues, not just in the history of science, but in science itself. For all that Newton accomplished, numerous questions remain—not just about gravity, but about the much broader issue of what science can or cannot do.

In the 2,400 years since Democritus argued that all matter was made of tiny particles called "atoms," or even since 2015, when Massachusetts Institute of Technology researchers "built an array of light detectors sensitive enough to register the arrival of individual light particles, or photons, and mounted them on a silicon optical chip,"[10] debate still exists over what science really is; what it does, or can do, or should do; or how well it achieves whatever it supposedly does.

Does science reveal nature as it really is (i.e., the truth), or does it simply tell us how nature acts under such and such conditions, which then enables us (among many other amazing things) to build nuclear reactors, grow genetically modified crops, construct smartphones, and get crippled spacecrafts home? "Scientific laws, properly formulated," wrote W. T. Stace, "never 'explain' anything. They simply state, in an abbreviated and generalized form, *what happens*."[11] Or, as some suggest, "Scientific theories cannot be said to 'explain the world'—they only explain the *phenomena* that are observed within the world."[12]

Some suggest that science neither describes nor even explains what nature is or does, but only how nature *appears* to us to be or to do. Science, the argument goes, never takes us beyond the subjective human experience. We know, wrote Arthur Schopenhauer, "not a sun and not an earth, but only an eye that sees a sun, a hand that feels an earth."[13] Sure, we create fantastic devices, from microscopes to space telescopes to particle accelerators, which open up aspects of reality that our dull and limited senses would otherwise never funnel into our heads. But do these devices show us what's really out there, or do they show us just how what's really out there appears to us in these devices?

"The astronomer Arthur Eddington," wrote Ian G. Barbour, "once told a delightful parable about a man studying deep-sea life using a net with a three-inch mesh. After bringing up repeated samples, the man concluded that there are no deep-sea fish smaller than three inches in length. Our methods of fishing, Eddington suggests, determine what we can catch."[14] Do the kinds of devices we create reveal only the kinds of reality we are looking for to begin with? And, if we created a different device, how different would reality then appear? And how does the appearance the device delivers to our senses differ from the reality itself?

On the other hand (some argue), if you need the device just to describe what you are looking at, and it does so, at least according to the parameters that your device allows for, then what more do you want? If you want to create something useful, and the device allows you to, Voilà! Who cares how twisted or distorted reality might appear to you through the filters, magnifiers, and assumptions built into the nuts, bolts, bars, sensors, and software of the contraption? If the device pulls out of reality, at least to some degree, what you welded and hammered into the device to begin with, and if from that you can make predictions, create new medicines, build better bridges, whatever—then science is doing what science does, and does best, and no more.

If, however, science is about finding truth, about revealing to us the real world, then these questions remain troublesome.

Scientific questions

Even after all the accomplishments of science—from showing us that the earth does move to creating the Large Hadron Collider—no clear definition of "science" has been agreed upon. What is science? How does one differentiate between good science, bad science, and pseudoscience? "The philosophy of natural science is basically the study of what natural science is, what it does, how it works, why it works and how far it works," wrote Del Ratzsch. "A reasonable place to begin would be with a definition of *natural science*. However, the term has no standard, accepted definition."[15] Here we are, more than four hundred years since Galileo's astronomical observations and the challenges they presented to almost two thousand years of "scientific" orthodoxy, and we still don't have a solid definition of "science" itself?

Then there's the vaunted "scientific method" with its mythic epistemic status. Apply the "scientific method" to any question, and isn't truth guaranteed at the other end? Isn't the method the modern age's Oracle of Delphi? When the "scientific method" reveals something, what mortal dare challenge it?

Yet contention exists on what the scientific method is, how it works, what it reveals, or if it even exists. Paul Feyerabend dissed the whole notion of the scientific method. "This book proposes a thesis," he wrote, "and draws consequences from it. The thesis is: *the events, procedures and results that constitute the sciences have no common structure*; there are no elements that occur in every scientific investigation but are missing elsewhere."[16] According to Feyerabend and others, no "scientific method" exists. It's a myth, intellectually akin to bigfoot or the Loch Ness monster.

Also, if one believes that science does explain reality, what entails a proper explanation? How far down does science have to go before we have a complete explanation of "the lining of the world"?[17] Because everything in the natural world is composed of atomic and subatomic entities, do we not fall short of understanding biology, astronomy, psychology, or anything until we can parse, predict, and extrapolate the actions of the lepton, mesons, and quarks in whatever we're studying, be it quasars or brain cells?

"Current biology," wrote chemist Michael Polanyi, "is based on the assumption that you can explain the processes of life in terms of physics and chemistry; and, of course, physics and chemistry are both to be represented ultimately in terms of the forces acting between atomic particles. So all life, all human beings, and all works of man, including Shakespeare's sonnets and Kant's *Critique of Pure Reason*, are also to be so represented. The ideal of science [is] . . . to replace all human knowledge by a complete knowledge of atoms in motion."[18]

"Imagine," wrote Leon Wieseltier, "a scientific explanation of a painting—a breakdown of Chardin's cherries into the pigments that comprise them, and a chemical analysis of how their admixtures produce the subtle and plangent tonalities for which they are celebrated. Such an analysis will explain everything except what most needs explaining: the quality of beauty that is the reason for our contemplation of the painting."[19]

Also, if science is so good at reaching truth, why does the truth change so often? "If the historical landscape is littered with discarded theological ideas," wrote Gary Ferngren, "it is equally littered with discarded scientific ones."[20] Why do the findings of science, the results of the "scientific method," often contradict each other? We're not talking only of contradictory speculations about 1×10^{-43} seconds after the big bang, but about things subject to real-time experimentation and observation. Why can scientists, using the same "scientific method," looking at the same reality, sometimes even through the same devices, derive different conclusions about what they see?

Myriad other unresolved questions remain. How do we know a scientific theory is right, especially when theories taught as dogma have later been trashed? Why are scientific certitudes of the past not the same ones of the present? And, no doubt, won't some current ex cathedra scientific truths be mocked as myth just as some past ex cathedra scientific truths are today?

Even a hard-core scientism aficionado as Michael Shermer admits, "All facts in science are provisional and subject to challenge and change, therefore science is not a 'thing' per se; rather it is a *method* of discovery that leads to *provisional* conclusions."[21]

How are those provisional conclusions derived, anyway? How do scientists prove, or disprove, a theory? What is a scientific theory as opposed to a pseudo-scientific one? Why can opposing theories sometimes make the same accurate predictions, or why can theories believed to be wrong nevertheless make correct predictions? What assumptions must be made in order to do science, and how do we know those assumptions are right? What other factors—personal, political, social, and monetary—influence those assumptions, and thus the theories that morph out of them? ("Tell me who paid for the scientific research, and I'll tell you the results" might be a joke but, as with most jokes, some truth often exists.) Also, how is it possible that successful technology can be based on scientific theories now believed to be wrong?

Science has created incredible fruit, and who can debate that science has given humans astonishing new views of the world (or at least how the world appears to us)? Who can doubt the progress, the utility, the success of science in so many practical components of human life? And the technology that has arisen from science, that is still arising, and that will arise has amazed, amazes now, and will amaze in the future. At a certain level, one can easily understand the claim that science is humanity's greatest intellectual achievement.

Yet science is still, inevitably and necessarily, a human endeavor, shackled, weighed down, and distorted by the shackles, weights, and distortions that qualify all beliefs. The idea persists that science stands at some Archimedean point, what Thomas Nagel has called "a view from nowhere,"[22] and thus delivers us an objective window on what's real. That's a myth, on par with Romulus and Remus being nursed by a she-wolf.

Science is a historical enterprise. It unfolds in time and in history and, as such, is affected by the culture and society in which it is practiced. Scientific concepts, theories, and assumptions are inextricably bound up with culture, history, and language, because scientists are inextricably bound up with culture, history, and language. "Science, like any other human affair," said leftist Terry Eagleton at a Yale lecture series, "is indeed shot through with prejudice and partisanship, not to speak of ungrounded assumptions, unconscious biases, taken-for-granted truths, and beliefs too close to the eyeball to be objectified. Like religion, science is a culture, not just a set of procedures and hypotheses."[23] Thus, whatever scientists experience, or think they experience, comes filtered through all the things that filter human knowledge.

"What science says the world is like at a certain time is affected by the human ideas, choices, expectations, prejudices, beliefs, and assumptions holding at that time," wrote philosophers of science Peter Machamer, Marcello Pera, and Aristides Baltas.[24]

Science and faith

The questions about how accurately science delivers truth, or if it even can, or what it means to deliver "truth," become especially pertinent in the issue of faith and science. A barrage of books by the "new atheists"[25] portray faith and science as irreconcilable enemies—one (science) the objective pursuit of truth, the other (faith) the promulgation of superstition and ignorance. Yet this dichotomy is a distortion, even a caricature. Natural philosophy, or "science," has rarely conflicted with faith. Many of the early scientific giants—Copernicus, Kepler, Galileo, Newton—were believers in God and didn't see their work as denying faith. "The chief aim of all investigations of the external world," wrote Johannes Kepler, "should be to discover the rational order and harmony which has been imposed on it by God and which He revealed to us in the language of mathematics."[26]

Ian G. Barbour wrote: "The 'virtuosi,' as the English scientists of the second half of the seventeenth century called themselves, were religious men, predominantly from Puritan backgrounds. The Charter of the Royal Society instructed its fellows to direct their studies 'to the glory of God and the benefit of the human race.' Robert Boyle said that science is a *religious task*, 'the disclosure of the admirable workmanship which God displayed in the universe.' Newton believed that the universe bespeaks an all-powerful Creator."[27]

Though battles were fought (see chapter 2), the common view of science and religion in constant conflict has been greatly exaggerated. "For nearly a century," wrote Colin A. Russell, "the notion of mutual hostility . . . [between science and religion] has been routinely employed in popular-science writing, by the media, and in a few older histories of science. Deeply embedded in the culture of the West, it has proven extremely hard to dislodge. Only in the last thirty years of the twentieth century did historians of science mount a sustained attack on the thesis, and only gradually has a wider public begun to recognize its deficiencies."[28]

Nevertheless, one area of crucial contention exists, and that deals with origins. *Who are we? Where did we come from? Why do we exist? Where are we going?* We're at the basement level here, the foundation upon which all existence and all human knowledge about existence rests. Everything humans have ever written, spoken, or even thought arises from our origins. The clash here isn't over the perceived benefits of resveratrol in red wine or the mating habits of *Megascops hoyi*. The clash is over human identity, which arises as directly from our origins as musical notes do from strummed harp strings.

Despite endless attempts from almost every conceivable angle, evolution and the Bible cannot be melded into any coherent account of origins, at least not without bowdlerizing both. It takes the most bone-breaking theological contortions (see chapter 10) to try to fit the "neo-Darwinian synthesis" (basically the latest incarnation of Darwin) into the biblical account of origins.

The names alone of the two grand mechanisms in the Darwinian scheme, *random* mutation and *natural* selection, reveal their incompatibility with the Genesis account. Even in the widest, broadest reading possible, the Genesis Creation is a supernatural event, as opposed to a merely *natural* one, and the

origins

Genesis Creation hints at nothing *random*, much less *mutational*. The language used to express evolution excludes anything related to the Bible and its supernatural, ends-driven Creation. However, these inconvenient truths have not stopped Christians from the dubious endeavor of trying to meld Charles Darwin with Jesus Christ.

"So," writes evolutionist Richard Dewitt, "if one adds a supernatural involvement into the account of evolution by natural selection, say by allowing a God to meddle in the evolutionary process, then it is no longer natural selection. One is no longer taking natural science, and evolutionary theory, seriously. In short, taking natural science seriously means that an account of evolutionary development that is importantly influenced by a supernatural being is not an intellectually honest option."[29]

The compromise

Why, then, the irresistible lure among so many Christians to "baptize the devil" by seeking to harmonize evolution with Scripture? Though we can't know individual motives, the overarching answer is tied to the overarching contemporary belief that evolution must be true, because science says it is. After all, *It's science!*

Also, when the world's greatest thinkers; the best and brightest; the feted experts; the Nobel laureates in biology, chemistry, economics, physics, literature, and medicine; the most educated, knowledgeable, and informed among us; the PhDs; the fellows; the postdocs; the Rhodes scholars; the renowned; the famous; the brilliant—when all these believe in evolution, teach evolution, promote evolution, and just assume evolution, many Christians think that they must do the same. When every discipline—biology, astronomy, medicine, political theory, psychology, literary criticism, history, chemistry, ethics, economics, geology, sociology, even theology—either openly promotes a neo-Darwinian worldview or just presumes it, these Christians feel pressure to follow suit. When "our interpreted world," as Rilke called it,[30] is interpreted through the assumptions of evolution, when every aspect of earth's life—from the antelope placenta, to cucumbers, to the invention of mathematics—is filtered, parsed, and explained in terms of evolutionary theory, it's no wonder that many people, including Christians, get swept up in the fervor. It's crowd psychology spilled over from the streets and seeping into the pulpit.

Baptizing the Devil seeks to show that this capitulation (and that's what it is, a capitulation) is not only unnecessary but misguided. It's just another unfortunate example of well-meaning Christians compromising their faith to the prevailing culture,[31] the ethos of our age, which is science dressed in the philosophical garb of scientism. And not just the science of experiment, testing, and verification (which has brought us so much), but a speculative branch of science rooted in layer upon layer of unproven assumptions, retrodictions, and leaps of epistemological faith across hypothesized millions, even billions, of years. By looking at the questions (and others) about science raised earlier in this chapter, *Baptizing the Devil* hopes to free people from the knee-jerk reaction that the only logical, rational reaction to the phrase *It's science!* is to surrender to it one's beliefs, even religious ones. In some cases, that might be prudent (the science of meteorology, as opposed to witchcraft, to explain crop failures being one powerful case in point), but not in every case, and certainly not when it comes to replacing the Genesis account with the latest incarnation of the neo-Darwinian synthesis or, worse, trying to meld them.

Science has provided humanity with powerful methods and tools for converting matter into practical wonders, everything from vaccines, to smartphones, to nuclear submarines. Its technological successes speak for themselves. But that's hardly the same thing as finding truth; it might even have nothing to do with truth, except in the very narrow spheres needed to create vaccines, smartphones, and nuclear submarines. And though the argument still exists regarding whether science reveals reality as it is or only as it appears to us, it's not just a happy coincidence that the moon's gravity gave the crippled Apollo 13 spacecraft some of the requisite oomph to return home. The science of Newton said that it would, and it did, which means that there was some truth in the mix—regardless of all the unknowns, mistakes, and false assumptions that bedeviled the theory itself.

Science does, then, reveal insights into reality itself, regardless of how limited or even distorted those insights may be. And that's the major point of this book: to show just how limited those insights are and how greatly they are influenced by the inescapable subjectivity that slants all human knowledge, which is precisely why Christians shouldn't compromise such a foundational belief as origins just because science, or rather the claims of some scientists, teach something contrary.

An atheist, in Italy, scribbled these words on a wall: *There is no God!—and Mary is his mother.* However ridiculous, this scribbling reveals something primal about humanity's quest for truth. We're hopelessly subjective. Whatever we seek, and however we seek it, it's only through the icons, axioms, and presuppositions of our culture, genetics, and education that we probe, view, interpret, and express the results of our quests. We can no more escape these filters than we can our thought, because it's through these filters that we think and, indeed, do science as well.

1. Isaac Newton, *The Principia: Mathematical Principles of Natural Philosophy*, trans. I. Bernard Cohen and Anne Whitman, assisted by Julia Budenz (Berkeley: University of California Press, 1999).

2. "Sir Isaac Newton," Westminster Abbey, www.westminster-abbey.org/our-history/people/sir-isaac-newton. Pope had hoped this epitaph would be placed on Newton's monument, but it was not allowed. Instead, the following, which was inscribed there, though not as eloquent as Pope's lines, makes the point nonetheless:

> Here is buried Isaac Newton, Knight, who by a strength of mind almost divine, and mathematical principles peculiarly his own, explored the course and figures of the planets, the paths of comets, the tides of the sea, the dissimilarities in rays of light, and, what no other scholar has previously imagined, the properties of the colours thus produced. Diligent, sagacious and faithful, in his expositions of nature, antiquity and the holy Scriptures, he vindicated by his philosophy the majesty of God mighty and good, and expressed the simplicity of the Gospel in his manners. Mortals rejoice that there has existed such and so great an ornament of the human race! He was born on 25th December 1642, and died on 20th March 1726 (ibid.).

3. Austin L. Hughes, "The Folly of Scientism," *The New Atlantis*, no. 37 (Fall 2012): 32. For a recent powerful critique of scientism, see Richard N. Williams and Daniel N. Robinson, eds., *Scientism: The New Orthodoxy* (London: Bloomsbury Academic, 2015).

4. Alex Rosenberg, *The Atheist's Guide to Reality: Enjoying Life Without Illusions* (New York: W. W. Norton, 2011), Kindle edition, chap. 1.

5. Attributed to Russell in Ted Peters, *Cosmos as Creation: Theology and Science in Consonance* (Nashville: Abingdon Press, 1989), 14, with a note that it was "told [to] a BBC audience [earlier this century]" (ibid.). The other version of the statement attributed to him is "What science cannot discover, mankind cannot know."

6. John W. Loftus, ed., *The Christian Delusion: Why Faith Fails* (New York: Prometheus Books, 2010), Kindle edition, chap. 4.

7. Newton, *Principia*, 943. "I have not as yet been able to deduce from phenomena the reason for these properties of gravity, and I do not feign hypotheses. For whatever is not deduced from the phenomena must be called a hypothesis; and hypotheses, whether metaphysical or physical, or based on occult qualities, or mechanical, have no place in experimental philosophy. In this experimental philosophy, propositions are deduced from the phenomena and are made general by induction" (ibid.).

8. Newton to Richard Bentley, 189.R.4.47, ff. 7, 8, Trinity College Library, Cambridge, UK, published October 2007, http://www.newtonproject.sussex.ac.uk/view/texts/normalized/THEM00258.

9. Alexander Bird, *Philosophy of Science*, Fundamentals of Philosophy (Routledge, 2006), Kindle edition, chap. 4. Some might argue that calling it "false" is too strong; it might better be said that it was incomplete, or viable only under certain conditions.

10. Massachusetts Institute of Technology, "Toward Quantum Chips: Packing Single-Photon Detectors on an Optical Chip Is Crucial for Quantum-Computational Circuits," Science Daily, January 9, 2015, https://www.sciencedaily.com/releases/2015/01/150109101047.htm.

11. W. T. Stace, "Science and the Physical World," in *Introductory Readings in the Philosophy of Science*, ed. E. D. Klemke, Robert Hollinger, and David Wÿss Rudge, with A. David Kline (Amherst, NY: Prometheus Books, 1998), 355 (italics in the original).

12. Alister McGrath and Joanna Collicutt McGrath, *The Dawkins Delusion? Atheist Funda-*

mentalism and the Denial of the Divine (Downers Grove, IL: IVP Books, 2007), 38 (italics in the original).

13. Arthur Schopenhauer, *The World as Will and Representation*, vol. 2 (London: J. M. Dent, 2001), 3.

14. Ian G. Barbour, *When Science Meets Religion: Enemies, Strangers, or Partners?* (New York: HarperSanFrancisco, 2000), 14 (italics in the original).

15. Del Ratzsch, *Science and Its Limits: The Natural Sciences in Christian Perspective* (Downers Grove, IL: IVP Academic, 2000), 11 (italics in the original).

16. Paul Feyerabend, *Against Method*, 3rd ed. (London: Verso, 1993), 1; italics in the original.

17. Czeslaw Milosz, "Meaning," *New and Collected Poems, 1931–2001* (New York: Harper-Collins, 2003), 569.

18. Michael Polanyi and Harry Prosch, *Meaning* (Chicago: University of Chicago Press, 1977), 25 (italics in the original).

19. Leon Wieseltier, "Crimes Against Humanities," *New Republic*, September 3, 2013, https://newrepublic.com/article/114548/leon-wieseltier-responds-steven-pinkers-scientism?a&utm_campaign=tnr-daily-newsletter&utm_source=hs_.

20. Gary B. Ferngren, ed., *Science and Religion: A Historical Introduction* (Baltimore: Johns Hopkins University Press, 2002), xiii.

21. Michael Shermer, *The Moral Arc: How Science and Reason Lead Humanity Toward Truth, Justice, and Freedom* (New York: Henry Holt, 2015), 15 (italics in the original).

22. Thomas Nagel, *The View From Nowhere* (New York: Oxford University Press, 1986), Kindle edition, chap. 5, sec. 1. The full quote, in context, is worth reading, because it is applicable to the challenges of science as well: "The question is how limited beings like ourselves can alter their conception of the world so that it is no longer just the view from where they are but in a sense a view from nowhere, which includes and comprehends the fact that the world contains beings which possess it, explains why the world appears to them as it does prior to the formation of that conception, and explains how they can arrive at the conception itself" (ibid.).

23. Terry Eagleton, *Reason, Faith, and Revolution: Reflections on the God Debate* (New Haven, CT: Yale University Press, 2009), 132.

24. Peter Machamer, Marcello Pera, and Aristides Baltas, eds., *Scientific Controversies: Philosophical and Historical Perspectives* (New York: Oxford University Press, 2000), 6.

25. Some familiar titles are Richard Dawkins, *The God Delusion* (2006); Daniel C. Dennett, *Breaking the Spell: Religion as a Natural Phenomenon* (2006); Sam Harris, *The End of Faith: Religion, Terror, and the Future of Reason* (2004); and Christopher Hitchens, *God Is Not Great: How Religion Poisons Everything* (2007).

26. Quoted in Noson S. Yanofsky, *The Outer Limits of Reason: What Science, Mathematics, and Logic Cannot Tell Us* (Cambridge, MA: MIT Press, 2013), 262.

27. Ian Barbour, *Issues in Science and Religion* (New York: Harper Torchbooks, 1966), 37 (italics in the original).

28. Colin A. Russell, "The Conflict of Science and Religion," in Ferngren, *Science and Religion*, 4. Two of the most popular books in the past pushing this warfare idea were Andrew Dickson White, *A History of the Warfare of Science With Theology in Christendom* (New York, 1896); and John William Draper, *History of the Conflict Between Religion and Science* (New York, 1874).

29. Richard DeWitt, *Worldviews: An Introduction to the History and Philosophy of Science*, 2nd ed. (West Sussex, UK: Wiley-Blackwell, 2010), 312, 313.

30. Rainer Maria Rilke, "The First Elegy," in *The Selected Poetry of Rainer Maria Rilke*, trans. and ed. Stephen Mitchell (New York: Vintage International, 1989), 151.

31. An argument, it has been said, breaks down as soon as someone brings in the Nazis or Hitler. Maybe. But we do have the tragic example of how readily the Christian church in the

Third Reich compromised with the National Socialists. No one is paralleling evolution with Nazism; the parallel below simply reveals how easily Christians can compromise with the prevailing *zeitgeist*, even with something as abhorrent as the Nazi regime: "The German Christians always painted Jesus as a non-Jew and often as a cruel anti-Semite. As Hitler had called him 'our greatest Aryan hero,' this was not much of a leap. Before the German Christians were through with him, the Nazarene rabbi would be a goose-stepping, strudel-loving son of the Reich." Eric Metaxas, *Bonhoeffer: Pastor, Martyr, Prophet, Spy* (Nashville, TN: Thomas Nelson, 2010), 172.

CHAPTER 2

GALILEO'S HERESY

Almost every schoolchild in the post-Enlightenment West has learned about the heresy trial of Galileo Galilei by the Roman Inquisition in the seventeenth century. Though depicted as the paradigmatic illustration of ignorant and dogmatic religionists fighting the rational and logical progress of science, the story is, instead, an illustration of what happens when dogmatic science becomes mainstream and, worse, what happens when religious believers incorporate that dogmatism into their faith.

"The *leitmotif* which I recognize in Galileo's work," wrote Albert Einstein in the foreword to a twentieth-century publication of Galileo's *Dialogue Concerning the Two Chief World Systems*, "is the passionate fight against any kind of dogma based on authority."[1]

Einstein was right. Galileo's work was a fight against "dogma based on authority." But the dogma was based on the authority of science, a dogma as intolerant in the seventeenth century as it is today. Far from revealing the dangers of religion battling science, the Galileo trial reveals the dangers of religion capitulating to science. The church wasn't defending the Bible, but a false interpretation of the Bible created by an unfortunate conflation of faith with science. If they were smart, theistic evolutionists would shun the Galileo controversy and not parade it as the archetypal example of why Christians must meld evolution with Scripture.

A crucial difference, however, exists between what the church did then with the earth-centered Ptolemaic-Aristotelian cosmos, and with what theistic evolutionists do today. The earth-centered view of the cosmos isn't addressed in the Bible, so that model could have been correct without contradicting Scripture. But evolution contradicts the Bible *in every way*. The mistake that Christian evolutionists make today in regard to evolution is qualitatively worse than what their spiritual and intellectual ancestors in the Roman Inquisition did with Galileo's "heresy."

With "unfeigned faith"

As with everything in life, it's complicated. Regardless of one's spin, numerous factors from multiple directions congealed into the Galileo episode. Besides Vatican court intrigues, other aspects included political tensions between Rome and the Italian city-states, and between Rome and Spain; internecine fighting among the clergy (Dominicans versus the Jesuits, Jesuits versus Jesuits); intellectual rivalries between Galileo and other scientists; church dogmatism; the influence of philosophy on faith; and the stresses of the battle with the Reformation, which put great pressure on Rome to maintain "biblical orthodoxy." Not helping matters was the fact that some of Galileo's arguments weren't so strong (some were, in fact, wrong), and his personal character flaws didn't help either (Galileo was hardly a saint). Also, aside from the scriptural issues, some impressive logical and empirical reasons to question Galileo's position existed. All these factors led to some of the most infamous words in intellectual, scientific, and religious history, Galileo's recantation.

It reads, in part:

I, Galileo Galilei, son of the late Vincenzio Galilei of Florence, aged 70 years, tried personally by this court, and kneeling before You, the most Eminent and Reverend Lord Cardinals, Inquisitors-General throughout the Christian Republic against heretical depravity, having before my eyes the Most Holy Gospels, and laying on them my own hands; I swear that I have always believed, I believe now, and with God's help I will in future believe all which the Holy Catholic and Apostolic Church doth hold, preach, and teach.

But since I, after having been admonished by this Holy Office entirely to abandon the false opinion that the Sun was the centre of the universe and immoveable, and that the Earth was not the centre of the same and that it moved, and that I was neither to hold, defend, nor teach in any manner whatever, either orally or in writing, the said false doctrine; and after having received a notification that the said doctrine is contrary to Holy Writ, I did write and cause to be printed a book in which I treat of the said already condemned doctrine, and bring forward arguments of much efficacy in its favour, without arriving at any solution: I have been judged vehemently suspected of heresy, that is, of having held and believed that the Sun is the centre of the universe and immoveable, and that the Earth is not the centre of the same, and that it does move.

Nevertheless, wishing to remove from the minds of your Eminences and all faithful Christians this vehement suspicion reasonably conceived against me, *I abjure with sincere heart and unfeigned faith, I curse and detest the said errors and heresies, and generally all and every error and sect contrary to the Holy Catholic Church.* . . .

I Galileo Galilei aforesaid have abjured, sworn, and promised, and hold myself bound as above; and in token of the truth, with my own hand have subscribed the present schedule of my abjuration, and have recited it word by word. In Rome, at the Convent della Minerva, this 22nd day of June, 1633.

I, GALILEO GALILEI, have abjured as above, with my own hand.[2]

After this abjuration, Galileo supposedly muttered under his breath *eppur si muove*, "still it moves," though many historians question whether this happened.[3]

Either way, his recantation came in direct response to the formal charge brought by the Roman Inquisition.

It reads, in part:

Whereas you, Galileo, son of the late Vincenzio Galilei, of Florence, aged seventy years, were denounced in 1615, to this Holy Office, for holding as true a false doctrine taught by many, namely, that the sun is immovable in the center of the world [i.e., the universe], and that the earth moves, and also with a diurnal motion . . . and whereas thereupon was produced the copy of a writing, in form of a letter professedly written by you to a person formerly your pupil, in which, following the hypothesis of Copernicus, you include several propositions contrary to the true sense and authority of the Holy Scriptures; therefore (this Holy Tribunal being desirous of providing against the disorder and mischief which were thence proceeding and increasing to the detriment of the Holy Faith) by the desire of his Holiness and the Most Emminent [*sic*] Lords, Cardinals of this supreme and universal Inquisition, the two propositions of the stability of the sun, and the motion of the earth, were qualified by the Theological Qualifiers as follows:

1. The proposition that the sun is in the center of the world and immovable from its place is absurd, philosophically false, and formally heretical; because it is expressly contrary to Holy Scriptures.
2. The proposition that the earth is not the center of the world, nor immovable, but that it moves, and also with a diurnal action, is also absurd, philosophically false, and, theologically considered, at least erroneous in faith.

Therefore . . . , invoking the most holy name of our Lord Jesus Christ and of His Most Glorious Mother Mary, We pronounce this Our final sentence: We pronounce, judge, and declare, that you, the said Galileo . . . have rendered yourself vehemently suspected by this Holy Office of heresy, that is, of having believed and held the doctrine (which is false and contrary to the Holy and Divine Scriptures) that the sun is the center of the world, and that it does not move from east to west, and that the earth does move, and is not the center of the world; also, that an opinion can be held and supported as probable, after it has been declared and finally decreed contrary to the Holy Scripture, and, consequently, that you have incurred all the censures and penalties enjoined and promulgated in the sacred canons and other general and particular constituents against delinquents of this description. From which it is Our pleasure that you be absolved, provided that with a sincere heart and unfeigned faith, in Our presence, you abjure, curse, and detest, the said error and heresies, and every other error and heresy contrary to the Catholic and Apostolic Church of Rome.[4]

No wonder that Galileo, with "unfeigned faith," cursed, detested, and abjured "the said error and heresies." The Inquisition warned that he would be tortured if he didn't, and—for a man at his age and with fragile health— torture could have meant death. "Galileo," wrote Albert Camus centuries later, "who held a scientific truth of great importance, abjured it with the greatest ease as soon as it endangered his life. In a certain sense, he did right."[5]

How easily he abjured it, or if he did right in doing so, is debatable. What is not debatable is what he was charged with and what he abjured. Or maybe that *is* debatable. Galileo's heresy wasn't, in fact, "contrary to the Holy and Divine Scriptures," but contrary to a pagan Greek philosopher dead for more than nineteen centuries—a crucial point often snuffed out of popular accounts.

The *Dialogue Concerning the Two Chief World Systems*

Galileo's troubles, especially with certain Jesuits and Dominicans, began decades before the abjuration, when he aimed his telescope into the heavens and saw things that, according to time-honored and long-established science, were not supposed to be there. Though Galileo had been under suspicion for years, what brought Rome's wrath was his book *Dialogue Concerning the Two Chief World Systems*, first published in 1632. Having already been warned about teaching some of his views (one concerned friend told him that Rome was not the place to talk about things on the moon[6]), Galileo had hoped to obviate the blows by writing the book as a spirited intellectual debate between three protagonists, Salviati, Sagredo, and Simplicio.

What follows are excerpts from the *Dialogue Concerning the Two Chief World Systems*:

> This [a circular motion is more perfect than straight] is the cornerstone, basis, and foundation of the entire structure of the Aristotelian universe, upon which are superimposed all other celestial properties—freedom from gravity and levity, ingenerability, incorruptibility, exemption from all mutations except local ones, etc.[7]

> I might add that neither Aristotle nor you can ever prove that the earth is *de facto* the center of the universe; if any center may be assigned to the universe, we shall rather find the sun to be placed there, as you will understand in due course.[8]

> But seeing on the other hand the great authority that Aristotle has gained universally; considering the number of famous interpreters who have toiled to explain his meanings; and observing that the other sciences, so useful and necessary to mankind, base a large part of their value and reputation upon Aristotle's credit; Simplicio is confused and perplexed, and I seem to hear him say, "Who would there be to settle our controversies if Aristotle were to be deposed?"[9]

> I do not mean that a person should not listen to Aristotle; indeed, I applaud the reading and careful study of his works, and I reproach only those who give themselves up as slaves to him in such a way as to subscribe blindly to everything he says and take it as an inviolable decree without looking for any other reasons.[10]

> You are only angry that Aristotle cannot speak; yet I tell you that if Aristotle were here he would either be convinced by us or he would pick our arguments to pieces and persuade us with better ones.[11]

Who is the focus of the dialogue? Moses? Jesus? Paul? No, the focus is Aristotle, whose teachings (and Galileo's refutation of those teachings) are a key component of the *Dialogue*. Moses, Jesus, and Paul are never mentioned. The phrase "Holy Scriptures" appears only twice in the book, in contrast to "Aristotle," who appears in the pages about one hundred times.

The Darwin of that day

Galileo wasn't fighting against the Bible but against *an interpretation* of the

Bible dominated by the prevailing scientific dogma, which for centuries had been Aristotelianism. The importance of this point cannot be overestimated. Aristotle (384–322 B.C.) was the Darwin of that era, all but deified in ways that even Darwin is not today. Many intellectuals, no matter how much they may remain under the Englishman's spell, will criticize his work. Even such a Darwinian jihadist as Richard Dawkins could write, "Much of what Darwin said is, in detail, wrong."[12]

In contrast, in the era of Galileo, people were less ready to contradict Aristotle, whose writings intellectually plundered and pillaged the culture of the time. Students entering colleges in the Middle Ages were told to discard any teaching that went against "The Philosopher," as Aristotle had come to be known. "The writings of Aristotle," wrote William R. Shea, "that had earlier stimulated lively discussion were increasingly turned into rigid dogma and a mechanical criterion of truth. Other philosophical systems were viewed with suspicion."[13]

Just like today's mania to interpret everything in a Darwinian context—from the shape of a dog's ear, to our "natural tendency to be kind to our genetic relations but to be xenophobic, suspicious, and even aggressive toward people in other tribes"[14]—back then, Aristotle's teaching was the filter through which everything was to be understood, from the motion of the stars, to the nature of the bread and wine in the Eucharist.

In the sixteen hundreds, about two thousand years after Aristotle, René Descartes could complain about him: "How fortunate that man was: whatever he wrote, whether he gave it much thought or not, is regarded by most people today as having oracular authority."[15]

The Arabs introduced Aristotle's writings to Europe in the eleventh and twelfth centuries. By the thirteenth century, however, Aristotle had fallen into disfavor, especially with churchmen. After all, this pagan Greek taught that the universe had always existed, that God had no interest in or knowledge of humanity, and that natural causes alone explained happenings on earth. Such beliefs made him suspect with more traditionally minded scholars and clerics; bans on his "scientific" works were issued in 1210 and 1215, including an attempt in 1231 to eradicate them. "All such attempts were in vain," wrote Edward Grant, "and by 1255 Aristotle's works were not only officially sanctioned but constituted the core of the arts curriculum."[16]

Nevertheless, medieval scholars had to twist, turn, distort, and obfuscate in order to meld Aristotle's science, philosophy, and cosmology with biblical doctrine, much in the same way people do today as they try to harmonize Jesus with Darwin. No one worked at it more "successfully" than the Italian Dominican friar and priest, Thomas Aquinas (c. 1225–1274), who all but converted the pagan Aristotle into a mass-going, indulgence-offering, Mary-adoring Roman Catholic. Although at the time of Galileo some opposition existed (and was growing)[17] against the Aristotelian worldview, Aristotle's writings were still the filter through which the works of God in nature were to be viewed. "With the Church's gradual acceptance of that work," wrote Richard Tarnas, "the Aristotelian corpus was elevated virtually to the status of Christian dogma."[18]

Aristotle's universe

Other elements of Aristotle's teaching reverberated through the Galileo saga, but his cosmology—his understanding of the universe—became ground zero. Some of these teachings predated Aristotle and could be found among the Babylonians, Egyptians, and Pythagoreans, who certainly influenced Galileo's thought, but Aristotle had developed his own systematic understanding of the universe's structure, which the church had adapted and then adopted (at least in part) for centuries.

Aristotle divided creation into two distinct regions: the terrestrial and the celestial. He taught that the terrestrial, everything below the moon, is composed of four basic elements: earth, air, fire, and water. This realm suffered from change, decay, birth, generation, and corruption—everything from ice storms to roadkill. In contrast, the celestial realm—the moon and above—remained eternal, changeless, and perfect. The stars and planets were composed of a fifth element (from which we get the word *quintessence*) known as "aether." Unlike earth, air, fire, and water, aether was pure, eternal, immutable.

And though one set of laws and principles governed the celestial sphere and another the terrestrial, the celestial greatly influenced events on earth. "The substance and the motion of the celestial spheres," wrote philosopher of science Thomas Kuhn in describing Aristotle's view, "are the only ones compatible with the immutability and majesty of the heavens, and it is the heavens that produce and control all variety and change on earth."[19]

In Aristotle's system, the stars orbited the earth in circles, deemed the most perfect of all geometrical forms. He envisioned the universe itself as fifty-five concentric crystalline spheres, one nestled inside the other, from the smallest, closest to the earth, to the largest, the farthest away. Each crystalline sphere, on which the various planets and stars sat, rotated at its own constant speed around the earth, which was itself immobile in the center, like a dot in the middle of tree rings.

The centrality and immovability of the earth was crucial to Aristotle's cosmos, and in his work *On the Heavens,* he argued for the earth as the immovable center of the universe. Although he used different rationales, one argument was that the earth must sit at the center of all that exists, because if you throw anything up in the air, it automatically falls to the earth.

"It is clear, then," Aristotle wrote, "that the earth must be at the centre and immovable, not only for the reasons already given, but also because heavy bodies forcibly thrown quite straight upward return to the point from which they started, even if they are thrown to an infinite distance. From these considerations then it is clear that the earth does not move and does not lie elsewhere than at the centre."[20]

Ptolemy, Dante, Copernicus

Besides the obvious problems we see today with this system, people in the days of Aristotle looked up at the night sky and saw, quite easily, that the stars do not move the way they should according to his model. The beliefs and assumptions upon which his view was built did not match the phenomena; it was as if the heavens themselves hadn't read *On the Heavens*. For instance, if the stars and planets orbit the earth at constant speeds and in perfect circles, why do some planets at times stop their movement, go backward, and then go forward again? Aristotle's theory does not easily explain the retrograde motion seen in the night sky.

Nevertheless, with various tweaks and modifications, that geocentric model of planets and stars orbiting in perfect spheres at uniform speeds around a stationary earth existed until the seventeenth century (though it took Rome until 1992—359 years after the condemnation of Galileo—before the Vatican under John Paul II formally admitted its error).[21] The longevity of this theory reveals the propagandizing power of scientific tradition and dogma, even in the face of powerful conflicting evidence.

At the same time, thinkers through the ages tried to make the model fit the facts. *Save the phenomena* was the idea. In other words: "Here's the theory; now make what we see, the phenomena, match it." (Today, especially in evolutionary biology, little has changed.)

In the second century A.D., Greco-Egyptian astronomer Claudius Ptolemy wrote a thirteen-part treatise, the *Almagest*, in which he tried to better describe the motion of the cosmos in an Aristotelian, earth-centered universe. Though quite complex, the Ptolemaic system was a precise mathematical description (based on the model of celestial bodies moving in perfect spheres around an immovable earth) of what eyes on earth saw in the heavens. And, to some degree, it worked. That is, one could make accurate predictions based on the false science that undergirded the *Almagest*, which put an immovable earth as the center of the universe. Though the book was written about A.D. 150, the *Almagest*'s influence lasted into the sixteen hundreds.

"Ptolemy," wrote Anthony Gottlieb, "was the most influential astronomer until the scientific revolution: his version of Aristotle's earth-centred universe went virtually unquestioned for 1,200 years."[22]

Another crucial text wasn't even science, but a poem: Dante's *Divine Comedy*, written in the early thirteen hundreds. A long epic narrative, the poem describes Dante's guided tour through hell, purgatory, and heaven. He starts on the surface of the earth and then descends into the nine circles of hell (*Inferno*) under the earth, where he found written the famous words "ABANDON ALL HOPE YE WHO ENTER HERE."[23] Dante comes back to the surface, into the mount of purgatory (*Purgatorio*), with its base on earth and its top extending into the sky. Finally, he ascends into the celestial realms (*Paradiso*) of this Aristotelian universe.

With the *Divine Comedy*, Dante did with poetry what Aquinas did with philosophy—he integrated Aristotle's cosmos with Christian theology, putting the immovable earth and humanity at the center of God's creation.

"Dante's use of the Ptolemaic-Aristotelian cosmology," wrote Richard Tarnas, "as a structural foundation for the Christian world view readily established itself in the collective Christian imagination, with every aspect of the Greek scientific scheme now imbued with religious significance. In the minds of Dante and his contemporaries, astronomy and theology were inextricably conjoined, and the cultural ramifications of this cosmological synthesis were profound: for if any essential physical change were to be introduced into that system by future astronomers—such as, for example, a moving Earth—the effect of a purely scientific innovation would threaten the integrity of the entire Christian cosmology."[24]

And yet a moving earth is, precisely, what Nicolaus Copernicus, in 1543, postulated with his *On the Revolutions of Heavenly Spheres*. In this work of six sections ("books"), Copernicus argued for the circular motion of the earth around a motionless sun at the center of the universe. Though others, such as Aristarchus of Samos (third century B.C.), had argued for a similar cosmology, Copernicus knew that, because of the theological implications of this position, he might be rushing where angels feared to tread. In the first line of his dedication of the book to Pope Paul III he wrote, "I can reckon easily enough, Most Holy Father, that as soon as certain people learn that in these books of mine which I have written about the revolutions of the spheres of the world I attribute certain motions to the terrestrial globe, they will immediately shout to have me and my opinion hooted off the stage."[25]

Though Copernicus wasn't exactly hooted off the stage (he was on his deathbed when *On the Revolutions of Heavenly Spheres* left the press), in 1616 the treatise was placed on the Catholic Index of Forbidden Books, despite his attempt to placate the powers-that-be by dedicating it to none other than the vicar of Christ himself. Sixteen years after the ban, Galileo was condemned by

Rome for "having believed and held the doctrine (which is false and contrary to the Holy and Divine Scriptures) that the sun is the center of the world, and that it does not move from east to west, and that the earth does move, and is not the center of the world." In other words, the cosmology of Copernicus.

The devil's device

Whatever was going on in the heavens, such was the scientific and intellectual atmosphere in which Galileo's storm broke on earth. For the medieval mind, the universe was a strict hierarchy in which the sky, starting with the moon and moving outward, was perfect and harmonious. All the heavenly bodies—sun, moon, planets, stars—each perfect spheres themselves, orbited the earth in perfect circles, the supreme geometrical form, the only motion worthy of Yahweh's cosmos. Amid it all, at the immovable center, sat the earth. Here was the scientific model that dominated Western intellectual thought for more than 1,500 years, the one that the church had worked hard to incorporate into its theology as well.

After all, *It's science!*

However, when Galileo started aiming his telescope into the night sky, people could see that what happened in the heavens didn't fit what the science here on earth said. Suddenly, the phenomena and the science that explained the phenomena became irreconcilable. As Shakespeare wrote in *Hamlet*, "There are more things in heaven and earth, Horatio, than are dreamt of in your philosophy."[26] Not only were there more things (at least in the heavens), there were things that, according to the best science, shouldn't have been there to begin with.

With his telescope Galileo could see sunspots, which—according to Aristotle—should not exist in a perfect and unchanging cosmos. "His proof that the sunspots were on the surface of the sun," wrote Galileo biographer David Wootton, "and that consequently the Aristotelian doctrine of the immutability of the heavens was simply false, would, he believed, prove decisive. This would be the funeral, as he put it—he meant the *coup de grâce*—for the 'pseudo-philosophy' of his adversaries."[27]

Galileo's discovery of mountains, valleys, and plains on the moon struck another blow to the Aristotelian cosmos, whose heavenly orbs were composed, supposedly, of perfect spheres only. Galileo wrote in his 1610 *Sidereal Messenger* that "the Moon's surface is dotted everywhere with protuberances and cavities; it only remains for me to speak about their size, and to show that the ruggednesses of the Earth's surface are far smaller than those of the Moon's."[28]

Galileo then aimed his magnified eyes at Venus. Much to his surprise, he saw that it went through phases, just as our moon does. "But, the nature of these phases could only be explained by Venus going around the Sun, not the Earth. Galileo concluded that Venus must travel around the Sun, passing at times behind and beyond it, rather than revolving directly around the Earth."[29]

Even more astonishing, and unexpected—considering the scientific dogma of the time—were the four previously unknown "planets" orbiting Jupiter. Wrote Galileo: "But that which will excite the greatest astonishment by far, and which indeed especially moved me to call the attention of all astronomers and philosophers, is this, namely, that I have discovered four planets, neither known nor observed by any one of the astronomers before my time, which have their orbits round a certain bright star, one of those previously known, like Venus and Mercury round the Sun, and are sometimes in front of it, sometimes behind it, though they never depart from it beyond certain limits."[30]

According to established scientific thinking, that couldn't be; after all, more than three hundred years before Christ, Aristotle had said the bodies in heaven orbited only the earth, nothing else. To quote a famous twentieth-century physicist upon the discovery of a hitherto unknown subatomic particle, "Who ordered that?"

Even before Galileo aimed the telescope heavenward, some feared it might be demonic. A text from 1575 warned that the devil taking Jesus up into a high mountain and showing Him all the kingdoms of the world could have been a reference to something like the newly developed telescope. "No Christian dared," wrote John Heilbron, "to develop the Devil's device for another three and thirty years."[31]

But once the "devil's device" was developed and aimed upward, the light that shone out the end that met the eye exposed centuries of scientific dogma and assumption as false. At first, scientists and theologians were skeptical, even hostile, toward the things Galileo was finding. "Among the general literate public," wrote Stillman Drake, "they created great excitement, while philosophers and astronomers for the most part declared them optical illusions and ridiculed Galileo or accused him of fraud."[32] (How ironic that even today the "general literate public" remains much more skeptical of evolution than do biologists and philosophers.) Some experts, even Jesuit astronomers, were won over; others were not, at least not fully. And though accusations, arguments, and condemnations volleyed back and forth for years, Galileo was able to freely promote his views—that is, until 1632 and the publication of the *Dialogue Concerning the Two Chief World Systems.*

Galileo's heresy

Among the charges that the Inquisition hurled at Galileo because of his book was this: "The proposition that the sun is in the center of the world [i.e., the universe] and immovable from its place is absurd, philosophically false, and formally heretical; because it is expressly contrary to Holy Scriptures."

Technically, the Inquisition was right and Galileo wrong. The sun is not the center of the universe, but only of our solar system, which itself hovers in the outer burbs of the Milky Way, one of billions of galaxies careening across the universe. And far from being "immovable from its place," the sun is hurling through the cosmos at fantastic speeds along with the rest of the stars and planets in our galaxy. The sun is just not moving in the manner that the church, in the thrall of science, taught that it was, and this is the view that Galileo rejected. Thus his claims, both about the location and about the immobility of the sun, were deemed "formally heretical" and "expressly contrary to Holy Scriptures."

The only problem? Where does Scripture address the location of the sun in relation to the cosmos? What inspired words say that it is, or is not, the center of anything, much less the universe? Even if Galileo were right (which, in the immediate context, he was), how could something never touched on in Scripture be deemed heresy?

The answer is easy: Galileo's heresy wasn't against the Bible but against an interpretation of the Bible based on Aristotle. It didn't matter that the Bible never said that the sun was at the center of the universe. Aristotle did, and because the Bible was interpreted through this prevailing scientific theory, an astronomical point never addressed in Scripture had become a theological position of such centrality that the Inquisition threatened to torture an old man for teaching contrary to it.

What about the sun as "immovable"? Here, at least, the church had texts to work with. But do these texts teach that the sun orbits the earth as the church insisted they do?

The heavens declare the glory of God;
And the firmament shows His handiwork.
Day unto day utters speech,
And night unto night reveals knowledge.
There is no speech nor language
Where their voice is not heard.
Their line has gone out through all the earth,
And their words to the end of the world.
In them He has set a tabernacle for the sun,

Which is like a bridegroom coming out of his chamber,
And rejoices like a strong man to run its race.
Its rising is from one end of heaven,
And its circuit to the other end;
And there is nothing hidden from its heat (Psalm 19:1–6).

Don't these verses prove the motion of the sun across the sky, similar to a bridegroom coming "out of his chamber," or a strong man ready to run a race? These metaphors mean nothing if not motion. Thus, the Bible teaches that the sun, not the earth, is moving, right?

To begin with, we are dealing with metaphors in a poem, and so how closely and literally does one press metaphors in poetry? The psalmist also wrote "Day unto day utters speech" and "There is no speech nor language where their voice is not heard." *The day speaks in every human language? And so we hear that heavenly speech in our own tongue?* Either the world in King David's time was radically different than it is today, or the poet was using poetic imagery to express truths deeper than the imagery itself.

Psalm 19 is a poetical expression of the power of God as revealed in the heavens. This is theology, not cosmology, and to use these texts to promote an Aristotelian worldview is to pull out of them what wasn't put into them to begin with.

What about texts like these? "The sun also rises, and the sun goes down, and hastens to the place where it arose" (Ecclesiastes 1:5)? Or, "The sun had risen upon the earth when Lot entered Zoar" (Genesis 19:23)? Or, "When the sun was setting, all those who had any that were sick with various diseases brought them to Him; and He laid His hands on every one of them and healed them" (Luke 4:40)?

What about them? Does our present use of the terms "sunrise" and "sunset" reflect the reality that is taking place—the earth's daily rotation on its axis causing the sun to appear in the sky in the morning and then to look like it's moving across the sky all day, and finally to disappear behind the horizon later? That reality is certainly not what our words imply. But we are expressing what *appears* to be happening, not what is actually happening. "Sunrise" and "sunset" are just quick, easy ways to express what humans see, not what is causing the sights themselves.

Otherwise, how should sunrises and sunsets be expressed? Suppose, instead of saying, "What a beautiful sunset," we said, "What a beautiful spin of the earth on its axis that makes the sun appear to dip behind the horizon in such a colorful way."

Should Ecclesiastes 1:5 have been written like this? "The rotation of the earth on its axis also brings the sun into our view, and then hides the sun from our view. And then the rotation of the earth on its axis brings it back into our view again." Wouldn't that have been a more accurate depiction of the celestial phenomena themselves, if in fact that was what the Word of God was intending to express?

And what about Joshua 10:12, 13?

> Then Joshua spoke to the LORD in the day when the LORD delivered up the Amorites before the children of Israel, and he said in the sight of Israel:
> "Sun, stand still over Gibeon;
> And Moon, in the Valley of Aijalon."
> So the sun stood still,
> And the moon stopped,
> Till the people had revenge
> Upon their enemies.
> Is this not written in the Book of Jasher? So the sun stood still in the midst of heaven, and did not hasten to go down for about a whole day.

It's not easy to explain this passage, even given our current understanding of cosmology. Yet the issue is not *how* God did it, but that He did do it, whatever means He used. Here, too, the Bible is using human language to explain appearances. If the Lord wanted us to derive cosmology from these texts, should the texts not have said something like, "O earth, stop your rotation on your axis so that the sun will remain over Gibeon"?

Why is it not "contrary to the Holy Scriptures" to teach that the brain is the seat of our thoughts? After all, didn't Jesus say, "Why are you thinking these things *in your hearts*?" (Luke 5:22, NIV; italics added)? Jesus knew that we don't think with our hearts. Jesus' point was theological, not physiological, just as the point in Joshua (and Ecclesiastes and Psalms) was theological or historical, not cosmological.

The language of "sunrise" and "sunset" took on the importance that it did only because of the incorporation of false science into theology. Had the church not adopted Aristotle's cosmology and not made a theological issue out of what the Bible never addressed, it might have been spared the embarrassment of the Galileo affair.

Besides condemning Galileo's ideas about the motion and position of the sun, the church charged that his "proposition that the earth is not the center of the world, nor immovable, but that it moves, and also with a diurnal action, is also absurd, philosophically false, and, theologically considered, at least erroneous in faith."

But where does Scripture locate the earth in relationship to the cosmos, much less plop it into the center? That was Aristotle's view, not Scripture's. How ironic: supposedly defending the faith, the church accused a man of heresy for opposing a long-held scientific theory, a theory not only never addressed in Scripture but that turned out to be wrong!

What about the motion of the earth? Don't the following texts show that it is, indeed, not moving?

> The Lord reigns, He is clothed with majesty;
> The Lord is clothed,
> He has girded Himself with strength.
> Surely the world is established, so that it cannot be moved (Psalm 93:1).

> Tremble before Him, all the earth.
> The world also is firmly established,
> It shall not be moved (1 Chronicles 16:30).

> Say among the nations, "The Lord reigns;
> The world also is firmly established,
> It shall not be moved" (Psalm 96:10).

Even Protestant Reformers Luther and Calvin saw such texts as evidence of an immovable earth; neither had much time for the new astronomy. Yet, what does one do with texts like the following?

> And the foundations of the earth are shaken.
> The earth is violently broken,
> The earth is split open,
> The earth is shaken exceedingly.
> The earth shall reel to and fro like a drunkard,
> And shall totter like a hut (Isaiah 24:18–20).

> Therefore I will shake the heavens,
> And the earth will move out of her place (Isaiah 13:13).

> The Lord also will roar from Zion,
> And utter His voice from Jerusalem;
> The heavens and earth will shake (Joel 3:16).

For in My jealousy and in the fire of My wrath I have spoken: "Surely in that day there shall be a great earthquake in the land of Israel" (Ezekiel 38:19).

The words of Amos, who was among the sheepbreeders of Tekoa, which he saw concerning Israel in the days of Uzziah king of Judah, and in the days of Jeroboam the son of Joash, king of Israel, two years before the earthquake (Amos 1:1).

Then you shall flee through My mountain valley,
For the mountain valley shall reach to Azal.
Yes, you shall flee
As you fled from the earthquake (Zechariah 14:5).

And there will be great earthquakes in various places, and famines and pestilences; and there will be fearful sights and great signs from heaven (Luke 21:11).

He shakes the earth out of its place,
And its pillars tremble (Job 9:6).

The earth is, obviously, not immovable. Earthquakes, which existed in the time of the Bible writers, alone prove that point, so whatever these texts mean, they can't mean that the earth doesn't move in any way at all.

The motion described in these texts about the earth reeling "to and fro like a drunkard" and tottering and being shaken isn't referring to the motion of the earth's orbit or its rotation on its axis. But neither are the texts that speak about God establishing the earth so that "it cannot be moved" dealing with terrestrial orbits or the earth's rotation on its axis. These verses are talking about the power and majesty of God as Creator and as Judge; they aren't about cosmology any more than Peter's words to Ananias, "Why has Satan filled your heart to lie to the Holy Spirit?" (Acts 5:3), are about anatomy and physiology.

Theological objections

Though Aristotelian science was the background, the template, in which Galileo's saga unfolded, the church had other reasons, theological and scientific, to reject his defense of the Copernican hypothesis.

First, many feared what a Copernican universe would do to the gospel. If the earth, and hence humanity, were at the center of the cosmos, as opposed to some far-off orb in the cosmic boondocks, it would make much more sense for God to send His Son to die here at the apex of His creation. If the earth were just one tiny planet among billions, the idea of the Creator coming here to save humanity becomes more implausible.

One could retort, of course, as people did even back then that our smallness amid the "eternal silence" and "infinite spaces"[33] of the creation only enhances the gospel: God's love was so great that, in the person of Jesus Christ, it reached across those "infinite spaces" to us here even in the cosmic boondocks.

Imagine having been taught your whole life—and knowing that many previous generations before you were taught—that the earth sat in the center of the cosmos, only now to be told that this view is wrong. We are not at home plate. We're not even in the ballpark. We're in the outer edges of the parking lot. Far from the center of anything, we suddenly discover that not only are we just one of a number of other planets orbiting the sun, but that the sun is just one of billions of other suns in our own galaxy, which is itself one of billions of other galaxies. As far as cosmic geography goes, Copernicus pulled us out of the center of the circle where Aristotle had placed us since antiquity and exiled us to who knew where.

Though writing about an era after Galileo, Richard Tarnas captured what these earlier church fathers feared from the Copernican implications: "The sheer improbability of the whole nexus of events was becoming painfully obvious—that an infinite eternal God would have suddenly become a particular human being in a specific historical time and place only to be ignominiously executed. That a single brief life taking place two millennia earlier in an obscure primitive nation, on a planet now known to be a relatively insignificant piece of matter revolving about one star among billions in an inconceivably vast and impersonal universe—that such an undistinguished event should have any overwhelming cosmic or eternal meaning could no longer be a compelling belief for reasonable men."[34] Though wrong about Copernicus' theory, the Inquisitors were right about its potential implications.

Another fear: What would a Copernican universe do to the ascension of Christ? With the earth immobile at the center of everything and heaven spread about above in all directions, Christ's ascension seemed fairly easy to envision, at least geographically. "The factual basis," wrote William R. Shea, "of Christ's ascension seemed also to be imperiled by the motion of the earth. Here again the diagrammatic representation of theory that placed the sun at the center of the universe and the earth above or below it added to the difficulty of visualizing Christ ascending into the uppermost region of the heavens."[35]

Scientific objections

It's easy today to mock the ignorance of the ancients (in this case the "ancients" being the medievals), especially on something as rudimentary as the motion of the earth. (After all, what's more obvious and commonsensical than the earth's yearly orbit around the sun and its diurnal rotation on its axis?) But, from the medievals' perspective, the motion of the earth was not so obvious as it is to us, who have been taught it since childhood.

Philosopher Ludwig Wittgenstein (1889-1951), the story goes, asked a student in the halls of Cambridge University, "Tell me, why do people always say that it was natural for men to assume that the sun went around the earth, rather than the earth was rotating?"

"Well, obviously," the student responded, "because it looks as if the sun is going around the earth."

"OK," responded Wittgenstein, "but what would it look like if the earth were rotating?"

Wittgenstein's point reveals an important truth, not just about the Galileo affair but about science in general: Science can present good reasons for believing false theories. So much established science has later been deemed false even despite years of strong confirming data and validating evidence painstakingly accumulated by experts using the most advanced tools and the most highly acclaimed methodologies.

In fact, intelligent and educated people in the time of Galileo had good "scientific" reasons to reject the Copernican hypothesis. It wasn't just religion or Aristotle, but science and the tools of science that helped justify the initial rejection of Galileo's *Dialogue Concerning the Two Chief World Systems.*

To begin, what about the earth suggests that it not only spins on its axis, but also orbits the sun, as well as treks through the Milky Way at 792,000 kilometers per hour? Who ever felt these motions? If the earth spins, why don't birds get blown in the opposite direction of the spin? Or why do objects dropped from heights fall straight down to a spot right below, as opposed to somewhere else depending upon the direction of the earth's rotation? Although even in Aristotle's day people had answers to these questions, the idea of the earth moving seemed as counterintuitive, irrational, and contrary to simple sense perception to people back then as does the scientific claim today that physical reality is made up, not of subatomic particles, but of quantum fields.[36]

Other powerful scientific evidence against Copernicus dealt with the lack of any stellar parallax. If the earth were in a vast orbit around the sun, its position relative to the stars would change. A simple example is to place your thumb about four inches in front of your nose and look at it through one eye. Then shut that eye and look at your thumb through the other. Your thumb seems to have moved from where it was when you looked at it with the first eye. The change came not in the location of your thumb but in the place from where you viewed it. The argument in Galileo's day was that if the earth were moving as Copernicus suggested, the position of the stars at one point during the earth's orbit around the sun should appear in a different place six months later in that orbit. It was called the stellar parallax, and it was never observed. This suggested that the earth was not moving; if it were, the place of the stars in the sky should be different at different times during the year.

"The problem," wrote Marcelo Gleiser, "is that the stars are so far away, that the angular variation in the position of the nearest star is tiny, impossible to measure with the naked eye. Stellar parallax, the definitive proof that we orbit the Sun, would be detected only in 1838 by Friedrich Bessel. Had it been detected by the Greeks, possibly the entire history of astronomy and science would have been different."[37]

The irony of it all

How easy, in hindsight, to mock the Roman Church, not just for its condemnation of Galileo but for centuries of bungling the aftermath. Not until the early 1800s was Galileo's *Dialogue Concerning the Two Chief World Systems* removed from the Index of Forbidden Books and Catholics could freely teach Copernicanism. And not until almost two more centuries after that did Rome formally and publically (and finally) admit its error.

And although the story has been gleefully transformed into the archetypical example of ignorant religionists fighting intellectual progress, the reality remains more complicated. It wasn't just the stark binary of religion versus science; the Galileo disaster is an example of the tyranny of dogmatic science and scientific tradition over every other means of acquiring knowledge.

"The ignoble affairs," wrote Gerhard and Michael Hasel, "associated with the famous trial of Galileo in the seventeenth century could have been avoided had the church's theological consultants recognized that their interpretation of certain Bible texts was conditioned by tradition based on the cosmology of the pagan mathematician-geographer Ptolemy."[38] It wasn't just tradition, but a tradition that arose from the acceptance of prevailing scientific dogma.

"Lest we forget," wrote David Bentley Hart, "the birth of modern physics and cosmology was achieved by Galileo, Kepler, and Newton breaking free not from the close confining prison of faith (all three were believing Christians, of one sort or another) but from the enormous burden of the millennial authority of Aristotelian science."[39]

"We need to remember," wrote Charles Singer, "that the rigidity of the Aristotelian scheme lay not in itself but in the interpretation given to it, especially in the Middle Ages. By linking the theories of Aristotle with their own religious views, men of those times introduced a bitterness into the debate concerning the validity of the Aristotelian scheme that had nothing to do with its philosophical or scientific value."[40]

In the *Dialogue* Galileo sought to liberate the noosphere of his time from the neural patterns that centuries of Aristotle (the Darwin of his time) and his science had woven into medieval minds. "I do not mean," Galileo wrote, "that a person should not listen to Aristotle; indeed, I applaud the reading and careful study of his works, and I reproach only those who give themselves up as slaves to him in such a way as to subscribe blindly to everything he says and take it as an inviolable decree without looking for any other reasons."[41]

Galileo was fighting against a slavish devotion to ancient texts written by a man who, at the core of his philosophy, believed in studying the world on its own terms. In contrast to his great teacher, Plato, who believed that truth existed only in an idealistic nonmaterial world of ideas and forms, Aristotle believed that we need to use our senses, here on earth, to study the world itself. "All men by nature desire to know," he wrote. "An indication of this is the delight we take in our senses; for even apart from their usefulness they are loved for themselves; and above all others the sense of sight."[42]

The irony shouldn't be missed. A man in antiquity who promoted studying the world itself eventually became codified and canonized into an authority in his own right—even to the point where, as Galileo discovered, if you had experimental evidence (from study of the world itself) that contradicted him, or seemed to contradict him, then you had to chuck the experimental and experiential and go with Aristotle, the old authority. Everything had to be filtered through the lens of Aristotelianism, much like everything today is interpreted through the lens of whatever the latest incarnation of Darwin happens to be, regardless of any evidence that defies it.

Stomach-dwelling dwarfs

The Galileo saga, even centuries later, remains filled with lessons, not just about faith and science, but also about the human quest for truth, for knowledge, especially about the natural world. The world, the cosmos, the disputed territory in the Galilean saga is complicated. Nature doesn't give up her secrets easily, at least to us humans, who come out of the womb prepackaged with limitations (that seem to get only worse as we age) regarding how well we can discern the reality that we find ourselves immersed in. We are like a man "constantly being squeezed between the world and his idea of the world."[43] And for most of history, our ideas of the world have had a bad habit of being wrong.

Comedian Steve Martin portrayed Theodoric of York, a medieval barber who also practiced medicine. Theodoric tells the mother of a patient not to worry, that even though medicine is not an exact science, "we are learning all the time. Why, just fifty years ago they thought a disease like your daughter's was caused by demonic possession or witchcraft. But nowadays we know that

Isabelle is suffering from an imbalance of bodily humors, perhaps caused by a toad or a small dwarf living in her stomach."[44]

Because we believe we have been etched out of finer, more advanced stuff than were previous generations, we smugly mock their ignorance. But the vast gap between what we know and what can be known should help us realize that even with the Large Hadron Collider, the Human Genome Project, and the Hubble space telescope, we're only a few notches up the intellectual food chain from either Theodoric of York or even Galileo's inquisitors.

Whatever lessons can be milked from Galileo's "heresy," one should be that science never unfolds in a vacuum but always in a context that, of necessity, influences its conclusions. Whether seeking the Higgs boson or dissing Galileo's *Dialogue*, scientists work from presuppositions and assumptions. Ideally, over time, they assume that their later assumptions are closer to reality than were the earlier ones—perhaps with good reasons—but they are still just that, assumptions. The story of science, in Galileo's day and in ours, is rife with scientists who had good reasons for theories and the assumptions behind those theories, which are now believed to be wrong.

1. Galileo Galilei, *Dialogue Concerning the Two Chief World Systems: Ptolemaic and Copernican*, trans. Stillman Drake (New York: Modern Library, 2001), xxviii (italics in the original).

2. *The Crime of Galileo: Indictment and Abjuration of 1633*, Modern History Sourcebook, Fordham University, last modified January 1999, http://legacy.fordham.edu/halsall/mod/1630galileo.asp (italics added).

3. J. L. Heilbron, *Galileo* (Oxford: Oxford University Press, 2010), 317.

4. *Crime of Galileo.*

5. Albert Camus, *The Myth of Sisyphus, and Other Essays*, trans. Justin O'Brien (New York: Vintage International, 1991), 3.

6. William R. Shea, "Galileo and the Church," in *God and Nature: Historical Essays on the Encounter Between Christianity and Science*, ed. David C. Lindberg and Ronald L. Numbers (Berkeley: University of California Press, 1986), 127.

7. Galilei, *Dialogue*, 20.

8. Ibid., 37, 38 (italics in the original).

9. Ibid., 64.

10. Ibid., 131.

11. Ibid., 152.

12. Richard Dawkins, *The Selfish Gene* (Oxford: Oxford University Press, 2006), 195.

13. Shea, "Galileo and the Church," 115.

14. Shermer, *Moral Arc*, 25.

15. Quoted in Anthony Gottlieb, *The Dream of Reason: A History of Western Philosophy From the Greeks to the Renaissance* (New York: W. W. Norton, 2000), 222.

16. Edward Grant, "Science and Theology in the Middle Ages," in Lindberg and Numbers, *God and Nature*, 53.

17. "Between 1605 and 1644 a series of books appeared in rapid succession in England, Italy, and

France which laid waste the Aristotelian natural philosophy of the universities. The authors were Francis Bacon, Galileo, and René Descartes. The only conspicuous matter of agreement among them was that Aristotelian natural philosophy was not good science." Stillman Drake, *Galileo: A Very Short Introduction*, Very Short Introductions (Oxford: Oxford University Press, 2001), 3.

18. Richard Tarnas, *The Passion of the Western Mind: Understanding the Ideas That Have Shaped Our World View* (New York: Ballantine Books, 1991), 193.

19. Thomas S. Kuhn, *The Copernican Revolution: Planetary Astronomy in the Development of Western Thought* (Cambridge, MA: Harvard University Press, 1985), 91.

20. Aristotle, *On the Heavens*, trans. J. L. Stocks, in Daniel C. Stevenson, Internet Classics Archive, http://classics.mit.edu/Aristotle/heavens.html; book 2, part 14, para. 2.

21. " 'This subjective error of judgment, so clear to us today, led them to a disciplinary measure from which Galileo "had much to suffer." These mistakes must be frankly recognized, as you, Holy Father, have requested,' Cardinal Paul Poupard, the commission chairman, told the Pope." William D. Montalbano, "Earth Moves for Vatican in Galileo Case," *Los Angeles Times*, November 1, 1992, http://articles.latimes.com/1992-11-01/news/mn-1827_1_galileo-galilei.

Meanwhile, only in 1820 did the Catholic Church formally permit the teaching of Copernicanism, even if restrictions on the discussion of his work had slowly broken down over the years. And not until 1835 were Copernicus and Galileo removed from the Index of Forbidden Books.

22. Gottlieb, *Dream of Reason*, 363.

23. Dante Alighieri, *Inferno*, trans. John Ciardi (New York: Modern Library / W. W. Norton, 1996), 20.

24. Tarnas, *Western Mind*, 195, 196.

25. Nicolaus Copernicus, *On the Revolutions of Heavenly Spheres*, trans. Charles Glenn Wallis, Great Minds Series (New York: Prometheus Books, 1995), 4.

26. William Shakespeare, *Hamlet*, act 1, scene 5.

27. David Wootton, *Galileo: Watcher of the Skies* (New Haven, CT: Yale University Press, 2010), 190 (italics in the original).

28. Galileo Galilei and Johannes Kepler, *The Sidereal Messenger of Galileo Galilei*, trans. Edward Stafford Carlos (London: Rivingtons, 1880), 28.

29. Stanford Solar Center, "Galileo Challenge," http://solar-center.stanford.edu/gal-challenge /gquiz6c.html.

30. Galilei and Kepler, *Sidereal Messenger*, 9.

31. Heilbron, *Galileo*, 148.

32. Drake, *Galileo: A Very Short Introduction*, 48.

33. Blaise Pascal, *Pensées*, trans. A. J. Krailsheimer (London: Penguin Classics, 1995), 66.

34. Tarnas, *Western Mind*, 305.

35. Shea, "Galileo and the Church," 125.

36. Sean Carroll, "The Higgs Boson and Beyond," The Great Courses, http://www.thegreat courses.com/courses/the-higgs-boson-and-beyond.html.

37. Marcelo Gleiser, *The Dancing Universe: From Creation Myths to the Big Bang* (Hanover, NH: Dartmouth College Press, 2005), 52.

38. Gerhard F. Hasel and Michael G. Hasel, "The Unique Cosmology of Genesis 1 Against Ancient Near Eastern and Egyptian Parallels," in *The Genesis Creation Account and Its Reverberations in the Old Testament*, ed. Gerald A. Klingbeil (Berrien Springs, MI: Andrews University Press, 2015), 15.

39. David Bentley Hart, *Atheist Delusions: The Christian Revolution and Its Fashionable Enemies* (New Haven, CT: Yale University Press, 2009), 68.

40. Charles Singer, *A Short History of Science to the Nineteenth Century* (Mineola, NY: Dover Publications, 1997), 50.

41. Galilei, *Dialogue*, 131.

42. Aristotle, *Metaphysics*, trans. W. D. Ross, in Daniel C. Stevenson, Internet Classics Archive, http://classics.mit.edu/Aristotle/metaphysics.html; book 1, part 1, para. 1.

43. Stephen Dobyns, "Spiritual Chickens," *Cemetery Nights* (New York: Viking, 1987), 37.

44. Quoted in Shermer, *Moral Arc*, 103.

CHAPTER 3

MIND AND COSMOS

A t the Hirshhorn Museum in Washington, DC, I entered an exhibit, a small room so dark that an usher had to guide me in. The only light was a dimly lit wall opposite my seat. Though I often reach out in faith regarding "modern art," that faith began to waver as I sat, staring at the wall. Within a few minutes, the wall got brighter and, fascinatingly enough, light started to emerge from the bottom of the wall into a kind of shelf that stopped about a foot off the floor and halfway across the room.

As I sat there, still wondering what it was all about, the usher guided another man to a seat, as she had done me. But why? There was plenty of light now.

Then it hit me: the room, to my mind, which had adjusted to the light, seemed bright enough. But to the man who just entered, in his mind, the room was so dark that he needed an usher. In other words, the reality of the room appeared one way to me and another to him.

There was only one room and one light in it, so whose view (mine or his) of the room and light was the true one, the one that accurately corresponded to the immediate environment around us both?[1]

Whatever is extractable from this anecdote about culture in general or about modern art in particular, what shouldn't be missed is what it says about the limits inherent in all human attempts to understand the world. We're not granted unmediated access to reality. We are part of the reality that we want to investigate, made (at the deepest levels) of the same quantum fields and existing in the same dimensions as is what we are studying. Maybe, like the narrator of Edwin Abbot's 1884 *Flatland*, our minds have "been opened to higher views of things,"[2] but we can't get into that "higher view" and look down from there to our view here. (Or perhaps this "higher view" is just another angle on the same reality that we're already in?) Talking about the limits inherent in studying the world, Paul Feyerabend wrote that "we cannot discover it from the *inside*. . . . We need a dream-world in order to discover the features of the real world we think we inhabit."[3] We can know the world only through our minds, which, part of the reality that they study, are inseparably entangled with that reality and, thus, hopelessly subjective about it.

"But since we are who we are," writes Thomas Nagel, "we can't get outside of ourselves completely. Whatever we do, we remain subparts of the world with limited access to the real nature of the rest of it and of ourselves. There is no way of telling how much of reality lies beyond the reach of present or future objectivity or any other conceivable form of human understanding."[4] In other words, paradoxes and limits will, of necessity, constrain whatever we can know about reality. These constraints include scientific endeavors, which explains why so often science—like all human attempts at knowledge—gets things wrong.

Losing truth?

And science gets it wrong more often than most people realize. In 2013, *The Economist* magazine published an article called "How Science Goes Wrong,"[5] a candid look at some dirty secrets of science that mere mortals aren't supposed to be privy to.

"Too many of the findings that fill the academic ether," the article says, "are the result of shoddy experiments or poor analysis. A rule of thumb among biotechnology venture-capitalists is that half of published research cannot be replicated. Even that may be optimistic. Last year researchers at one biotech firm, Amgen, found they could reproduce just six of 53 'landmark' studies in cancer research. Earlier, a group at Bayer, a drug company, managed to repeat just a quarter of 67 similarly important papers. A leading computer scientist frets that three-quarters of papers in his subfield are bunk."[6]

This is what happens in science, the objective and unbiased explanation of reality?[7]

And replication of only six out of "53 'landmark' studies"? How could that be? Replication of research is a foundation of scientific verification. Someone makes a claim about results in an experiment or a study, and what better way to verify the results than to replicate the experiment or study and, ideally, the results?

Yet many supposedly well-established and reconfirmed findings look increasingly uncertain. "It's as if our facts were losing their truth," said an article in *The New Yorker* on a similar topic. "Claims that have been enshrined in textbooks are suddenly unprovable. This phenomenon doesn't yet have an official name, but it's occurring across a wide range of fields, from psychology to ecology."[8] Stanford epidemiologist John Ioannidis was so concerned about the problem he wrote an oft-cited paper: "Why Most Published Research Findings Are False."[9]

The Economist article continued, saying, "In 2000-10 roughly 80,000 patients took part in clinical trials based on research that was later retracted because of mistakes or improprieties."[10]

How comforting.

What about "peer review"? Isn't that supposed to protect against false science?

Again, *The Economist*: "The hallowed process of peer review is not all it is cracked up to be, either. When a prominent medical journal ran research past other experts in the field, it found that most of the reviewers failed to spot mistakes it had deliberately inserted into papers, even after being told they were being tested."[11]

Besides, if one's peers dogmatically share the same scientific paradigm, the same model, the same assumptions as the author, then what does peer review do other than make sure the author stays faithful to the party line, regardless of whether the party line is correct? Peer review ensures (supposedly) the validity of work within a set of assumptions; it says nothing about the validity of the assumptions themselves (see chapter 7).

Writing in the *Atlantic*, author Bourree Lam told about a recent spate of scientific findings retracted because all had been shown to be wrong. Apparently, the problem is more widespread than most people realize. "A study in the *Proceedings of the National Academy of Sciences*," she wrote, "reviewed 2,047 retractions of biomedical and life-sciences articles and found that *just 21.3 percent stemmed from straightforward error, while 67.4 percent resulted from misconduct*, including fraud or suspected fraud (43.4 percent) and plagiarism (9.8 percent)."[12]

Plus, if rampant problems exist in experimental science, which is being done on what's alive and kicking now (such as on those 80,000 patients), should we be expected to bow down in intellectual obsequiousness when science makes bold pronouncements about what happened supposedly 250 million years ago when the *Coelurosauravus* (we have been told) evolved wings before vanishing into the Paleozoic ozone?

How about this lead in an article in the *New York Times*? "Do studies show that soft drinks promote obesity and Type 2 diabetes? It depends on who paid for the study."[13]

It depends upon who paid for the study?

The article discussed how the results of scientific research on the health hazards of soft drinks varied, and how scientific studies funded by the soft drink industry downplayed the health hazards in contrast to independent research. Nevertheless, the soft drink industry claims that it is doing the finest in science. "The research we fund," declared the industry, "adheres to the highest standards of integrity for scientific inquiry based on recognized standards by prominent research institutions."[14] In fact, the industry charged that those funding the research that pointed out health hazards of soft drinks were paid by those who had a vested interest in making such products appear worse than they really were.

We're not talking about literary critics on Cormac McCarthy or music critics on Max Richter. These are scientific researchers, supposedly adhering "to the highest standards of integrity for scientific inquiry," looking at the same objective reality but coming up with different scientific conclusions.

How could this be? After all—*It's science!* Could there really be bias among scientists that affects their conclusions, not just in research on things that exist now—soft drinks and diabetes—but also on the study of life-forms that supposedly existed millions or even billions of years ago?

This isn't a new question. Writing about the relationship between the early church and science, David Lindberg argued like this: "True science, . . . [a critic] might maintain, cannot be the handmaiden of anything, but must possess total autonomy; consequently, the 'disciplined' science that Augustine sought is no science at all. In fact, this complaint misses the mark: totally autonomous science is an attractive ideal, but we do not live in an ideal world. And many of the most important developments in the history of science have been produced by people committed not to autonomous science, but to science in the service of some ideology, social program, or practical end; for most of its history, the question has not been whether science will function as handmaiden, but which mistress it will serve."[15]

Multiple reasons exist for these problems in scientific research: cherry-picked data, competition for money, outcome bias, the influence of big business, rivalry among researchers, the lack of resources, and so forth. But these reasons sound like what one expects in theology or literary criticism or feminist studies or political theory. *But should we find such issues in science, supposedly the purest and most objective means of finding truth about reality?*[16]

The reasons go much deeper than just cherry-picked data or grant money, however. They go, instead, to the problem of how humans (including scientists)—subjective beings trapped within limited receptors that allow only radically narrow perspectives on what's outside themselves—can accurately explain the "highly complex, multifaceted, multilayered reality"[17] that not only surrounds them but of which they are part.

Mind and cosmos

Imagine our universe the way many contemporary scientists insist that it once was: only electrons, positrons, neutrinos, photons, and then later helium and hydrogen that, "under the influence of gravitation to form clumps . . . would ultimately condense to form the galaxies and stars of the present universe."[18]

But suppose that this universe was also (as many believe it to be) godless, without awareness, with no life at all. Nothing but energy, gases, stars, and rocks composed of the subatomic entities currently believed to form all matter and energy.

Suppose it were that way still, now?

In such a universe, could knowledge exist? Photons, electrons, stars, cosmic rays, yes. But *knowledge*? The idea of "knowledge" itself demands not just consciousness (after all, an Egyptian fruit bat has "consciousness") but a higher level of consciousness, a mind able to contain rational thought. Knowledge without mind is as impossible as thought without mind, for what is knowledge but a form of thought? If there were no God, or gods, and no intelligent life anywhere else in the cosmos other than humans, then the only knowledge in all creation would be what is in human minds. And if all humans were to die, all knowledge would die with them.

We have knowledge only because we have minds; no minds, no thoughts, no knowledge. And because we have *human* minds, all human knowledge is limited by the kind of thought human minds can have. Whatever we as humans know, or think we know, including scientific knowledge, we know only as human thoughts.

Which leads to, arguably, the most foundational question we can ask: *How do we know that our thoughts are correct?* How can we be sure that what we know, or think we know, is true? Whatever we know (or think we know), we know (or think we know) only through the processes that create knowledge in our minds to begin with. So to ask how we know if the processes that we use for gaining knowledge are correct is to hurl oneself into a self-referential labyrinth, the intellectual equivalent of an Escher sketch. How do we know that our methods of gaining knowledge are correct when we need some method of gaining knowledge in order to judge those methods? But if the issue of how we gain knowledge is what we are questioning from the start, then how can we trust our judgment of that method itself? We must assume the very thing that we are questioning. This is another example of the limits of human knowledge, not just about what we know (or think we know), but about the process itself of knowing. This process is called *epistemology*.

Epistemology

Anyone interested in the creation-evolution debate needs to understand the concept behind the word *epistemology*. Like biology, geology, theology, the word *epistemology* contains its own meaning. But instead of the study of life (*bios*), or of the earth (*geo*), or of God (*theos*), epistemology is the study of *episteme*, of knowledge itself. It is "the branch of philosophy concerned with enquiry into the nature, sources and validity of knowledge."[19]

Epistemology is not the study of knowledge, in the sense of *what* we know (at least not directly)—such as two plus two equals four, or that Jesus Christ died for humanity, or that blood feeds oxygen to our cells, or that you have a toothache, or that Françoise Mitterrand was president of France. Rather, epistemology is the study of *how* we come to make the knowledge claims that we do about two plus two, or about Jesus, or about oxygen in blood, or about a toothache, or about Françoise Mitterrand, or about anything that we claim to know.

You say, "I *know* that two plus two equals four." You say, "I *know* that Jesus died for my sins." You say, "I *know* that Françoise Mitterrand was president of France." You say, "I *know* that I have a toothache." In each case the verb *know* is being used similarly, in that you are certain of the veracity of each sentence.

Yet you came to this knowledge and to the use of the verb *know* through different methods. How you know that you have a toothache is quite different from how you know that two plus two equals four, or how you know Jesus Christ died for your sins. You didn't feel in your mouth the sensation two plus two equals four, just as you didn't learn from reading Paul and other Scripture that you have a toothache. You might know these things, just as you know that the sun will rise tomorrow, or that John F. Kennedy was assassinated, or that God loves the world. But, again, you came to this knowing, this knowledge, through different methods.

Epistemology looks at those methods.

Empiricism

One of those methods, one of central importance in the creation-evolution debate, is *empiricism*, the theory that we get our knowledge from our senses. In the above statements, the one about knowing that you have a toothache (as opposed to knowing that two plus two equals four) would be deemed *empirical* knowledge. Your senses, in this case the sense of pain, gave you the knowledge that you have about your tooth.

If someone were to say to you, "There are ten people in the room," a logical response would be, "OK, let me go see for myself." You get up, you go to the room, and, with your eyes, your sense receptors, you reach a conclusion regarding the truth or falsity of the statement about the number of people in the room. That is empiricism.

Now, suppose someone were to say to you, "If there are ten people in the room, then there are three more persons there than there would be if there were only seven people in the room." If you answered, "OK, but let me go in and see for myself," that response would be strange. Rationality alone reveals that when ten people are in the room, there are three more persons there than when there are seven in the room. No need exists, as in the first example, to go to the room and count the people there. The statement itself, on its own terms, shows its truthfulness. You don't need to go outside the statement, to your senses, or to history, or to revelation to know it is true.

An empiricist epistemology

The crucial point is this: science, including all the branches that teach evolution, is an *empiricist epistemology*. Whatever else is involved, science at the core is a human attempt—through the use of our senses—to understand, interpret, describe, and, ideally, explain the world. Whether or not it is Aristotle 2,300 years ago looking at bugs, or Darwin in the Galapagos studying birds, or chemists working for the Philip Morris tobacco company, or astronomers using the Hubble telescope to examine stars, or biologists claiming that life began on earth between 3.8 and 4 billion years ago—science is an empirical endeavor. It is human beings, sometimes with the aid of devices, using their senses to explore the natural world.

Which is fine. How else would scientists study the world? After all, we do learn much from our senses. One could argue that most of what we know, at least about the natural world, we know *only* from our senses. Even knowledge that is revealed to us, things that we couldn't know otherwise, such as our birthday, we know only through our senses—our ears (someone told us) or our eyes (we read it). And if we know that John F. Kennedy was assassinated or that Julius Caesar held the title *Pontifex Maximus*, how do we know these things other than, again, by either our eyes or ears or both?

Sensory deprivation

Yet for thousands of years, people have struggled with the difficult question about how accurately, or inaccurately, our senses funnel the world to us. What's the difference between the reality that is outside our brains and how that reality appears to us *in* our brains? When you look at a tree, for example, what you see is not the tree itself, but an image of the tree that exists in your mind. If your mind stopped functioning, the image of the tree existing in your head would cease to exist—*not the tree itself*. This is proof that they are two different things. Whatever is in your head, which appears to you as the tree, is certainly not the tree itself.

What transformation, then, takes place as our senses capture whatever is external to us and convert it into the chemical-electrical impulses in our bodies and brains that underlie all our experience? In short, what's the difference between the tree image existing in your head and the tree itself? A lot, because whatever is in your head is certainly not real bark, leaves, and wood.

As the museum example showed, our senses can give conflicting views of what's out there. To one person the room appeared well lit; to the other it appeared dark. If science studies what's really out there, then it should not be concerned with how the room appears to different people. The issue is the reality of the room itself. Why would a geologist, studying a shale cliff, care about how the cliff appears to the eyes of bats or in the lens of a Canon camera or to someone who is color-blind? In the same way, science is concerned only with what the room is really like in and of itself, regardless of the pupil size in the eyes of, or what's going on in the brain of, the sentient beings in the room.

If the science were physiology or psychology, then the subjective sensations of the beings in question would be the specific focus.[20] But if the science is dealing with such things as air pressure or the structure of the Tadpole Galaxy or the first flowering of plants in the Cretaceous period—supposedly 146 to 65 million years ago—then the gap between how things appear in our brains and what they really are in and of themselves becomes crucial.

Why? Because this question gets to one of the many inherent limitations of science, a limitation that becomes exponentially more problematic when science is dealing not only with what's right before us now, but with what it claims happened millions or billions of years ago to things that were, supposedly, long gone before our senses even existed.

Come back to the example about how many people are in a room. Someone says that ten people are there. So you walk in and count. Yes, ten people are in the room. Isn't that a solid, certain conclusion? Can't one be as certain about that as about the claim that if ten people are in the room, then there are three more persons than there would be if only seven people were in the room?

Suppose, however, a woman was hiding under the table and you missed her in the count. Or suppose three more people were in the rafters above your head and out of sight. Or suppose someone's definition of the word *room* included the closet, where two more people were hiding. Or suppose you were an American who lived during the Confederacy, when slaves were considered as only two-thirds of a person, and four of the people in the room were slaves.

So you really can't be as certain about how many people are actually in the room as you can be about the claim that when ten people are in the room there are three more persons than when seven people are there.

"The nub of the problem," wrote A. C. Grayling, "is that if we are acquainted only with our own perceptions, and never with the things which are supposed to lie beyond them, how can we hope for knowledge of those things, or even be justified in asserting their existence?"[21]

Wrote Iris Murdoch, "It is a *task* to come to see the world as it is."[22] This, however, is easier said than done, if even possible.[23]

Again, if this foundational epistemological limitation holds true with things that we believe exist now (such as the number of people in a room), then how much greater will the problem be with those things that don't exist now, such as all the billions of years of evolutionary history that we are told predated us and our senses?

"Our studies," wrote Sir James Jeans decades ago, "can never put us into contact with reality; we can never penetrate beyond the impressions that reality implants in our minds."[24]

Writing about sight, Nobel Prize winner Francis Crick argued that "the brain combines the information provided by the many distinct features of the visual scene (aspects of shape, color, movement, etc.) and settles on the most plausible interpretation of all these various visual clues taken together."[25] He went on to argue that "what you see is not what is *really* there; it is what your brain *believes* is there. . . . Your brain makes the best interpretation it can according to its previous experience and the limited and ambiguous information provided by your eyes."[26]

Different brains, different realities, then?

"Seek out reality," wrote William Butler Yeats, "leave things that seem."[27] Fine, but how does one do it, if it can be done at all?

Hilary Putnam wrote that "the enterprises of providing a *foundation* for Being and Knowledge—a successful description of the Furniture of the World . . . —are enterprises that have disastrously failed, and we could not have seen this until these enterprises had been given time to prove their futility."[28]

The cave

The contrast between what is real and how these real things seem to us is nothing new. About 2,400 years ago Plato, in *The Republic*, used a metaphor to describe this problem.

"Imagine," wrote Plato, "an underground chamber like a cave, with a long entrance open to the daylight and as wide as the cave. In this chamber are men who have been prisoners there since they were children, their legs and necks being so fastened that they can only look straight ahead of them and cannot turn their heads."[29]

He then says that outside the cave is a fire, and between the fire and the cave is a road on which various objects pass. According to his metaphor, all that the people in the cave would see would be shadows on the cave wall of the things on the road that passed behind them. They would mistake the shadows, which were all that their sense perceptions revealed to them, for reality. Would they not, wrote Plato, "assume that the shadows they saw were the real things?"[30]

Though only a metaphor, Plato's cave expressed this difference between what we perceive with our senses and what's really out there—that is, the difference between a tree and the image of that tree in our minds. In the 2,400 years since Plato, this question still haunts those who ponder it. It does so with even more ferocity than ever, because in the past few hundred years we have learned of the existence of whole aspects of reality (germs, subatomic particles, the Higgs field, radio waves, etc.) completely beyond unaided senses. It's bad enough that we can't be sure about the nature or existence of what we grasp with our senses, but what about all those things we believe exist that our senses can't grasp at all, at least not without the help of machinery, which itself raises a host of other questions?

Red or blue glasses

Through the millennia, people have come to different conclusions regarding empiricism and knowledge in general (remember, knowledge exists only if mind does). Some people deny "the possibility of any and all knowledge, and even justified belief."[31] Others acknowledge the gap we've been discussing but don't seem concerned about it. As far as they are concerned, the real world is the world of our experiences, and it's fruitless to think otherwise.

About two thousand years after Plato, the German philosopher Immanuel Kant argued that our minds alone construe the reality that we experience. Our minds are not passive recipients of sense data, like hot wax that sense impressions mold into their own image. Rather, our minds are complicated filters that categorize, organize, and ultimately create the reality that we see, hear, smell, taste, and touch. Not that our minds create the world, but only how the world appears to us.

A popular, if crude, metaphor is this: imagine that you wore red-colored glasses. Everything you saw would, of course, be tinted red because of the glasses on your face. If the glasses were blue, the same reality would look blue. In a similar way, we know only the world that our minds allow us to know. This is what Kant called the "phenomenal" world: the image of the tree in our minds or the room in the museum as it appeared to those in it. These images are the phenomena in our minds, in contrast to the tree itself or to the room itself, which exists outside our minds. Now, were our minds made differently, both the tree and the room would appear differently to us as well.

This distinction leads back to a fundamental weakness in all empirical endeavors, including (and maybe even especially) science. Unless the objects of study are the mind and cognition themselves, science, ideally, is not concerned with how the world appears to subjective beings such as humans, chimps, or mantis shrimp (which have four times as many photoreceptors as humans), but with the world as it is itself *independently of how it appears to us*. A paleon-tologist studying a fossil cares about the fossil itself and what he or she thinks it reveals, not about how the fossil appears in a human mind.

But, according to Kant, true knowledge of the world in and of itself—the tree, the room, the fossil—is impossible. The question "What are objects considered as things in themselves?" wrote Kant, "remains unanswerable even after the most thorough examination of the phenomenal world."[32] That is, no matter how much we study the world of our experiences, we can never get beyond those experiences to the world as it is in and of itself.

"Thus," wrote Alfred North Whitehead, somewhat facetiously, "nature gets credit which should in truth be reserved for ourselves: the rose for its scent: the nightingale for his song: and the sun for his radiance. The poets are entirely mistaken. They should address their lyrics to themselves, and should turn them into odes of self-congratulation on the excellency of the human mind. Nature is a dull affair, soundless, scentless, colourless; merely the hurrying of material, endlessly, meaninglessly."[33]

Yet, the question still remains: How do we step out of our eyes or ears or skin or mouths or noses in order to experience stimuli apart from how these tissues—with their various cells, chemicals, and nerve endings—respond to external stimuli? At one level, everything we experience is just biology; even when scientists do science, it is biology at work. "I would like to point out," wrote Bas C. van Fraassen, "that science is a biological phenomenon, an activity by one kind of organism which facilitates its interaction with the environment."[34] Our only contact with the external world is through the tissues that make up our sense receptors and the biology at work in them. It is not unreasonable to assume that if these tissues were differently constructed and functioned differently biologically, then how they interact with the world would be different too. Which would mean that they would give us a different conception of the world than they do now (think red glasses versus blue glasses).

Which is why, even today, this issue remains one of many unresolved problems in regard to the difference between what people think science reveals to us and what it really reveals. Science is supposed to tell us what is really out there, as opposed to how what is out there appears to us.

Can it?

"Physical science is after all," wrote Thomas Nagel, "just an operation of our minds, and we have no reason to assume that their capacities in these respects, remarkable as they are, correlate fully with reality."[35]

In a book regarding the great and still unresolved debate about what color actually is, M. Chirimuuta wrote: "To be a color realist is to hold that colors are perceiver-independent properties that are instantiated on the surfaces of things, whether or not anybody is there to look. What the realist denies is that color is in any way a by-product of neural activity. . . . Vision scientists have variously claimed that color is identifiable with states of the brain, or that it is created or constructed by the brain."[36]

Does color truly exist "out there," or is color simply a product of the mind responding to whatever is out there? For those who care about this issue, it remains as unresolved as do many questions about what science can or cannot reveal to us about reality. And if a host of questions remain about whether the color red, for example, is real, how dogmatically should we accept what science tells us about how tortoises supposedly evolved their hard shells millions of years ago? And if we are limited in what we can know about the color red or about tortoise shells that exist today, how seriously should we take what evolutionists declare to us about what tortoise shells were supposed to be like millions of years ago?

Object X

Contrary to popular opinion, the controversies in science are not only about the truth or falsity of specific scientific claims—Is light a wave or a particle? Do vaccines cause autism? Is fat good or bad for us? Do parallel universes exist? Did a meteorite kill the dinosaurs? The issues go much deeper than any one theory; they go to the whole idea of *theory* itself. The question is not so much about whether a specific theory is true or false (though this does come into play), but about what it means to say that a scientific theory is true or false or whether it is even possible to know with any certainty that a theory is or is not true.

"One of the most lively and persistent debates in twentieth century philosophy of science," wrote Martin Curd and J. A. Cover, "is that between empiricists and realists concerning the status of scientific theories. Are scientific theories to be understood as offering (or at least intending to offer) a true account of the world? And if we accept scientific theories as true, should we believe that the entities they appear to postulate really exist?"[37]

Are scientific theories understood as offering "a true account of the world?" What kind of question is that? Isn't the whole point of scientific theories to offer a true account of the world? What's the purpose of science were it to do anything else? What good is a scientific theory that offers a false account of the world?

And if we accept a theory as true, "should we believe that the entities they appear to postulate really exist?" What kind of question is that? If a theory about object X is believed to be true, then isn't it assumed that object X itself exists? What is the sense of even talking about object X if we don't believe object X exists in the first place?

Are accepted scientific theories true? Do entities that science says exist really exist?

Issues as basic as these remain hotly debated questions that don't have easy answers.

And for this reason, among others (all of which *Baptizing the Devil* will explore), Christians shouldn't be so ready to throw down their weapons and lift their arms in surrender to every claim science makes, especially in regard to origins, where science's claims about a reality that they can only posit exists clearly contradict God's Word.

---

1. Clifford Goldstein, "The Room and the Light," *Adventist Review,* September 15, 2011, 17.

2. Edwin A. Abbott, *Flatland: A Romance of Many Dimensions* (Mineola, N.Y.: Dover, 1992), 3.

3. Feyerabend, *Against Method,* 22 (italics in the original).

4. Nagel, *The View From Nowhere,* Kindle edition, chap. 1.

5. "How Science Goes Wrong," *The Economist,* October 21, 2013, https://www.economist .com/news/leaders/21588069-scientific-research-has-changed-world-now-it-needs-change -itself-how-science-goes-wrong.

6. Ibid.

7. For instance, when the tobacco industry hired scientists to study the effects of tobacco, were these scientists doing real science, especially when for years they were telling us that their scientific research showed that tobacco smoking wasn't harmful? Or what about the meat industry scientists studying the health effects of eating meat and time and again concluding that a meat diet is really good for you? And they had scientific evidence to back it up too. Was this real science, bad science, or pseudoscience? One year they tell us that it's good to drink wine. They have the scientific evidence that it's good for you. Two years later, they have scientific evidence that it's bad for you. Science tells us one thing; then later science tells us the opposite. This doesn't mean science is bad or evil, but it's clear that whatever science is, it's not certain.

8. Jonah Lehrer, "The Truth Wears Off," *The New Yorker,* December 13, 2010, http://www .newyorker.com/magazine/2010/12/13/the-truth-wears-off.

9. John P. A. Ioannidis, "Why Most Published Research Findings Are False," August 30, 2005, http://journals.plos.org/plosmedicine/article?id=10.1371/journal.pmed.0020124; see also his article "An Epidemic of False Claims," *Scientific American,* June 1, 2011, http://www .scientificamerican.com/article/an-epidemic-of-false-claims/.

10. "How Science Goes Wrong."

11. Ibid.

12. Bourree Lam, "A Scientific Look at Bad Science," *The Atlantic,* September 2015, https:// www.theatlantic.com/magazine/archive/2015/09/a-scientific-look-at-bad-science/399371/ (italics in the original).

13. Anahad O'Connor, "Studies Linked to Soda Industry Mask Health Risks," *New York Times,* October 31, 2016, http://www.nytimes.com/2016/11/01/well/eat/studies-linked-to -soda-industry-mask-health-risks.html?_r=0.

14. Ibid.

15. David C. Lindberg, *The Beginnings of Western Science: The European Scientific Tradition in Philosophical, Religious, and Institutional Context, Prehistory to A.D. 1450,* 2nd ed. (Chicago: University of Chicago Press, 2007), 150.

16. The Center for Scientific Integrity runs a website, retractionwatch.com, that follows the retractions of scientific claims. "The mission of the Center for Scientific Integrity, the parent

organization of Retraction Watch, is to promote transparency and integrity in science and scientific publishing, and to disseminate best practices and increase efficiency in science" (http://retractionwatch.com/the-center-for-scientific-integrity/).

17. McGrath and McGrath, *The Dawkins Delusion?* 34.

18. Steven Weinberg, *The First Three Minutes: A Modern View of the Origin of the Universe*, updated ed. (New York: Basic Books, 1993), 8.

19. A. C. Grayling, "Epistemology," in *The Blackwell Companion to Philosophy*, ed. Nicholas Bunnin and E. P. Tsui-James, 2nd ed. (Oxford: Blackwell, 2003), 37.

20. Of course, certain interpretations of quantum theory challenge this strong subject-object distinction.

21. A. C. Grayling, *Skepticism and the Possibility of Knowledge* (London: Continuum, 2008), 5.

22. Iris Murdoch, *The Sovereignty of Good* (London: Routledge Great Minds, 2014), 89 (italics in the original).

23. And not just with sight but with any of our senses. Quantum physicist Erwin Schrödinger, writing about sound, expressed it like this: "We can follow the pressure changes in the air as they produce vibrations of the ear-drum, we can see how its motion is transferred by a chain of tiny bones to another membrane and eventually to parts of the membrane inside the cochlea, composed of fibres of varying length, described above. We may reach an understanding of how such a vibrating fibre sets up an electrical and chemical process of conduction in the nervous fibre with which it is in touch. We may follow this conduction to the cerebral cortex and we may even obtain some objective knowledge of some of the things that happen there. But nowhere shall we hit on this 'registering as sound,' which simply is not contained in our scientific picture, but is only in the mind of the person whose ear and brain we are speaking of." Erwin Schrödinger, *What Is Life?* (Cambridge, UK: Cambridge University Press, 2012), 157, 158.

24. Sir James Jeans, *Physics and Philosophy* (New York: Dover Publications, 1981), 15.

25. Francis Crick, *The Astonishing Hypothesis: The Scientific Search for the Soul* (New York: Touchstone, 1995), 30.

26. Ibid., 31 (italics in the original).

27. William Butler Yeats, *The Collected Poems of W. B. Yeats*, ed. Richard J. Finneran, rev. 2nd ed. (New York: Scribner, 1996), 252.

28. Hilary Putnam, *Realism With a Human Face*, ed. James Conant (Cambridge, MA: Harvard University Press, 1992), 19 (italics in the original).

29. Plato, *The Republic*, trans. Desmond Lee (London: Penguin Books, 2003), 241.

30. Ibid.

31. Charles Landesman, *Skepticism: The Central Issues* (Oxford: Blackwell, 2002), 4.

32. Immanuel Kant, *Critique of Pure Reason*, trans. J. M. D. Meiklejohn (Mineola, NY: Dover, 2003), 36.

33. Alfred North Whitehead, *Science and the Modern World* (Cambridge, UK: Cambridge University Press, 1953), 68, 69.

34. Bas C. van Fraassen, *The Scientific Image* (Oxford: Clarendon Press, 1980), 39.

35. Nagel, *The View From Nowhere*, Kindle edition, chap. 2, sec. 2.

36. M. Chirimuuta, *Outside Color: Perceptual Science and the Puzzle of Color in Philosophy* (Cambridge, MA: MIT Press, 2015), 102.

37. Martin Curd and J. A. Cover, *Philosophy of Science: The Central Issues* (New York: W. W. Norton, 1998), 1049.

CHAPTER 4

GOOD—BUT NOT TRUE

I magine the audacity: Claiming to overturn thousands of years of received wisdom, even the scientific wisdom of the world's greatest minds, ancient and modern? Daring to refute the Philosopher himself, Aristotle? Daring to question what the senses undeniably taught?

In a book filled with charts, geometric figures, tables, and numbers, this upstart rattled the scientific foundations that the most advanced civilizations had believed and used in their daily lives for millennia—from discerning when to plant crops to when to wage war. He kicked hard at the edifice upon which most of the world for most of known human history had built its sense of identity and place in the cosmos. This man, a mere bureaucrat in a local church in Poland, had the chutzpah to challenge the pillars, the assumptions, the accepted scientific beliefs held by "the world's greatest thinkers; the best and brightest; the feted experts; . . . the most educated, knowledgeable, and informed . . . ; . . . the renowned; the famous; the brilliant"?[1]

His moves were as radical, as heretical, and as dangerous as a scientist today publicly rebutting Darwinism.

The man was Nicolaus Copernicus, and his book *De revolutionibus orbium coelestium* (*On the Revolutions of Heavenly Spheres*), published in 1543, was one of the first and most forceful fingers in the eye of Aristotle and the worldview based upon his science and the beliefs emanating from it. Though Copernicus was not the first to hold the view that the earth orbited the sun, and though his book had numerous errors (for instance, he believed the sun sat motionless in the center of the universe and that the orbits of the planets were perfect circles), nothing like *De revolutionibus* had so thoroughly and convincingly challenged the prevailing scientific consensus. When, in the next century, Galileo was intellectually lynched by the Roman Inquisition, it was because he was "following the hypothesis of Copernicus."[2]

Copernicus, though, never faced the Inquisition or any other tribunal for challenging the cultural, scientific, and intellectual establishment. Why? Did he live in an age when scientific dissent was tolerated more than it was in Galileo's day, or in ours?

Hardly. He escaped trouble only because he died on May 24, 1543, the same time his book began leaving the press.

Osiander's introduction

Was that timing coincidence? Although Copernicus had been sick, maybe what pushed him over the edge was the introduction to the book—an introduction that he hadn't written and that didn't reflect his views.

As far back as 1508, Copernicus had been toying with the idea of a heliocentric universe, thus challenging the intellectual and scientific status quo. A German Lutheran clergyman and friend, Andreas Osiander, had taken over the printing and publication of Copernicus' work on the subject. Worried about the reaction and what it could mean for Copernicus (who, as a loyal son of the church, had been hesitant for years to promote his radical and controversial ideas), Osiander penned an unsigned introduction that accompanied *De revolutionibus'* first printing.

Osiander's introduction began by saying, "Since the newness of the hypotheses of this work—which sets the earth in motion and puts an immovable sun at the centre of the universe—has already received a great deal of publicity, I have no doubt that certain of the savants have taken grave offense and think it wrong to raise any disturbance among liberal disciplines which have had the right set-up for a long time now."[3]

Osiander argued that all Copernicus had done was to study the celestial motions and then work out whatever "causes or hypotheses"[4] he theorized could explain those motions. However, wrote Osiander, "it is not necessary that these hypotheses should be true, or even probably; but it is enough if they provide a calculus which fits the observations."[5] Copernicus' ideas, he claimed, were not presented to "persuade anyone of their truth but only in order that they may provide a correct basis for calculation."[6]

Finally, Osiander ended the introduction: "And as far as hypotheses go, let no one expect anything in the way of certainty from astronomy, since astronomy can offer us nothing certain, lest, if anyone take as true that which has been constructed for another use, he [will] go away from this discipline a bigger fool than when he came to it. Farewell."[7]

Osiander's message was, essentially: *Look, Copernicus isn't saying that the earth, really, actually, goes around the sun. No, he has created a hypothetical model only, one that (to use a phrase from the twentieth century) is "empirically adequate."*[8] *That is, his model merely presents another way to explain what we see. Copernicus is simply saying: "Suppose we were to pretend that the earth went around the sun; look at how this hypothesis could be used in a way that fits the observations. This book wasn't written to persuade anyone of the truth of the hypothesis it presents; no, the hypothesis is a mere tool to help describe the revolution of the moving bodies in the sky."*

The Copernican preface

Whether Osiander's introduction helped put Copernicus in the grave, we don't know. We do know, however, that the book's preface, written by Copernicus himself, contradicted Osiander's introduction, which immediately preceded it. Writing to Pope Paul III, to whom he dedicated the book, Copernicus made clear his intentions—and they weren't what Osiander said.

Because, Copernicus wrote, "I attribute certain motions to the terrestrial globe," he expected to have "me and my opinion hooted off the stage."[9] (Has anything changed in five hundred years?) He said if he were to assert that the earth moves, he knew "how absurd this 'lecture' would be held by those who know that the opinion that the Earth rests immovable in the middle of the heavens as if their centre had been confirmed by the judgments of many ages."[10]

Nevertheless, through the encouragement of friends, Copernicus decided to "bring to light my commentaries written to demonstrate the Earth's movement,"[11] despite the inevitable controversy.

"But perhaps Your Holiness will not be so much surprised at my giving the results of my nocturnal study to the light—after having taken such care in working them out that I did not hesitate to put in writing my conceptions as to the movement of the Earth—as you will be eager to hear from me what came into my mind that in opposition to the general opinion of mathematicians and almost in opposition to common sense I should dare to imagine some movement of the Earth."[12]

"And so," he wrote to the pope, "having laid down the movements which I attribute to the Earth farther on in the work, I finally discovered by the help of long and numerous observations that if the movements of the other wandering stars are correlated with the circular movement of the Earth, and if the movements are computed in accordance with the revolution of each planet, not only do all their phenomena follow from that but also this correlation binds together so closely the order and magnitudes of all the planets and of their spheres or orbital circles and the heavens themselves that nothing can be shifted around in any part of them without disrupting the remaining parts and the universe as a whole."[13]

The quantum fields of Fido

Contrary to Osiander's introduction, *De revolutionibus* was not a hypothetical model. Copernicus wasn't positing a *what if* or a *suppose that* situation. He was attempting to prove what he believed to be actualities: that the earth really was moving around the sun in perfect circles, and that the sun really did sit still in the center of the universe. And it was, Copernicus argued, because of these actualities, these facts, that we see the motions in the sky as we do.[14] This system, Copernicus claimed, fits the phenomena so well "that nothing can be shifted around in any part of them without disrupting the remaining parts and the universe as a whole."

Osiander's attempt to blunt Copernicus' assault on dogmatic Aristotelianism was a pragmatic and political move. He was trying to protect his friend from the backlash that such a bold challenge to the prevailing scientific and religious consensus would bring. He was employing philosophy in an attempt to diffuse what would have (as the Galileo trial later showed) degenerated into a criminal and ecclesiological issue.

Nevertheless, the story of Osiander's introduction to *De revolutionibus* and Copernicus' intentions for his book reveals what continues to be an unresolved question about the limits of scientific truth. And that question returns us to the previous chapter, which dealt with the gap between what we perceive and what really is out there *regardless of how we perceive it* (or even if we can perceive it)—a gap that science has, in some cases, only widened.

For instance, science has shown us the vast gap between how a dog appears to our senses and what scientists now think the beast is really made of—atomic and subatomic particles manifested as different expressions of quantum fields, all of which are inaccessible to our senses. Whatever Fido would look like if we could see him as subatomic particles or quantum fields (impossible), he would look nothing as he appears to our eyes now. Though Fido can be analyzed, scientifically, at a number of levels—biological, chemical, atomic, subatomic, quantum—which level reveals the "truth" about him, especially when we reach levels where we can't see what we are theorizing about?

Or, is everything that science says to us about Fido nothing but theoretical models, anyway? As Osiander said about Copernicus' work, does science give us only mere helpful descriptions of what's out there—or, at least how what's out there appears to our senses—that enable us, as in the case of Fido, to interact with the beast at levels where, for instance, we can treat his ringworm?

As quoted in chapter 3, "One of the most lively and persistent debates in twentieth century philosophy of science is that between empiricists and realists concerning the status of scientific theories. Are scientific theories to be understood as offering (or at least intending to offer) a true account of the world?

And if we accept scientific theories as true, should we believe that the entities they appear to postulate really exist?"[15]

Again, these questions seem redundant, like asking if lifeguards should know how to swim or if airplanes should fly. Of course scientific theories should be understood as giving a "true account of the world." Isn't that what science is about? When scientists posit a theory, isn't that theory stating what the scientists believe is really happening? Also, when science talks about certain entities in its theories, why question if those entities exist? How could the theory be correct if the entities didn't actually exist?

When science, for instance, tells us that millions of years ago a primeval pre-lobster life-form outwitted its competitors through random mutation, natural selection, and survival of the fittest to eventually evolve into the lobster we see today, the scientist means just that: a real primeval pre-lobster had, through random mutation, natural selection, and survival of the fittest really evolved into today's lobster with real shells, claws, eyes, the whole shebang. It's not just a helpful or symbolic model; it's what, they claim, really happened.

Of course, no scientist has ever observed a primeval pre-lobster, though some might claim to have observed a pre-lobster fossil, or a whole host of other scientific ideas, concepts, and entities, some of which are now thought never to have existed to begin with. Observable or not, some of these entities have been (and some still are) promoted as existing. After all, why would scientists posit entities in a theory if they didn't believe that the entities were real?

Good—but not true

Nevertheless, these questions about the truth of theories or the existence of postulated entities continue. Scientific "realists" argue that science does give us, if not an absolute, true account of the world, then at least an approximate one. Realists argue that, though resting on experience, science goes deeper than experience to the truth about reality itself, a reality that exists independently of human beings and their contingent limitations. Science must be discovering what's really out there, which is why realism, said Hilary Putnam, is "the only philosophy of science that does not make the success of science a miracle."[16]

In contrast, scientific "empiricists" (we should know that word) argue that science gives us only our own subjective experiences of how the world appears to us and that it never gets to the real world, the truth itself. The most science can do is explain, even somewhat superficially, why observable things appear as they do. The senses, wrote Aristotle, "do not tell us the 'why' of anything"[17] but are, instead, only descriptive. Meanwhile, empiricists often remain agnostic about the existence of many of the "unobservable"[18] entities that science posits. "As an empiricist," wrote W. V. Quine, "I continue to think of the conceptual scheme of science as a tool, ultimately, for predicting future experience in the light of past experience. Physical objects are conceptually imported into the situation as convenient intermediaries—not by definition in terms of experience, but simply as irreducible posits comparable, epistemologically, to the gods of Homer."[19]

The point here isn't to explore the convoluted, word-peeling philosophical and intellectual slugfest between realists and empiricists, especially over the existence of entities deemed as unobservable. Each side rolls out arguments and examples to buttress its position while pummeling opponents. The point, instead, is this: If philosophers can't agree whether science is giving us "a true account of the world" or if the entities it posits in its theories even exist, then why do so many people, including Christians, lie down and play dead before almost every scientific declaration, especially about hypothetical events that supposedly occurred millions of years ago, as if what science says must be true, because science is the most trustworthy and reliable form of knowledge?

The truth about what science does is nowhere near so simple—the controversy between scientific realists and scientific empiricists is one of many examples. It's pretty heavy when this brooding question hovers over all science. The question isn't just about whether theory X is true or not (even the concept of what it means to be "true" in science is, also, disputed). No, the bigger question lingers in the background: Can we ever know *for certain* if any theory—theory X, or Y, or Z, or 345bbtt3q, or any theory—is true?[20]

"All of us," wrote Larry Laudan, "would like realism to be true; we would like to think that science works because it has got a grip on how things really are. But such claims have yet to be made out."[21]

What? Science—which split the atom, decoded the genome, and detected the Higgs boson—doesn't have a "grip on how things really are"? Why would as renowned a thinker as Larry Laudan say that? Whether he's right or wrong, the existence of the question implies, if nothing else, that science isn't as straightforward and objective as we plebes believe.

Sean Carroll quoted Niels Bohr, one of the twentieth century's great physicists, regarding Bohr's views of reality, especially at the quantum realm: "There is no quantum world. There is only an abstract physical description. It is wrong to think that the task of physics is to find out how nature *is*. Physics concerns what we can *say* about nature."[22]

It's not just in the elusive, bizarre world of quantum reality that we face crippling limits about what science does or even can do theoretically.

"The most common misunderstanding about science," wrote physicist Neil Gershenfeld, "is that scientists seek and find truth. They don't—they make and test models."[23]

A vast conceptual divide exists, does it not, between finding out what nature really is as opposed to simply finding ways to talk about it or model it? Who cares, one could argue, what we can say about reality or what models we make to describe it? What matters, one would think, is finding out what's really out there. Unfortunately, that's not so easy; it may even be impossible.

This debate is crucial. When evolutionists (theistic, atheistic, agnostic, whatever version) espouse their theories, they are not talking mere models or modes of communication. When they declare that we evolved over billions of years of random mutation and natural selection, they mean just that: We evolved over billions of years of random mutation and natural selection. Even when admitting that many facets of the process remain unknown, they still take the process literally, as bona fide truth, not as a hypothetical model that represents a deeper reality that could be much different from the biological processes espoused.

One of the last century's most influential philosophers of science, Bas C. van Fraassen, wrote in *The Scientific Image* that scientific "theories need not be true to be good."[24]

How can a theory be "good," but not true? Again, isn't the whole point of a scientific theory to be true?

As the first chapter in this book showed, NASA scientists employed a scientific theory, Newton's law of gravitation, in order to get the crippled Apollo 13 spacecraft back to terra firma. In that sense, the theory was "good." Using it, scientists made predictions about what events would occur in the real world, and sure enough, those predicted events occurred just as the theory predicted.

Yet, besides giving accurate descriptions regarding the gravitational pull between objects in the universe, how true was the theory, or was it true at all? Remember, Newton had no idea what causes this pull between objects in the universe. Second, he had founded his theory on false assumptions about the most basic aspects of the physical world—space and time. And, finally, much of his theory was superseded or even overturned by Albert Einstein.

This is truth? But even if it weren't, the theory has borne *practical* fruit, which makes it "good." Thus Van Fraassen could argue that "the aim of science can well be served without giving such a literally true story, and acceptance of a theory may properly involve something less (or other) than belief that it is true."[25]

What?

Our minds have not been trained to think that a scientific theory can be "good" without being "true." What good is a false theory? We tend to equate scientific success—explanation, accurate predictions, workable technology, and so on—with *truth*. When events, based on a theory, happen as predicted by the theory, we therefore reason that the theory must be a true and accurate description of the real world. Otherwise, how could the predictions have been foreseen? When devices conceived, designed, and built based on a theory work as the theory said they would, we believe the theory must be a true depiction of the world. Otherwise, how could the devices have worked?

These are reasonable assumptions that could even, at times, be the case. But accurate predictions or even workable technologies don't guarantee the truth of the theory behind the predictions or the technologies. And this point is crucial for Christians to understand, especially as they confront the prevailing scientific consensus of our era—the neo-Darwinian synthesis and its full-frontal assault on the most foundational and basic Christian belief: Creation.

Ptolemy's cosmos

As we have already seen, for much of recorded Western history, the best and brightest, the smartest and most educated, the wined and dined intellectual movers and shakers believed in Aristotle's cosmos in one form or another—a stationary earth in the center of the universe, around which the sun, moon, and stars orbited in perfect circular motions at constant speeds. For decades after the publication of *De revolutionibus* in 1543, the idea of an orbiting and revolving earth was deemed so contrary, not only to everyday experience but to the received wisdom (scientific and ecclesiological) of the ages, that most educated people paid it little heed.

And why should they have heeded it? Besides the reasons for belief in the old view, in the second century A.D. Claudius Ptolemy had worked out a very detailed and complex exposition of the sun-centric model. For *twelve centuries* his system reigned as the prevailing scientific consensus about cosmology (pretty amazing when you think that the present prevailing scientific consensus about origins, the neo-Darwinian synthesis, is less than one hundred years old). Working with what was bequeathed to him from Aristotle and thinkers even before Aristotle—such as the idea that the planets orbit the earth in perfect circles and at constant speeds—Ptolemy wrote the *Almagest* (Greatest), called in the twentieth century "the first systematic mathematical treatise to give a *complete*, *detailed*, and *quantitative* account of all the celestial motions."[26]

However (and here's an incredible point revealing just how powerful assumptions and preconceptions are, even in science), Aristotle knew, as did Ptolemy, that when you look up in the night sky, the planets and stars certainly don't seem to move around the earth in circular paths at constant speeds. The appearances didn't appear to match the theory. Some of the celestial objects in the sky appear to stop, to go backward, and then to go forward again, motions hard to square with the assumption that all these bodies were booking through the heavens in a circular motion at a constant speed around an immobile earth.

Ptolemy's predecessors, Ptolemy himself, and those who followed him had conjured up all sorts of geometrical and mathematical add-ons to make the data fit the model—such as epicycles (the idea that, along with circling the earth, many of these bodies also went in much smaller circles themselves, kind of like circles within circles). If Ptolemy assumed that the prevailing theory had to be right, because so much evidence pointed to it (and, to some degree, it did), then he had to make the phenomena fit the theory.

"Recall the epicycles, the imaginary circles that Ptolemy used and formalized around A.D. 150 to describe the motions of planets," wrote physicists Adam Frank and Marcelo Gleiser. "Although Ptolemy had no evidence for their existence, epicycles successfully explained what the ancients could see in the night sky, so they were accepted as real. But they were eventually shown to be a fiction, more than 1,500 years later. Are superstrings and the multiverse, painstakingly theorized by hundreds of brilliant scientists, anything more than modern-day epicycles?"[27]

Hundreds of brilliant scientists painstakingly theorizing, even writing PhD theses, about what might not exist? Not an idea that has reached the public consciousness about science, to be sure. And if these writers have such concerns about experimental science, science that can be done today in the lab with tangible, real things—from rocks to sea horses—one can only imagine what equivalents to "modern-day epicycles" are conjured up to explain events supposedly occurring millions, even billions, of years ago about objects that don't exist now.

In other words (and this practice is much more common in science than most people realize), instead of working from what he saw, and then devising a theory based on what he saw, Ptolemy—assuming the theory to be true—interpreted what he saw through the lens of the theory that he already believed. He didn't look up at the sky, see what was happening, and then devise his model. No, he looked up and viewed the sky only through his model, which is why he saw what he did.

Some argue that scientists can't even know what data to look at without first having a theory that guides them in what data to look for and then, of course, in how to interpret that data once they find it. Assuming circular motions at constant speed around an immovable earth,[28] Ptolemy worked out the math and science to make the bodies in the sky fit the theory as much as he could.

And the thing is—it worked! If you wanted to sail a ship from Lisbon to Venice, you could use the Ptolemaic system to guide your voyage. If you wanted to predict the motion of Venus, you could do it using this theory—and successfully too.

This means, then, that a theory based on an immovable earth (false), sitting at the center of the universe (false), orbited by all the bodies in the sky (false), in perfect circles (false) at constant speeds (false), nevertheless enabled people to make accurate predictions and even bore tangible fruit, such as guiding ships at sea. A scientific theory about as accurate as flat-earth geography still enabled people to make accurate predictions and to navigate land and seas—and to do so from the time of Aristotle up through the age of Copernicus and beyond.

No wonder "theories need not be true to be good."[29]

But it works!

This point is important for those concerned with the challenges that the speculative theories of science about origins present to biblical faith. Besides the phrase *It's science!* one also hears the phrase *But the science works!* The implication is that, because the science works then the theory behind that science must be true. For instance, according to this common line of thinking, if some macroevolutionary concept is based on, or even related to, a scientific theory that works, then that evolutionary concept is likely to be correct.

Owen Gingerich, an astronomer and a Christian, criticized Christians who don't accept the science behind the theory of evolution: "Folks who take in stride," he wrote, "the modern technology of cell phones, laser scanners, airplanes, and atomic bombs nevertheless show reluctance to accept the implications of the science that lies behind these awesome inventions of the past century."[30]

Maybe, or maybe they realize that technology doesn't mean that all the implications of a theory are correct. Plus, one could humbly ask: What is the link between a cell phone working and, for instance, the claim that birds evolved from small carnivorous dinosaurs called theropods?

Yes, a theory that works—in that it allows for accurate predictions or can be used to create successful technology—is more likely to be "true" than would be a theory that doesn't lead to successful predictions or workable technology. But "more likely" to be true doesn't mean that it is. It's more likely that ancient Babylonian astrological charts, as opposed to aliens from Pluto, guided Christopher Columbus on his voyage to the New World. But it's still not likely that Babylonian astrology got him there.

"When I walk across the street," wrote Peter Achinstein, "I increase the probability that I will be hit by a 2001 Cadillac, but the fact that I am walking across the street is not evidence that I will be hit by a 2001 Cadillac. When Michael Phelps goes swimming he increases the probability that he will drown, but the fact that he is swimming is not evidence that he will drown."[31]

Despite the flat-out falsity of the geocentric theory, it reigned as the prevailing scientific-mathematical consensus for about two thousand years (give or take a century or two), and it was believed and accepted by the world's most educated and smartest people for just about as long. History has other examples of scientific theories (which came with lots of empirical and/or logical evidence to back them) that bore fruit or made accurate predictions, and that were accepted by the best and the brightest, even though they are now believed to be wrong.

Stephen Goldman, a professor of philosophy and history at Lehigh University, wrote that many scientific theories reaping great technological rewards in the 1800s were, by the 1900s, being overturned. "Science was being productive for society based on theories that," wrote Goldman, "the scientists themselves were in the process of disproving as knowledge."[32] What an irony. They're making a widget based on a certain theory only to be told, *Oh, by the way, the theory you have used to make that widget is, we now believe, not an accurate reflection of reality.*

"An electrician," wrote David Lindberg, "with only the most rudimentary knowledge of electrical theory can successfully wire a house. It is possible to differentiate between poisonous and therapeutic herbs without possessing any biochemical knowledge that would explain poisonous or therapeutic properties. The point is simply that practical rules of thumb can be effectively employed even in the face of total ignorance of the theoretical principles that lie behind them. You can have 'know-how' without theoretical knowledge."[33] Or you can have "know-how" even with wrong theoretical "knowledge."

In the seventeenth and eighteenth centuries, debate ensued among researchers over the nature of heat. Some argued that heat was the escape of a mysterious fluid, a weightless substance called "caloric." According to that model, everything had caloric in it, and when an object was hot the heat was simply caloric escaping from the object. The other theory was that heat was the motion of tiny particles that made up whatever element was being heated, and the hotter something became the faster the particles were moving. Heat was, merely, the movement of these particles.

Goldman lectured about a book, *The Analytical Theory of Heat*,[34] published in 1822, by Frenchman Joseph Fourier. Coming out amid this debate over the nature of heat, Fourier's book was a detailed mathematical treatise describing the flow of heat and how it behaves. However, Fourier made a startling announcement. Goldman paraphrased the essence of what he called "Fourier's Move" like this: "Who cares what heat is? That's not a scientific question at all. It's a metaphysical question. My equations tell you how heat behaves. . . . What else do you want from a theory of heat? . . . I don't want to be involved in the ontological questions of what heat is. I'm not giving you a picture of reality.

I'm giving you a picture that describes heat behaviorally."[35]

Fourier wanted to separate the fact that a theory worked (it was "good" in that it provided some form of description, made accurate predictions, and even led to technology) from the question about how accurately, if at all, the theory reflected the real world (it was "true").

And even today, almost two centuries later, that distinction remains. Paul Feyerabend argued that empiricism can function "only if you are prepared to work with many alternative theories rather than with a single point of view and 'experience.' The plurality of theories must not be regarded as a preliminary stage of knowledge which will at some time in the future be replaced by the One True Theory. Theoretical pluralism is assumed to be an *essential feature* of all knowledge that claims to be objective."[36]

In other words, forget trying to know which is the "One True Theory." Feyerabend seems to be saying that even if there is one true theory, we will never know it for sure, anyway.

General relativity versus quantum mechanics

One powerful example from contemporary science helps illustrate that a scientific theory could be good but not true.

General relativity and quantum mechanics are the two foundational pillars of modern physics. General relativity, to quote Stephen Hawking, is about "the force of gravity and the large-scale structure of the universe, that is, the structure on scales from only a few miles to as large as a million million million million (1 with twenty-four zeros after it) miles, the size of the observable universe. Quantum mechanics, on the other hand, deals with phenomena on extremely small scales, such as a millionth of a millionth of an inch."[37] In other words, the two theories cover just about all the *known* material world, the world of scientific discovery.

More so, the two theories are some of the most "successful" scientific theories ever. Both have been experimentally confirmed with incredible accuracy. Quantum mechanics can make predictions with the precision of a human hair compared to the length of the continental United States. Besides that, both (especially quantum mechanics) have borne technological fruit. Transistors, computers, lasers, Blu-ray players, and digital TVs use quantum mechanics; and the GPS on cell phones and cars and submarines uses general relativity. If ever two theories would qualify as "good," it would be general relativity and quantum mechanics.

However, one glitch persists that has baffled physicists for decades. "Through years of research," wrote physicist Brian Greene, "physicists have experimentally confirmed to almost unimaginable accuracy virtually all predictions made by each of these theories. But these same theoretical tools inexorably lead to another disturbing conclusion: As they are currently formulated, general relativity and quantum mechanics *cannot both be right*. The two theories underlying the tremendous progress of physics during the last hundred years— progress that has explained the expansion of the heavens and the fundamental structure of matter—are mutually incompatible."[38]

Or, as Stephen Hawking said concerning general relativity and quantum mechanics: "Unfortunately, . . . these two theories are known to be inconsistent with each other—they cannot both be correct."[39]

Two incredibly successful theories, two "good" theories, but both can't be correct? It would be like saying that our theories about the motion of the earth contradict our theories about the circulation of the blood in a human body. How could that be? It can be only because scientists' understanding of one of the theories, or both, is flawed. And yet, regardless of what is missing or misinterpreted in either one or both theories, both have powerful predictive power, and both are used to create technology.

In other words, the science works! And it works well enough for us to get practical benefit from it. (Of course, so did Aristotle's and Newton's science as well.) Yet the practical benefits from science prove only that we understand the science enough to, well, get practical benefits from it. Those gains prove nothing certain about the correctness of the science itself. A theory can make great predictions and produce fruitful technology, yet not be an accurate depiction of reality. In other words, no matter how "good" the theory, it might not be "true."[40] Hilary Putnam, in the context of cosmology, wrote that Nobel Prize–winning scientist "Steven Weinberg now appears to urge that sometimes it is more convenient to use one theory, and sometimes it is more convenient to use another, and there is no reason to ask which is really true."[41]

Some argue—contrary to what's commonly believed—that scientists can never know for certain if a scientific theory is true, regardless of how "good" or successful that theory is. Whether or not this notion is correct (as the next chapter explores), the mere existence of the question should arouse skepticism about hypothetical events a hypothetical three to four billion years ago—events that from this side of such a vast chronological divide can be merely speculated about, and then only by extrapolating backward from the present to a time whose existence is also an assumption.

1. See chap. 1.
2. *Crime of Galileo*.
3. Copernicus, *Revolutions of Heavenly Spheres*, 3.

4. Ibid.

5. Ibid.

6. Ibid., 4.

7. Ibid.

8. Van Fraassen, *Scientific Image*, 4.

9. Copernicus, *Revolutions of Heavenly Spheres*, 4.

10. Ibid.

11. Ibid.

12. Ibid., 5.

13. Ibid., 6.

14. We know today, however, that some of these "actualities," these "facts" (such as the perfect circular orbits of the planets), are not actually facts.

15. Curd and Cover, *Philosophy of Science*, 1049.

16. Hilary Putnam, *Philosophy in an Age of Science: Physics, Mathematics, and Skepticism*, eds. Mario De Caro and David Macarthur (Cambridge, MA: Harvard University Press, 2012), 55.

17. Aristotle, *Metaphysics*, book 1, part 1, para. 5.

18. A great deal of debate exists over the distinction between "observable" and "unobservable" entities, with some arguing that it's a false dichotomy, because what is presently unobservable to us might not be later or could be observable to beings with sensory devices different from ours.

19. W. V. Quine, "Two Dogmas of Empiricism," *Philosophical Review* 60, no. 1 (January 1951): 41. The rest of the quote is worth reading too: "Let me interject that for my part I do, qua lay physicist, believe in physical objects and not in Homer's gods; and I consider it a scientific error to believe otherwise. But in point of epistemological footing the physical objects and the gods differ only in degree and not in kind. Both sorts of entities enter our conception only as cultural posits. The myth of physical objects is epistemologically superior to most in that it has proved more efficacious than other myths as a device for working a manageable structure into the flux of experience."

20. This question is another version of what we looked at in chapter 3, regarding epistemology, which is not about whether certain specific things that one believes in actually exist but, rather, what does it mean to say that something is true. The question between realism and empiricism is, at the core, a question of epistemology—which means that, ultimately, it's unanswerable.

21. Larry Laudan, "A Confutation of Convergent Realism," *Philosophy of Science* 48, no. 1 (March 1981): 48.

22. Quoted in Sean Carroll, *The Big Picture: On the Origins of Life, Meaning, and the Universe Itself* (New York: Dutton, 2016), 167 (italics in the original).

23. Neil Gershenfeld, "Truth Is a Model," Edge, https://www.edge.org/response-detail/10395.

24. Van Fraassen, *Scientific Image*, 10.

25. Ibid., 9.

26. Kuhn, *Copernican Revolution*, 73 (italics in the original).

27. Adam Frank and Marcelo Gleiser, "A Crisis at the Edge of Physics," *New York Times*, June 5, 2015, https://www.nytimes.com/2015/06/07/opinion/a-crisis-at-the-edge-of-physics.html?mcubz=0.

28. This idea was so ingrained that Copernicus and, later, Galileo couldn't shake the idea of circular motion at constant speed. Even Kepler, who eventually rejected both, found the idea of noncircular motion abhorrent and worked very hard, though unsuccessfully, to retain noncircular motion.

29. To draw an analogy: a man is hiding three Jewish children in his basement during the Holocaust. The Gestapo appear at the door and ask, "Are you hiding Jews in here? People said that

they heard the sound of scurrying feet coming from your basement and thought you were hiding people there." The man denies it, saying the sound coming from the basement was, not from children, but from his dogs. The Gestapo leave, and the children's lives are saved. What the man accomplished, in terms of saving innocent lives, was "good." But how he did it wasn't "true."

30. Owen Gingerich, *God's Universe* (Cambridge, MA: Belknap Press of Harvard University Press, 2006), 11.

31. Peter Achinstein, *Evidence, Explanation, and Realism: Essays in Philosophy of Science* (Oxford: Oxford University Press, 2010), 9.

32. Steven L. Goldman, *Science Wars: What Scientists Know and How They Know It* (Chantilly, VA: Teaching Company, 2006), part 2, p. 11.

33. Lindberg, *Beginnings of Western Science*, 4.

34. Joseph Fourier, *The Analytical Theory of Heat*, trans. Alexander Freeman (Cambridge, UK: Cambridge University Press, 1878).

35. Goldman, *Science Wars*, part 1, pp. 141, 142.

36. Paul K. Feyerabend, *Knowledge, Science, and Relativism*, Philosophical Papers, vol. 3, ed. John Preston (Cambridge, UK: Cambridge University Press, 1999), 80 (italics in the original).

37. Stephen W. Hawking, *A Brief History of Time* (New York: Bantam Books, 1998), 12.

38. Brian Greene, *The Elegant Universe: Superstrings, Hidden Dimensions, and the Quest for the Ultimate Theory* (New York: W. W. Norton, 2003), 3 (italics in the original).

39. Hawking, *Brief History of Time*, 12.

40. Gingerich makes the mistake of assuming that just because technology works, the science behind it must be correct, even though that is not necessarily the case. (See quote earlier in this chapter.)

41. Putnam, *Philosophy in an Age of Science*, 46.

CHAPTER 5

SCIENCE IN A SWAMP

A mid all the 2010 World Cup hype, one sensation caught the world's attention: Paul the octopus, "the eight-armed oracle" at the Oberhausen Sea Life Center in Germany. This sea critter "predicted" eight out of eight World Cup matches, including Spain's victory in the final.[1]

Before a game, two boxes, with a mussel in each, were placed in Paul's tank. One box bore one team's flag, the other box the other team's flag. Paul, the "psychic cephalopod," chose the box with the flag of the team that did, eventually, win—eight out of eight times, a 100 percent success rate!

Of course, had Paul gotten it right only one out of one try, or even two out of two, he would have still had a perfect score. Had he done it forty-seven out of fifty times, Paul would have been even more impressive, even though he'd be below 100 percent, which shows just how tricky statistics can be. After all, whom would you rather trust: someone that gets it right one out of one time (100 percent) or forty-seven out of fifty (only 94 percent)?

The octopus's predictions, however, lead to an important concept for understanding the relationship between faith and science, especially when, like Paul, scientific theories make accurate predictions.

Suppose scientists in a research lab, flush with cash by, say, big pharma or big tobacco, propose a scientific theory. According to theory X, object Y under certain circumstances will always turn green. That is, if theory X is correct, Y under these circumstances will turn green. It must, at least according to the theory.

Scientists test theory X again and again, and Y not only turns green under the specified circumstances, but it does so (like Paul's predictions) 100 percent of the time. Other labs do the same experiment, based on the same theory, under the same circumstances, and all come up with the same results. Theory X has just been proven correct, right?

Not necessarily, and maybe not even at all, another reason why people shouldn't get caught in the illusion that just because science has "proved" something it must be true.

Personal testimony

But, first, a personal story.

Born in 1955, I grew up in a secular Jewish home in Miami Beach. For my family, the Jewish holidays could have been boiled down to this mantra: *They tried to kill us; they failed—let's eat!*

My secular education paralleled my secular Jewish upbringing. I remember, in the fifth grade, in public school in 1965, a science book that taught us the ages of the earth. To this day I remember the epochs: Azoic, Archeozoic, Proterozoic, Paleozoic, Mesozoic, and Cenozoic.

The book also presented a drawing that I remember like this (or something similar). It began with a shallow pool. Above it was a single-cell life-form; then above that, a jellyfish; above that, a fish; then a reptile; then an apelike creature, followed by a protohuman, and, finally, *Homo sapiens*. A line was drawn, starting from the shallow pool up through various stages until stopping at the *Homo sapiens*. The idea, of course, being that this diagram represented the story of human evolutionary origins.

Jump ahead four years, to Mrs. Rubin's ninth-grade biology class at Nautilus Junior High in Miami Beach. I thought I was hot stuff because I knew the meaning of the phrase *ontogeny recapitulates phylogeny*. This phrase, Mrs. Rubin explained, was the idea that the stages of an embryo echo our long evolutionary history. That is, "gills" could be seen on the developing fetus, one example of a primal echo from the epoch when our ancestors were fish.

Never mind that this idea, made popular through drawings etched by an early Darwinian paladin named Ernst Haeckel, had been debunked back in the late 1800s, when Haeckel first faked the sketches—ontogeny recapitulates phylogeny was still being taught in public school in the 1960s and beyond. Even a staunch evolutionist such as Stephen Jay Gould had railed against the continued promotion of what had long been known as a fraud. "But Gould, himself one of evolution's most prominent proponents," wrote Larry Caldwell, "had nonetheless exposed an undeniable and incredibly revealing historical fact: In 2000, many proponents of Darwin's theory were using the same known fraudulent drawings and claims to sell evolution to school children that Darwin's leading proponent had used to sell Darwin's theory to the general public in 1900."[2]

Jump ahead to the mid-1970s and the University of Florida in Gainesville. I took an anthropology course, and though today nothing in particular stands out, I do remember that Darwinism formed the background for all that we had been taught.

Then, in the fall of 1979, just before my twenty-fourth birthday, I had a born-again experience. Overnight (almost literally), I went from being an agnostic to being a believer in Jesus as the Messiah.[3] In those early days, I had no concept of sin, much less of any nuanced knowledge of New Testament soteriology or eschatology. I knew only that I had become a new person in Christ.

Overnight, the geometry of reality had changed for me. It was as if points and lines and space didn't really do all that I had been told that they did or as if all the axioms, postulates, and theorems I had been taught were overturned. The world that I walked in now seemed different from what it had been before. Reality had fleshed itself out as so much deeper, broader, and more multi-faceted than the parochial, materialistic worldview that I had been fed all but intravenously since kindergarten.

It was as if the only reality that I had known, or thought even existed, had been shown to me through one peephole alone. Not that I could now see all that was beyond the peephole—of course not. Instead, I realized for the first time that reality existed beyond what the single peephole could ever reveal.[4]

In one area I immediately sensed an irreconcilable disconnect between the old and the new. Without knowing the deeper issues and all the futile attempts to harmonize them, I saw a clash between my belief in evolution and my born-again faith in Jesus. I sensed then that they both couldn't be right. I harangued the Christians whom I had first met about my struggle with this contradiction. They didn't seem bothered by the issue, but they finally gave me a book on creationism. I'm not sure of the title, the author, or if the book was any good (let's face it, some books promoting creationism can be as speculative as those promoting evolution).

As I read it, though, I had a life-changing revelation (one of many at that time); another vista of reality opened before me. From that fifth-grade textbook right up through college and beyond, I had been shown the world through a Darwinian framework only. I had worn only one pair of glasses, because that was the only pair I had been given, the only pair that I was led to believe even existed. But now everything had changed—once I took off the glasses and put on another pair.

No one is going to deny the existence of fossils from creatures now extinct. The bones, the fossils, as evidence, are there. Yet for the first time in my life I was presented with *another way to look at the evidence, another way to interpret it.* Until then, not only had I never been shown any other way; I had never been presented with the idea that any other way, or other ways, existed.

The fossils don't say, *Created sixty million years ago in the early Cenozoic era,* do they? Nor do they come inscribed with the words, *Evolved from a Haik-ouichthys 550 million years ago.* These are *interpretations* based on a web of assumptions and speculations, none of which could be described as universal, necessary, and certain. In other words, not only was the evolutionary science with which I had been indoctrinated all my life nowhere near as certain as it had been presented; I now believed it to be wrong.

Besides astonishment, I felt anger. Not so much because I had been taught Darwinism. After all, if the door is closed by default to anything supernatural (a philosophical, not a scientific, assumption), what else would I have been taught other than the Aristotelianism of our time? I was angry, instead, at the closed-minded, dogmatic manner in which it had been presented to me—an attitude not justified by something as speculative as evolution.

Underdetermination of theory by evidence

Little did I know that the existence of alternative explanations represented a weakness in the whole scientific enterprise itself, at least when science claims to reveal truth about the real world. Again, some argue that science only describes what things in the real world do, but cannot explain *why* they do it; others argue that science can tell us about how the world appears to us only through our biological senses (different biology, different senses, different world), but never about the real world itself. Whatever one thinks of these positions, it's logical and reasonable to assume that science does reveal *some* "truth" about the real world, limited and contingent as those "truths" might be.

Yet, however logical and reasonable this realist view might be, it faces a challenge that still has not been solved.

Let's go back to the imaginary laboratory funded by big pharma and its experiments seeking to prove theory X. Again, theory X states that under certain conditions Y will turn green. As we saw, in every instance Y did turn green, just as theory X predicted. And it did so 100 percent of the time. Thus, theory X must be true, right?

Not necessarily. Y could turn green for reasons that have nothing to do with theory X. Maybe someone proposed theory R, which makes the same predictions as theory X and gets the same results. Or others propose theory W or theory G, each one making the same predictions, and each one getting the same results as theory X—even if theories R, G, W, and X contradict one another.

How could this be?

Take the statement "If A is true, then B is true." If A is true, then B must be as well. That's deduction, pure and simple. It means that if my premise (A) is true, then my conclusion (B) must be too. The conclusion must logically flow from the premise. Someone says (A) "If it is raining," then (B) "the picnic table in the backyard will get wet." If this statement is valid, then (A) when it rains, (B) the picnic table must get wet.

However, if we take the same statement, "If A is true, then B is true," and B turns out to be true, that doesn't mean that A is. B could be true for reasons that have nothing to do with A.

(A), "If it is raining," then (B) "the picnic table in the backyard will get wet." Suppose B is true; the picnic table is wet. But maybe it is wet because the neighbor accidentally sprayed the table while watering plants. Or perhaps some kids were playing on the picnic table and spilled water on it. Or an airplane, putting out a nearby forest fire, dumped water on the picnic table instead of the fire. Or a workman, digging in the backyard, hit a waterline and the water shot up onto the table. Or aliens from Pluto dropped water on it from a flying saucer. Or maybe it's wet for reasons that no one knows. An infinite number of potential explanations, besides A, could explain B.

Imaginary scientist Ziggy Bowie, funded by an organization seeking evidence for life elsewhere in the universe, proposes a theory: invisible spiders from Mars are pushing everything on earth toward the ground. Dr. Bowie does all sorts of experiments and makes all sorts of observation in nature. Again and again his theory is confirmed by both experiment and observation. He throws a rock in the air, and it falls to the ground. Here's evidence that corroborates his theory. He watches skydivers jump from an airplane and fall to the ground. Here is even more evidence that corroborates his theory. He watches rain fall to the ground. More corroboration. He fires a projectile in the air, and it falls to the ground. More evidence, still. No question, his theory about invisible spiders from Mars is corroborated by experiment and empirical data. Thus, what could one say other than that Dr. Bowie has a lot of evidence for his theory, right?

Not necessarily (obviously). Other theories make the same predictions citing different causes. Aristotle, whose view held sway among the best and brightest for 1,800 years, argued that objects fall toward the earth because by nature they love the earth and want to be near it. After all, the earth is the center of the universe, an idea confirmed by the fact that everything falls toward it. Einstein's general theory of relativity theorizes that objects fall because mass bends space and time, and thus objects fall because of the curvature of space-time. Thus the evidence confirms his theory, as it did Dr. Bowie's and Aristotle's. Numerous other scientists could have a host of other theories about gravity (other theories do exist), each with good reasons for them, including observational and experimental corroboration.

Hence, "for any finite body of evidence, there are indefinitely many mutually contradictory theories, each of which logically entails the evidence."[5] *Indefinitely many theories, even contradictory theories that fit the evidence?* How can we know, then, which one is right?

For sure, scientists ideally have "good" reasons for choosing some theories over others, such as general relativity over Dr. Bowie's spider theory. But, contrary to what most people have been taught, accurate predictions are not one of those good reasons. A host of crazy theories can produce accurate predictions.

This problem, dubbed the "underdetermination of theory by evidence," means that, for any given set of observations, more than one theory can be compatible with the evidence. Competing, even contradictory, theories can explain data. For almost two millennia, the Aristotelian-Ptolemaic system, though grossly wrong, made accurate predictions. The history of science is littered with theories that—regardless of their predictive success—were later piled into the trash heap. Prediction is not proof for a theory, and (some would argue) it is not even evidence for a theory. Predictions provide corroboration, but corroboration is not proof any more than a wet picnic table proves that kids spilled water on it.

When, for instance, scientists claim that they have observational data that corroborates the theory of evolution, they do, but in the same way that a wet picnic table corroborates (not proves) that it rained. Working from a host of assumptions, presuppositions, and social influences, these scientists could have very good reasons for their claim. But others scientists, working from the same host of assumptions, presuppositions, and social influences (or, in fact, different assumptions, presuppositions, and social influences), could have very good reasons, including the same corroborating experimental and observational data, for competing or even contradictory theories.

Scientists can make predictions even without a theory. Again, Newton's physics led to powerfully accurate predictions, even with no theory to explain them. For centuries ancient astronomers could predict solar eclipses or the motion of the planets without any idea of what caused the phenomena, other than such beliefs as a giant frog eating the sun in order to explain the eclipse, or Aristotle's notion "that the planets required forty-nine or perhaps fifty-five gods to keep on pushing them in their orbits."[6] Accurate predictions are fine but offer no more proof that a theory is true than Paul the octopus's accurate prediction proved that he knew beforehand which World Cup soccer teams would win.

Science in a swamp

In this context, one of the most influential philosophers of science, Karl Popper (1902–1994), claimed that we "can never give positive reasons which justify the belief that a theory is true."[7] Science is not, he argued, "a system of certain, or well-established, statements; nor is it a system which steadily advances towards a state of finality. Our science is not knowledge (*epistēmē*): it can never claim to have attained truth, or even a substitute for it, such as probability."[8]

Science never can claim to have attained truth? Or even a probability of truth? Haven't we been told all our lives that science is the *only* way to obtain truth, or at least the most certain way, effective above every other method or means? And yet perhaps the last century's most influential thinker on science throws out this whammy?

Popper's argument is linked directly to the issues already looked at regarding the observation to be explained (the picnic table is wet) and the theory explaining it (it rained). The picnic table's wetness does not necessarily flow back to the theory that it rained. It could, but it could also flow back to any of the other theories presented or to one or more of an infinite number of different theories not yet presented.

One could "ascribe," Popper wrote, "to the hypothesis a certain probability—perhaps not a very precise one—on the basis of an estimate of the ratio of all the tests passed by it to all the tests which have not yet been attempted. But this way too leads nowhere. For this estimate can, as it happens, be computed with precision, and the result is always that the probability is zero."[9]

In other words, since most everything that science seeks an explanation for potentially has an infinite number of theories to explain it, and since we can never test all of them, then there is a zero probability that one theory could be verified as true.

That's not the same as saying that there is a zero probability the theory *is* true. It's saying only that there is zero probability *it can be verified as true.* In other words, scientists can never know, with certainty, that a theory is true.

"Since we can never imagine all possible hypotheses," wrote Philipp Frank, "we cannot say that a certain hypothesis is the right one. No hypothesis can be 'proved' by experiment. The correct way of speaking is to say that experiment 'confirms' a certain hypothesis. If a person doesn't find his purse in his pocket, this confirms the hypothesis that there may be a thief about, but it doesn't prove it."[10]

But isn't proof what science is about? Don't people become scientists, as opposed to poets, truck drivers, or linguists because they want proof for their beliefs, and because what better way is there to find that proof than through science?

Though a theory cannot be verified, Popper argues that it can be falsified. This is his famous concept of "falsification," the argument that scientific observation and experiment can never prove a theory true. All they can do is *falsify it.* Though "falsification" arose as a way to demarcate between science and pseudoscience (yes, debate exists not only over how science is done, but even over the definition of "science" itself), it quickly reveals the limits of scientific explanation and verification.

For Popper, after proposing a theory, a scientist should do all that he or she can to prove the theory wrong. (Yeah, right, that's just what all scientists do, seek to falsify their own theories!) This method, if not promising truth (which, Popper says, is impossible, anyway), can at least root out error. Even if you can't be sure a theory is right, you can at least be sure it's wrong.

Take the theory that the picnic table was wet because it rained. You get convincing evidence (what constitutes evidence presents its own set of big challenges) that it didn't rain. Thus, the theory has been falsified. Or what about the theory that kids spilled water on it? You have evidence that no kids were there. Scratch that; another falsification. The aliens from Pluto? You have evidence that no aliens from Pluto were in the area, either. You can, according to Popper, declare that this theory has been falsified. Or suppose you have powerful evidence that no airplane putting out a forest fire dropped water on the table. Another theory, despite the corroborating evidence, is shown wrong.

Suppose the only theory left standing, not yet falsified, is that workmen digging in the yard broke a pipe, which shot up water that got the table wet? For now, this remains the best theory. Not that we know it's correct, but only that it has yet to be falsified.

After all, might not someone hypothesize a better theory, one that fits the facts more precisely and comes with all the other things that, supposedly, make for the best scientific theories (simplicity, novel and unexpected predictions, fewest assumptions, etc.)? No matter how long the theory has been accepted or all the accentuating corroborative evidence, according to Popper the possibility always exists that it can later be falsified and replaced. Just as past scientific theories have been falsified, what promises that today's sacred scientific cows won't be tomorrow's hamburger meat?

"Science does not rest upon solid bedrock," wrote Popper. "The bold structure of its theories rises, as it were, above a swamp. It is like a building erected on piles. The piles are driven down from above into the swamp, but not down to any natural or 'given' base; and if we stop driving the piles deeper, it is not because we have reached firm ground. We simply stop when we are satisfied that the piles are firm enough to carry the structure, at least for the time being."[11]

Science is built upon swamp?[12] How could that be? Science, we have been told, is built upon the solid foundation composed of objective research, double-blind procedures, peer review, open debate, replication, cooperation, painstakingly detailed study of the natural world, and finally that supremely unsurpassed mode of empirical certainty, the "scientific method"—all in a quest for a certainty not found in any other epistemic endeavor. And yet Popper argues that science never reaches a "natural" base, or even "firm ground"?

In the late 1800s a young student named Max Planck was advised by professors not to study physics, because pretty much everything about physics, he was told, was already understood. More research would push the decimal points a few places farther left, that's all. Within the early years of the nineteen hundreds, however, three of the most fundamental aspects of physics—determinism, continuity, and separability—were superseded by quantum physics (which Max Planck pioneered). Many of the basic assumptions and principles of "classical physics" were trumped by the quantum hypothesis, regardless of how long these assumptions had been believed, assumed, tested, tried, and verified. And though quantum physics makes amazingly accurate predictions (so what?), and is crucial to so much technology (so what?)—who knows its fate?

Finally, certitude!

"Fifty-seven years ago," said Alfred North Whitehead in 1939, "it was when I was a young man in the University of Cambridge. I was taught science and mathematics by brilliant men and I did well in them; since the turn of the century I have lived to see every one of the basic assumptions of both set aside. . . . And yet, in the face of that, the discoverers of the new hypotheses in science are declaring, '*Now at last, we have certitude.*' "[13]

Whitehead's complaint wasn't about the dismantling of a time-honored theory of mulberry wine fermentation or about details concerning how the *Phiomia*'s digestive system supposedly evolved forty million years ago. He saw, instead, "every one of the basic assumptions of both [math and science] set aside." *Basic assumptions of both math and science?* Foundational principles ideally so solid, so intuitive, and so certain that they were assumed true, especially after having in some cases (such as math) centuries of a proven track record behind them? And yet all were, to use the Popperian word, "falsified"?

And if foundational principles have been overturned, what about specific theories, often based on these principles?

Chemist Michael Polanyi wrote about the struggle to affirm scientific theories themselves: "Nor am I saying that there are no rules to guide verification, but only that there are none which can be relied on in the last resort. Take the most important rules of experimental verification: reproducibility of results; agreement between determinations made by different and independent methods; fulfilment of predictions. These are powerful criteria; but I could give you examples in which they were all fulfilled and yet the statement which they seemed to confirm later turned out to be false."[14]

"Not even the most realist and rationalist philosophers of science," wrote James Ladyman, "would argue that all established scientific theories are proven to be true beyond any doubt, nor even that they are *all* probably true. But how far should a healthy skepticism go?"[15]

Yet, can one imagine Richard Dawkins saying, *Well, we don't know if evolution is really true, but just that it has yet to be falsified?* Or, *Well, evolution is a theory built upon a swamp and is really not on firm ground*? Instead, Dawkins is a high-octane version of those who in Whitehead's day declared, "Now at last, we have certitude."

In fact, arguing that the truth of macroevolution is beyond doubt, Dawkins puts those who reject macroevolution in favor of creationism or who even advocate for equal time in the classroom, in the same intellectual class as Holocaust deniers.

"Imagine," Dawkins wrote, "that, as a teacher of European history, you are continually faced with belligerent demands to 'teach the controversy,' and to give 'equal time' to the 'alternative theory' that the Holocaust never happened but was invented by a bunch of Zionist fabricators. Fashionably relativist intellectuals chime in to insist that there is no absolute truth: whether the Holocaust happened is a matter of personal belief; all points of view are equally valid and should be equally 'respected.' "[16]

Oozing the "certitude" that Alfred North Whitehead cautioned against, Dawkins continued: "Evolution is a fact. Beyond reasonable doubt, beyond serious doubt, beyond sane, informed, intelligent doubt, beyond doubt evolution is a fact. The evidence for evolution is at least as strong as the evidence for the Holocaust, even allowing for eye witnesses to the Holocaust. It is the plain truth that we are cousins of chimpanzees, somewhat more distant cousins of monkeys, more distant cousins still of aardvarks and manatees, yet more distant cousins of bananas and turnips . . . continue the list as long as desired."[17]

Meanwhile, in a TV interview, in the context of how the universe began, Richard Dawkins said the following: "Lawrence Krauss, my colleague, we did a film together called *The Unbelievers*. And he has written a book called *A Universe From Nothing*. And he produces a physical theory, mathematically worked out, to show that you can get something from nothing. *That nothing and nothing in some strange way cancels itself out to produce something*. And quantum theory allows that to happen. Well, I'm humble enough to say I don't understand it, and I am not arrogant enough to say that because I don't understand it, therefore it can't be right."[18]

Dawkins equates those who don't think humans are distant cousins of bananas and turnips with Holocaust deniers, but sees no reason to deny the theory, "mathematically worked out" (mind you), that "nothing and nothing in some strange way cancels itself out to produce something," that is, the universe?[19]

Dancing with Darwin

Dawkins' rhetoric exposes, among other things, the inescapable subjectivism of science. This subjectivism, however, arises not just from human foibles but from something more fundamental, logic itself, as seen in the sentence, "If A is true, then B is true." As already shown, assuming A assumes B; however, assuming B doesn't (necessarily) assume A. The wet picnic table (B) does not prove it rained (A).

Thus, the existence of the universe (B) does not necessarily mean that it arose because "nothing and nothing in some strange way cancels itself out to produce something" (A), even if Krauss's theory was "mathematically worked out" and then espoused by such an intellectual eminence as Richard Dawkins. Another cosmologist, working from the same universe, mining the same data, and even producing impressive mathematics to boot, might come up with a contradictory theory without the need to posit nothing canceling out nothing and then "in some strange way" producing everything.

The universe exists, but according to underdetermination of theory by evidence, and its cousin, falsification, we can never know from science if we have the definitive theory explaining its cause. Whatever the theory or however successful its predictive power (remember Paul the octopus), it can always be falsified and/or usurped by any one of a potentially infinite number of other, even contradictory, theories that could, ideally, explain the same data better and with more of the attributes of "good" science.

Now, neither underdetermination nor falsification is without critics. Is it true that scientists have not verified the second law of thermodynamics, the oxygen theory of combustion, and the germ theory—only not yet been able to falsify them? (Of course, 150 years ago, one could have made the same argument about the aether, which was as firmly believed then as germ theory is now, even if today the word *aether* sounds as if lifted from Greek mythology.) Some argue, meanwhile, that just as no theory can be conclusively proven, none can be conclusively refuted either, a claim that (if true) undermines Popper's project. Larry Lauden argued against most forms of underdetermination, concluding "that no one has yet shown that established forms of Underdetermination do anything to undermine scientific methodology. . . . The relativist critique of epistemology and methodology, insofar as it is based on arguments from Underdetermination, has produced much heat but no light whatsoever."[20] Lauden's critique itself, however, has not been without critics as well.

The point is not to engage in the epistemological quarrels—splitting syllables and consonants and vowels—that such topics morph into. It's to show, again, that popular notions about scientific "proof" are paparazzi stuff. The problem, though, isn't science itself, but scientism, the philosophical assumption that because all reality is ultimately materialistic, science can, ideally, explain all that can be explained, from the motion of the stars to why some prefer Brahms over Dvořák—no matter how presumptive that assumption is.

"Then it hit me: An acoustical engineer could explain everything about the sounds, the decibels, the wavelengths, and the pitch of the music; a physiologist could explain everything about the eardrum—the hammer, the anvil, the nerves from the ear to the brain; a neurologist could explain everything about the neurons that fired as I listened, or the neurotransmitters that leapt from cleft to cleft. Yet everything that science could now explain or ever could explain would never get near what really mattered, which was why that music moved me so powerfully. Science's dogmatic materialism can't explain that element of reality any more than a flashlight in a dark room could reveal a sleeper's dream."[21]

Nevertheless, given the continued success of science, especially the incredible, and becoming even more incredible, technology spawned from its loins, the spell of scientism remains strong. So strong that many Christians feel compelled to fold before it, even on a doctrine as foundational as Creation. With the overwhelming barrage of voices, including the "best and the brightest," from most every discipline, all purporting to have discovered Bs that point back to A—A being macroevolution ("If A is true, then B is true")—it's no wonder that many Christians get entranced by the spell.

Ironically enough, in an article purporting to downplay the specific concerns that scientism causes, psychologist Steven Pinker displays those specific concerns in flagrante delicto. Even more revealingly, he shows why scientism contradicts Christianity. All Christians, especially those who dance with Darwin the way the medievals did with Aristotle, ought to read this evolutionist's words carefully:

To begin with, the findings of science entail that the belief systems of all the world's traditional religions and cultures—their theories of the origins of life, humans, and societies—are factually mistaken. We know, but our ancestors did not, that humans belong to a single species of African primate that developed agriculture, government, and writing late in its history. We know that our species is a tiny twig of a genealogical tree that embraces all living things and that emerged from prebiotic chemicals almost four billion years ago. We know that we live on a planet that revolves around one of a hundred billion stars in our galaxy, which is one of a hundred billion galaxies in a 13.8-billion-year-old universe, possibly one of a vast number of universes. We know that our intuitions about space, time, matter, and causation are incommensurable with the nature of reality on scales that are very large and very small. We know that the laws governing the physical world (including accidents, disease, and other misfortunes) have no goals that pertain to human well-being. There is no such thing as fate, providence, karma, spells, curses, augury, divine retribution, or answered prayers—though the discrepancy between the laws of probability and the workings of cognition may explain why people believe there are. And we know that we did not always know these things, that the beloved convictions of every time and culture may be decisively falsified, doubtless including some we hold today.

. . . The facts of science, by exposing the absence of purpose in the laws governing the universe, force us to take responsibility for the welfare of ourselves, our species, and our planet. For the same reason, they undercut any moral or political system based on mystical forces, quests, destinies, dialectics, struggles, or messianic ages.[22]

Though earlier in the article he seemed to distinguish between what we believe from what "we know," Pinker eventually conflates them all, thanks to science, into what "we know"—from our origins out of "prebiotic chemicals almost four billion years ago," to there being no "answered prayers" (a pretty direct line, actually). Of course, it's one thing to assert that no fate, no answered prayers, no mystical forces, no divine retribution, or no purpose in laws governing the universe exist. But to assert these positions based on science is as foolish as chemically analyzing an early copy of *Hamlet* to learn the secret of Shakespeare's poetry. Pinker is doing scientism, not science; these conclusions are drawn from metaphysics, not physics, and from philosophy, not from chemistry, biology, or anthropology.

"A skeptic," wrote Richard Williams about Pinker's article, "begins to suspect at this point that Pinker's declarations . . . are not really scientific, but conjectural and reflect a kind of intellectual orthodoxy. They arise from shared metaphysical, epistemological, and moral commitments and are not the necessary conclusions of scientific endeavor."[23]

Pinker does, however, concede the following: "And we know that we did not always know these things, that the beloved convictions of every time and culture may be decisively falsified, doubtless including some we hold today."

And among the beliefs of our time and culture that, he said, could be (á la Popper) "falsified" might be included the belief that "our species is a tiny twig of a genealogical tree that embraces all living things and that emerged from prebiotic chemicals almost four billion years ago." In other words, the Bs that now bring many back to A—*A* being prebiotic chemical origins—are still underdetermined by the evidence, which means they could be replaced with another theory, one that contradicts A. Some argue that it is already happening, that the Bs are not pointing back to A as dogmatically as Steven Pinker, Richard Dawkins, and others have assured us they were.

"Guess what?" wrote Ann Gauger. "It's happening right now, but it's happening slowly, not overnight. That's because more and more people are recognizing that evolutionary biology's explanatory power is inversely proportional to its rigor. Yet there is still an enormous amount of pushback from people strongly invested in the Darwinian story."[24]

Meanwhile, Pinker boldly declares that science has proven religious faith "factually mistaken" on crucial issues such as the "origins of life, humans, and societies." What experiments were conducted to reach this conclusion, what assumptions were made to do them, and what reasons scientists had for justifying their results—Pinker didn't specify. It would be fascinating, too, to know what scientific research program proved that there's no such thing as fate, providence, or divine retribution.

Pinker's scientism aside, the questions considered in this chapter deal with two manifestations of a larger issue regarding scientific knowledge. And though this chapter used Paul the octopus as a lead into a look at underdetermination and falsification, chapter 6 will begin with a chicken whose unfortunate demise points to another challenge regarding the limits of science, a challenge that provides more reasons why Christians shouldn't so quickly dance with Darwin.

---

1. Actually the question "How did Paul do that?" is exceedingly ambiguous and filled with an almost endless host of epistemological conundrums that have important implications in understanding the limits of not just science, but anything.

2. Larry Caldwell, "Lessons Learned From Haeckel and His Drawings: We Shouldn't Always Believe What the 'Leading Experts' Tell Us About Evolution," Evolution News, June 5, 2007, https://evolutionnews.org/2007/06/lessons_learned_from_haeckel_a/.

3. See Clifford Goldstein, *The Clifford Goldstein Story* (Hagerstown, MD: Review and Herald®, 1996).

4. Or one could use Plato's cave analogy. For the first time in my life I realized that a greater reality existed beyond the shadows on the cave wall.

5. Larry Lauden, "Demystifying Underdetermination," in Curd and Cover, *Philosophy of Science*, 323. Lauden was not arguing for this position; he was quoting it to show why he thought it was overstated, though it is a position that other philosophers of science hold.

6. Bertrand Russell, *Human Society in Ethics and Politics* (London: Routledge, 1992), 191.

7. Karl Popper, *Conjectures and Refutations: The Growth of Scientific Knowledge* (London: Routledge Classics, 2002), 310.

8. Karl Popper, *The Logic of Scientific Discovery* (London: Routledge Classics, 2002), 278 (italics in the original).

9. Ibid., 255.

10. Philipp Frank, *Philosophy of Science: The Link Between Science and Philosophy* (Mineola, NY: Dover, 2004), 16.

11. Popper, *Logic of Scientific Discovery*, 94.

12. An even more famous analogy is that of seeking to rebuild a ship, one plank at a time, while the ship is out at sea. Either way, the point is the same: there is no absolute, solid foundation upon which science (or any epistemological endeavor, including evolutionary biology) can rest.

13. Quoted in Matthieu Ricard and Trinh Xuan Thuan, *The Quantum and the Lotus: A Journey to the Frontiers Where Science and Buddhism Meet* (New York: Three Rivers Press, 2001), 238 (italics in the original).

14. Michael Polanyi, *Science, Faith and Society* (London: Oxford University Press, 1946), 16.

15. James Ladyman, *Understanding Philosophy of Science* (London: Routledge, 2002), 120 (italics in the original).

16. Richard Dawkins, *The Greatest Show on Earth: The Evidence for Evolution* (New York: Free Press, 2009), 4.

17. Ibid., 8.

18. Richard Dawkins, interview by Sally Quinn, *After Words*, C-SPAN2, October 1, 2013 (italics added).

19. Others have seen the silliness of this position about the universe arising from nothing. Curtis White wrote:

> Assuming Krauss is right about the science—and I assume he is right, fascinatingly so—the problem simply becomes "why are there quantum fields rather than nothing," or "why was there an 'irregular smoothness' in the beginning?" His "nothing" is not nothing nothing; it is the quite full space between somethings. It is free of matter but not free of field and so creates a "condition in space" that can exert force on particles. As the astrophysicist John Wheeler put it, "It occupies space. It contains energy. Its presence eliminates a true vacuum." Moreover, if string theory is to be believed, this "nothing" may even have extra dimensions (five!) that curl subtly back onto themselves, saturating space in proportions a trillion trillion times smaller than an atom.
>
> I get this, and I'm no astrophysicist. So, á la Thomas Frank, What's the Matter with Krauss? Curtis White, *The Science Delusion: Asking the Big Questions in a Culture of Easy Answers* (Brooklyn, NY: Melville House, 2013), chap. 1.

20. Lauden, "Demystifying Underdetermination," in Curd and Cover, *Philosophy of Science*, 346.

21. Clifford Goldstein, "Brahms' Symphony No. 2," *Adventist Review*, May 16, 2013, http://archives.adventistreview.org/issue.php?issue=2013-1514&page=23.

22. Steven Pinker, "Science Is Not Your Enemy," *New Republic*, August 6, 2013, https://newrepublic.com/article/114127/science-not-enemy-humanities.

23. Williams and Robinson, *Scientism: The New Orthodoxy*, 15.

24. Ann Gauger, "What If People Stopped Believing in Darwin?" Evolution News, August 27, 2015, https://evolutionnews.org/2015/08/what_if_people/.

CHAPTER 6

THE THORN ON THE ROSE

E very morning at dawn the farmer comes out and feeds a chicken. Thus, every morning when the farmer arrives, the chicken (to the degree that chickens can be thus programmed) opens its mouth in expectation of food. One morning, though, instead of feeding the chicken, the farmer lops off its head.

A cowboy buys a horse and decides to train it to live without food. For thirty days straight he keeps the equine from eating. The cowboy assumes that he has succeeded and the horse can live without food. On the thirty-first day, the horse dies.

Despite their triteness, both stories show that the link, the continuity, between the past, the present, and the future isn't as firm as we like, and even need, to think it is. These accounts teach that the past, or even the present, does not provide solid justification for conclusions that we draw about the future, regardless of how often those conclusions turn out to be correct. That is, although much of what we assume about the future is based on the past or the present, we often don't have definitively good reasons for those assumptions. And though we may have little choice but to live that way, when it comes to science, this long-acknowledged problem, known as the problem of induction, presents another reason why Christians should not bow in obsequiousness every time science declares that it has "proven" a theory true.

Deduction versus induction

Epistemology is the study of how we come to know what we believe we know. Empiricism is the epistemological theory that knowledge is derived from sense perceptions. And though empiricist epistemology is how most science is done, it comes with another unresolved issue regarding its trustworthiness: the problem of induction.

Take the following set of phrases:

(1) All men are mortal.

(2) Socrates is a man.

(3) Hence, Socrates is mortal.

This sequence of thought is an example of *deductive logic*. It means that for any given set of statements, such as the one above, if the premises, (1) and (2), are true, then the conclusion, (3), is guaranteed to be true. There is no way that (1) and (2) can be true and (3) not be. The conclusion follows, absolutely, from the premises.

Now, it's important to remember that the conditions requisite for a true conclusion in deductive logic are true premises. In deductive logic, a set of premises does not necessarily mean that the conclusion is true; it means only that the conclusion must follow from the premises and that the premises guarantee the conclusion, regardless of whether the premises are true.

Take the following statements:

(1') All men are green fish.

(2') Socrates is a man.

(3') Hence, Socrates is a green fish.

In the language of logic, the conclusion, (3'), is said to be "valid," in that it follows deductively from the premises (1') and (2'). But what is the obvious problem? The conclusion, "Socrates is a green fish," is false, even if the logic leading to that conclusion is valid. How could that be? Easy. One of the premises, (1'), is false too.[1]

"The specific concern of logic," wrote Peter Smith, ". . . is not the truth of initial premises but *the way we argue from a given starting point*. Logic is not about whether our premises are true, i.e. match up to the world, but about whether our inferences really do support our conclusions once the premises are granted. It is in this sense that logic is concerned with the 'internal cogency' of our reasoning."[2]

However tightly woven, deductive logic does come with a major flaw: it teaches nothing new. If the premises are true—(1) "All men are mortal," (2) "Socrates is a man"—then they already contain the conclusion—(3) "Socrates is mortal"—within them. By going to (3), we learn nothing not already contained in (1) and (2). Deduction is a powerful mode of thought but, in the end, it gets us nowhere.

Look, in contrast, at the following statements:

(1") Glasses of grape juice that look and smell fine haven't killed you in the past.

(2") The present glass of grape juice looks and smells fine.
(3") The present glass of grape juice won't kill you.

Given the premises, (1") and (2"), the conclusion, (3"), is reasonable. But it is reasonable in the same way that it was reasonable for the chicken to assume that the farmer was going to feed him on the day he lopped off its head instead. Or for the cowboy to think that his horse was just fine. Reasonable, even justifiable, is not the same as guaranteed, as the conclusions were in the Socrates examples. In those cases, which followed deductive logic, the conclusion was guaranteed, regardless of whether the statements were true.

In the case of the grape juice, one could argue that yes, there are good reasons for believing that "the present glass of grape juice" won't kill you. Maybe for the past thirty years you daily drank grape juice that smelled and looked good and never suffered ill effects, much less death. Maybe every person whom you knew your whole life did the same—drank grape juice and never died from it. Thus, given (1") and (2"), the conclusion, (3"), is reasonable.

But reasonable is vastly different from absolute. Someone might have slipped a tasteless poison into the juice, perhaps only to show the fallacy of this method of reasoning, which relies on the idea that the past resembles the future, a foundational principle by which so much science (as well as everyday life) functions.

The induction dilemma
This method of reasoning is called *induction*. Like deduction, it's a way of working from premises to conclusions. Unlike deduction, which doesn't lead to conclusions that tell us anything new about the world, to anything not already in the premises, induction does take us to something new, to something not in the premises.

The fact that previous cups of grape juice didn't cause death doesn't guarantee that the one in your hand won't, either. It gives reasons, even plausible reasons (though some would argue against that), to believe that it won't. But it still might. Thus, though the inductive method leads to conclusions that deduction can't, it doesn't provide certainty about those conclusions, even if the premises are true.

"Inductive inference," wrote Peter Lipton, "is thus a matter of weighing evidence and judging probability, not of proof."[3]

Thus, if epistemology is the study of knowledge, and if empiricism is a form of epistemology, then induction (though not easy to define) is how one draws conclusions from empiricist epistemological endeavors. The problem is that induction can't guarantee its conclusions. And this weakness presents another reason why science, which works by induction and inductive inference, hasn't earned the superstar *epistemic* status it has pilfered for itself, especially when it comes to its bold pronouncements about the certainty that all life on earth—from grapefruit trees to Madonna—arose from a primeval prokaryotic cell more than three billion years ago.

Most people have heard of a scientific statement like "All copper conducts electricity." Only problem? That is more a philosophical statement than a scientific one. How can scientists, with the limited amount of copper they have ever tested, know with certainty that all copper conducts electricity? They are inductively inferring from the particular (the copper tested) to the universal (all copper in the universe). The statement might be right, but *might be right* means that it might be wrong too. A vast divide exists between a conclusion derived inductively and one derived deductively—a divide that bedevils almost all of science, especially one as highly speculative as evolution.

This problem, that of induction and variants of it, has been brooding over science for centuries. In the eighteenth century, Scotsman David Hume argued that all we know are particulars and that any projection from the particular to the universal is not truly justified, especially in the area of cause and effect, which is fundamental to the whole idea of science.

Hume used his famous example of billiard balls. Every time one billiard ball hits another billiard ball, the second one moves, and thus we assume that the motion of the first ball hitting the second causes the second one's motion. Though that's a reasonable assumption based on empiricism (it has always done so in the past), it's not necessarily justified. The conjunction of events—the motion of the first ball, the striking of the second ball, and the movement of the second ball—doesn't necessarily show causation. These events just show, Hume argued, that we are used to one event following another, but we don't have any knowledge of a true causal connection between them.

"When I see," Hume wrote, "for instance, a Billiard-ball moving in a straight line towards another; even suppose motion in the second ball should by accident be suggested to me, as the result of their contact or impulse; may I not conceive, that a hundred different events might as well follow from that cause? May not both these balls remain at absolute rest? May not the first ball return in a straight line, or leap off from the second in any line or direction? All these suppositions are consistent and conceivable. Why then should we give the preference to one, which is no more consistent or conceivable than the rest? All our reasonings *a priori* will never be able to show us any foundation for this preference."[4]

All we have, Hume said, are "effects of custom, not of reasoning,"[5] when it comes to inductive experiences. In other words, we just assume that because such and such happened in the past in a certain way, it will do so in the future, regardless of whether we are justified in those assumptions.

If every day for five years you go outside, get into your car, put the key in the ignition, and start the engine, you assume that tomorrow when you go outside, sit in your car, and put the key in the ignition, the car will start, just as it always has for the past five years. You have good reasons, then, not only to assume that it will start but to act on that assumption.

Of course, it might not start, either. Sooner or later, it won't. The past resembles the future? Perhaps. But even if it does, for how long?

For thousands of years, people in the Old World believed that all swans were white, because all the swans that anyone ever saw in the Old World were, well, white. The empirical evidence was overwhelming: every swan was white. What more proof was needed? However, the first Westerners who arrived in Australia discovered black swans, thus proving that the belief that all swans were white was wrong, although held for millennia and with good reasons and justification. Despite the overwhelming empirical evidence existing for so long, all swans were not white.

This story (along with the stories of the chicken and the horse) illustrates the weakness of knowledge derived from empirical experience. No matter how often something happens in the past, no matter how many times it has been observed happening in the past, that's no guarantee the same will happen in the future.

"In particular," wrote Alexander Bird, "it is almost never true that what is future is just the same as what is past. Tomorrow is most unlikely to be exactly like today, and next month is certain to be radically different from last month. Tomorrow will be either colder or warmer than today, perhaps not a lot, but it will not be identical. Tomorrow I shall wear different clothes and the Moon will be in a different location. More leaves will have fallen from the trees and atoms that have been stable for millennia will have decayed. Many people will be dead who were for a long time alive, and others will come into existence. It is foolish to expect the future to resemble the past in a whole host of regards, and this fact is well known to us all, although it may be better known to good poker players than it is to most philosophers. The only way the future can perfectly resemble the past is for nothing to change."[6]

And yet not only in science but in almost everything we do, we do on the assumption of the past resembling the future. And that's because, in many and important ways, the past *does* resemble the future—at least close enough to be able to make decisions about the "here and now" based on the already "done and gone."

Yet as reasonable as this principle seems—that the future resembles the past (or vice versa)—it does so only because it *appears* that way to us. But because the question at issue is how much can we trust what appears to us (empiricism), the assumption that the future resembles the past is relatively weak, regardless of how well it works in actuality. We're assuming the question we are asking. The idea that the future resembles the past is an inductive inference, the very method itself that is being challenged. We justify inductive inference, which is based on the idea that the future resembles the past, but we do so based on the inductive inference that the future resembles the past.

Talk about circular reasoning! No wonder it has been called "the myth of inductive logic."[7] How does one break out of it? Or, why should one break out of it when it works so well, at least most of the time, both in life and in science?[8]

Yet if the principle that the future resembles the past is questionable even when science deals with daily observable and measureable phenomena, such as swans or billiard balls, how much more so when it extrapolates and retrodicts events that it claims took place millions, even billions, of years in the past? Looking at a fossil today, science often makes bold assertions about what happened to it, supposedly six hundred million years ago. But how does anyone today know much about anything that happened six hundred million years ago, other than by assuming that whatever happened six hundred million years ago in some way resembles reality today, at least closely enough so that, judging by what happens today, the scientist can speculate about six hundred million years ago? What happened today might reflect a hypothetical six hundred million years ago, but it might not—not even closely. Even six thousand years ago the world might have been quite different than it is today.

"The problem of induction," wrote David Papineau, "seems to pose a threat to all scientific knowledge." Talking about some of the most established scientific laws—Galileo's law of free fall, Newton's law of gravity, Avogadro's law of gases, Papineau writes that the "problem of induction calls the authority of all these laws into question. For if our evidence is simply that these laws have worked so far, then how can we be sure that they will not be disproved by future occurrences?"[9]

And if this poses a question for something that can be studied every day, in the here and now, what about something such as macroevolution, forever out of reach in the distant past?

If induction functions on the idea that the future resembles the past, one can also ask, *How far back (or how far forward) does this resemblance hold?* Every day the farmer fed the chicken? Every day the horse went without eating? How far back can one legitimately retrodict the present into the past or project the present into the future? The answer, no doubt, depends upon the context in which the questions are being asked. But in every case, the assumption of continuity is implied, regardless of how justified (or unjustified) that assumption is.

From the "here and now" to the "done and gone"

For instance, whatever claims science makes about the origins of the earth and life on it, it is retrodicting to the unreachable past based on what is existent today—DNA, fossils, trees, subatomic particles, canyons, birds, whatever. After all, what else but the "here and now" can science use to develop hypotheses about the "done and gone"?

However, science works from assumptions that are not necessarily scientific. "Most philosophers of science believe," says *The Oxford Handbook of Philosophical Theology*, "that science cannot function without some underlying de facto metaphysical principles that are not consequences of science itself."[10]

And it's not just science. Whatever humans do—theology, math, mechanics, literary criticism—philosophical reasoning is required. Science works from assumptions about the reality of the world, assumptions "about how things in the broadest possible sense of the term hang together in the broadest possible sense of the term."[11] All human inquiry, including science, assumes certain starting points that are philosophical in nature.

"Either we ought to philosophize," wrote Aristotle, "or we ought not. If we ought, then we ought. If we ought not, then also we ought [i.e. in order to justify this view]. Hence in any case we ought to philosophize."[12]

And one philosophical assumption central to science is an unwavering naturalism. Not just methodological naturalism (*OK, we can't figure this out, but we must not invoke the supernatural to explain it*) but an ontological naturalism (which deals with the nature of "being" itself). Science, even if it is not explicitly stated, assumes that reality is material only and that everything in this natural realm (everything that exists, actually) is always subject to natural law. It's another way of saying, without saying it, that nothing supernatural or divine exists. It's the assumption of atheism, expressed by Alex Rosenberg like this:

> *Is there a God?* No.
> *What is the nature of reality?* What physics says it is.
> *What is the purpose of the universe?* There is none.
> *What is the meaning of life?* Ditto.
> *Why am I here?* Just dumb luck.[13]

These are philosophical, not scientific, assumptions—even his claim that the nature of reality is what physics says it is. How much reality might exist that physics knows nothing about or could never learn about? Does the physics describing the reality we know about apply to all reality? And if the past does resemble the future, then a good chance exists that the physics of today will be relegated to the trash heap, as was the physics of the past. Thus, his assertion about the nature of reality being what physics says is an expression of cultural bias more akin to Kim Kardashian talking about Botox than to Einstein talking about gravity.

And even if Rosenberg's assumptions somehow led to correct conclusions, those conclusions wouldn't be justified by the assumptions used to get there. Science assumes, not proves, the naturalism that it bases itself on.

"So," asked John Lennox, "is naturalism actually demanded by science? Or is it just conceivable that naturalism is a philosophy that is brought to science, more than something that is entailed by science? Could it even be, dare one ask, more like an expression of faith, akin to religious faith? One might at least be forgiven for thinking that from the way in which those who dare ask such questions are sometimes treated. Like religious heretics of a former age they may suffer a form of martyrdom by the cutting off of their grants."[14]

In a famous (or infamous) quote, well-known biologist Richard Lewontin wrote,

> Our willingness to accept scientific claims that are against common sense is the key to an understanding of the real struggle between science and the supernatural. We take the side of science *in spite* of the patent absurdity of some of its constructs . . . *in spite* of the tolerance of the scientific community for unsubstantiated just-so stories, because we have a prior commitment . . . to materialism. It is not that the methods and institutions of science somehow compel us to accept a material explanation of the phenomenal world, but, on the contrary, that we are forced by our *a priori* adherence to material causes to create an apparatus of investigation and a set of concepts that produce material explanations, no matter how counter-intuitive, no matter how mystifying to the uninitiated. Moreover, that materialism is absolute, for we cannot allow a Divine Foot in the door.[15]

When Lewontin said that this sacred canon of science, naturalism, is based on philosophy, not science, he said nothing not already known. He just said it with an unabashed honesty. Nothing, he admitted, in "the methods and institutions of science somehow compel[s] us to accept a material explanation of the phenomenal world." It is, instead, a philosophical commitment that led to science's absolute materialism.

Even that wouldn't be so bad were it not for the shabby philosophy behind this commitment: *the refusal to "allow a Divine Foot in the door."* It's not science itself that calls for this materialist presupposition, but cultural and social biases—hardly the stuff of serious philosophical inquiry.[16] Thus, materialism, a sacred assumption of science, arises from a philosophical commitment that science itself cannot even address, a commitment that some (but not all) scientists and philosophers find questionable.

"My basic case against materialism," wrote Laurence BonJour, "is complete at this point: there is no good reason for any strong presumption in favor of materialism; and the main materialist view fails to offer any real explanation of a central aspect of mental states, namely their conscious character, meaning that there is no good reason to think that it is correct as an account of such states."[17]

In response to the common argument, echoed from the scientific-industrial complex, that science is precluded from making statements about the supernatural because it is outside of its provenance, well-known science writer Sean Carroll disagreed.

"Science," he responded, "should be interested in determining the *truth*, whatever that truth may be—natural, supernatural, or otherwise. The stance known as methodological naturalism, while deployed with the best of intentions by supporters of science, amounts to assuming part of the answer ahead of time. If finding the truth is our goal, that is just about the biggest mistake we can make."[18]

Discontinuity

No wonder faith and science clash on the issue of origins. If science refuses to acknowledge even the existence of the supernatural, it will bring *only error to any supernatural origins*. How could it do otherwise? What can a view that won't allow "a Divine Foot in the door" posit except a narrow, distorted, if not overtly *wrong* perspective on a reality whose every molecule was the result of the Divine not only with a foot in the door, but whose creative power made every nook and cranny of the structure itself? If Creation was a supernatural act, and if science refuses to accept any supernatural act, then science can lead to only false conclusions regarding Creation. It's like a detective in a murder case who, a priori, rules out as a suspect the guilty party. Whomever the detective charges with the murder will, of necessity, be innocent.

Making this error, Francis Collins, a Christian, wrote, "Science reveals that the universe, our own planet, and life itself are engaged in an evolutionary process. The consequences of that can include the unpredictability of the weather, the slippage of a tectonic plate, or the misspelling of a cancer gene in the normal process of cell division. If at the beginning of time God chose to use these forces to create human beings, then the inevitability of these other painful consequences was also assured."[19] In other words, because these forces are going on now, they must have always gone on, even way in the past. A seemingly reasonable assumption, but still only an assumption and one that Scripture overtly refutes.

Induction assumes continuity between the past and the future, so intractable trouble occurs, because the Genesis Creation account reveals a radical *discontinuity* between the past and the future. The first words of Genesis, "In the beginning God created the heavens and the earth" (Genesis 1:1), depict a supernaturalism that suffuses the creation of the earth and life on it. The entire Creation account is about the *supernatural* birth of the natural world. And this means, therefore, that natural processes now existent were not the means through which the Creation first arose, any more than the rules of chess alone, and not human beings, were the means through which the game of chess was first created. To use those rules, and those rules alone, to discern the origins of chess is likely to lead only to dead ends, especially if the search for the game's origins works from an underlying premise that whatever created the game of chess, *it could not have been human beings*. Like the hapless detective who rules out the guilty party as the murder suspect, whatever conclusions are drawn about the origins of chess under this dogmatic assumption will, of necessity, be wrong.

Given their own presuppositions, then, what can scientists teach about origins revealed to have occurred in the following manner?

> Then God said, "Let there be a firmament in the midst of the waters, and let it divide the waters from the waters." Thus God made the firmament, and divided the waters which were under the firmament from the waters which were above the firmament; and it was so. And God called the firmament Heaven. So the evening and the morning were the second day (Genesis 1:6–8).

> Then God said, "Let the earth bring forth grass, the herb that yields seed, and the fruit tree that yields fruit according to its kind, whose seed is in itself, on the earth"; and it was so. And the earth brought forth grass, the herb that yields seed according to its kind, and the tree that yields fruit, whose seed is in itself according to its kind. And God saw that it was good. So the evening and the morning were the third day (Genesis 1:11–13).

> Then God said, "Let Us make man in Our image, according to Our likeness; let them have dominion over the fish of the sea, over the birds of the air, and over the cattle, over all the earth and over every creeping thing that creeps on the earth." So God created man in His own image; in the image of God He created him; male and female He created them (Genesis 1:26, 27).

And the LORD God formed man of the dust of the ground, and breathed into his nostrils the breath of life; and man became a living being (Genesis 2:7).

And the LORD God caused a deep sleep to fall on Adam, and he slept; and He took one of his ribs, and closed up the flesh in its place. Then the rib which the LORD God had taken from man He made into a woman, and He brought her to the man (Genesis 2:21).

Not quite the process depicted in Richard Dawkins' *The Selfish Gene,* in which Dawkins proclaims that life on earth, including human life, arose only because by chance "unordered atoms could group themselves into ever more complex patterns until they ended up manufacturing people."[20]

Again, the materialist presupposition of science automatically excludes the Genesis account, which—from the Christian perspective—means that scientists working on those assumptions cannot be correct. If the truth about our origins demands the supernatural, but every scientific theory about origins excludes the supernatural, then every scientific theory about origins must be wrong.

Discounting the supernatural, some scientists argue that life came only through chemical and physical processes arising from an unknown combination of air, water, and rock about 3.8 billion years ago. Out of this combination, by chance, life is said to have arisen either in a shallow pool or in clay or in shale or in energy-rich hydrothermal vents at the bottom of the sea. Other scientists speculate that life began when either space dust or meteorites carrying biomolecules landed on the earth. Working from the meta-assumption of life arising only by chance, scientists admit they don't know how it happened. Wrote Stuart Kauffman, "Anyone who tells you that he or she knows how life started on the sere earth some 3.45 billion years ago is a fool or a knave. Nobody knows."[21]

Despite these myriad and conflicting speculations and extrapolations about how life first emerged, and despite the agreement that scientists don't know how it emerged, science still assures it does know how this life-form—whatever it was, wherever it formed, and however it got kick-started—became transformed into the variegated and exceedingly complex life-forms extant today. This self-replicating protolife went through a "very improbable"[22] (to use Richard Dawkins's own words) process taking billions of years of random mutation and natural selection and evolved into everything from amoebas to Euripides, even if no purpose, no intention, no design was involved in the process. Life is merely "complicated things that give the appearance of having been designed for a purpose"[23] when, in fact, life has no intentional design or purpose.

In other words, an iPhone, which looks designed, acts designed, reveals design in its innards and outwards, and works only through design is, of course, designed. But a human being, which looks designed, acts designed, reveals design in its innards and outwards, and works only through design cannot be designed. Why? Because design would imply a designer, and science as practiced now—working from social and cultural biases—automatically excludes the supernatural. When we stare design in the face, and when it stares back, and even when the most obvious explanation for the fact before us is design, according to the nonscientific limits that science has imposed upon itself, that explanation must be only an appearance, an illusion, a card trick (well, not a card trick, because that would take forethought and no forethought is allowed).

Thus, using inductive inference (a limited means of finding certainty), based on the concept of the past resembling the future (wrong, at least in case of origins), and working from the cultural and social assumption of naturalism (wrong), scientists have come up with a theory about the origins of life that contradicts the biblical account of the same origins in every conceivable way. Given the limits of induction and the gross error of naturalism, how could they have done anything but get it wrong?

The thorn on the rose (or discontinuity continued)

In the case of origins, the limits of induction become more problematic when the Fall complicates the equation, because the Fall constructs new layers of discontinuity between the past and the present.

Supernatural origins of the natural world as depicted in Genesis chapters 1 and 2 aside, Genesis presents Creation as a reality qualitatively different from what's real now. Once the acts of creating were complete, the resultant creation was different from today's world, a difference that makes inductive inference about the original creation, based on the present one, awkward at best.

First, the Bible depicts the newborn earth like this: "For the LORD God had not caused it to rain on the earth, and there was no man to till the ground; but a mist went up from the earth and watered the whole face of the ground" (Genesis 2:5, 6). *It had not rained on the earth; instead, a mist watered the whole face of the ground?* These texts (if not spiritualized, bowdlerized, and revised into meaning the opposite of what they say) reveal an environment that differed profoundly from the natural world as known for most of history and, certainly, today. An environment in which it never rained would have an ecosystem quite different from what exists now.

Second, the finished creation was described like this: "Then God saw everything that He had made, and indeed it was very good" (Genesis 1:31). Everything that God had made—which, according to the text, included the earth, the seas, the sky, the birds, all life, including humanity—was declared "very good." Though one must not read more into the Creation account than what is in the text itself, it's not unreasonable to assume that this pre-Fall world, deemed "very good," didn't have many or even any of the negative elements that are so inseparable from earth's present environment. Earthquakes, plagues, tsunamis, tornadoes, storms (especially if it never rained), volcanoes, forest fires, floods, drought—phenomena that arise now from the natural world like runny noses arise from toddlers—if not part of that pre-Fall existence, would mean a radical discontinuity between that early existence and the one that science now parses, picks apart, and analyzes in labs and particle accelerators. How certain can science be, inferring backward from the "here and now" to the "done and gone," when Scripture posits a "done and gone" greatly dissimilar to the "here and now"?

And then there's the specter of death. "Therefore, just as through one man sin entered the world, and death through sin, and thus death spread to all men, because all sinned" (Romans 5:12). For centuries scholars have debated every syllable, accent mark, and preposition of this verse. A big question, one of immense importance in the creation-evolution debate, deals with to whom and to what did sin bring death. The text says that sin brought death to "all men." But does that mean only humanity died as a result of sin, or does it mean that sin brought death to all life on earth, including humanity, but Paul was focusing solely on humanity given his context of the grace of Christ that saves "all men" from consequences of sin?

Many Christians, and with good reason, believe sin brought death to all life in the earthly creation. "For we know that the whole creation groans and labors with birth pangs together until now" (Romans 8:22). But even if Romans 5:12 means that only humanity died from sin, the Word of God still posits a past creation incomprehensibly divergent from the only one now known. A natural world in which humans did not die differs, unimaginably, from a world in which humans move inexorably toward death, what Martin Heidegger called "being-towards-death."[24] A vast qualitative chasm (*people not dying*) divides humanity's earliest existence from the only existence humanity has ever experienced since then. If one believes the biblical account of death, that it arose only after sin, then, again, science, working backward only from what's "here and now," would inevitably get the "done and gone" wrong.

The biblical account of the immediate results of the Fall unfold an even greater discontinuity between past and present. Immediately after the Fall, God said to the snake, who had lured Eve into sin:

"Because you have done this,
You are cursed more than all cattle,
And more than every beast of the field;
On your belly you shall go,
And you shall eat dust
All the days of your life" (Genesis 3:14).

For the first time the word *cursed* appears in the Bible. It is applied to the serpent. Though cryptic, the text implies that God supernaturally revised the snake's bodily form. This change in its physical structure occurred because of what it had done, not as a natural result of its actions (like obesity leading to diabetes), but as a *supernatural* act, a divine punishment. It was a direct judgment of God, manifested as a supernatural modification of the natural world.

What the snake, the serpent, looked like before the curse, the text does not say, except to imply, by declaring that the animal would now crawl on its belly, that it previously didn't crawl on it. Through the ages speculation about what the snake was like before the curse has been rife—it stood upright or had feet or had wings. But the point is that God, supernaturally, made a structural change in the physical world, in this case, the serpent, a change that would affect all snakes since then. In other words, this curse reached even to the level of genetics.

The discontinuity continues. "Unto the woman he said, I will greatly multiply thy pain and thy conception; in pain thou shalt bring forth children; and thy desire shall be to thy husband, and he shall rule over thee" (Genesis 3:16, ASV).

For millennia people have mulled over this text. First, the word translated "pain" (*itzevon*) in the first clause, "multiply thy pain," though closely related to the word "pain" (*etzev*) in the next clause, "in pain thou shalt bring forth children," is not precisely the same. The reason for the difference can be only speculated about. The crucial clause, in this immediate context, is the second one: "in pain thou shalt bring forth children." Though the word can also be used to denote mental anguish, not just physical pain, given what we know about childbirth, physical pain was certainly included. The Lord says "in pain thou shalt bring forth children," implying in this immediate context (the results of their sin) that such wouldn't have been the case otherwise. Whatever a woman would have experienced in childbirth before the Fall, giving birth would now be experienced with great pain.

As with the snake, this change wasn't a natural result of Eve's actions; it was a supernatural transformation of her body, or at least part of it. Whatever she had been physically that would have allowed her to bear children without pain (or without much, anyway; see Genesis 3:16), that physical structure was revamped. And, as with the serpent, this revision was wired so deep into her genes that it was passed on to all succeeding generations.

There's more:

> Then to Adam He [God] said, "Because you have heeded the voice of your wife, and have eaten from the tree of which I commanded you, saying, 'You shall not eat of it':
> "Cursed is the ground for your sake;
> In toil you shall eat of it
> All the days of your life.
> Both thorns and thistles it shall bring forth for you,
> And you shall eat the herb of the field.
> In the sweat of your face you shall eat bread
> Till you return to the ground,
> For out of it you were taken;
> For dust you are,
> And to dust you shall return" (Genesis 3:17–19).

Scripture points here to another supernatural change of the natural world, and very early in the earth's history too. Directly because of what Adam had done, the ground was cursed. God said, "In toil you shall eat of it," meaning that whatever Adam had done in Eden, working in the garden to "tend and keep it" (Genesis 2:15), that work would be different from now on. Exactly what changed in the ground itself, in its chemical or molecular or atomic structure, the text does not say. That this change would be the result of a curse and that Adam would have to "toil" (the word for *toil* is the same word translated "pain" in Genesis 3:16—"In pain you shall bring forth children") and to do so "in the sweat of . . . [his] face" (Genesis 3:19) indicate that agriculture would be different than it had previously been. At the level of the literal ground itself, the natural world underwent a supernaturally wrought change in its physical nature that made it different from its original structure.

"Both thorns and thistles it shall bring forth for you." These thorns and thistles, results of the curse, weren't there previously. Scripture says that at the end of the Creation week, "the heavens and the earth, and all the host of them, were finished" (Genesis 2:1), a completed work that included plant life. The addition of the "thorns and thistles" came afterward; they were not in the original creation. Instead, they somehow arose afterward, adding another level of discontinuity, one that went to the genetic structure of the plants themselves, the results of which remain with us today.

Notice, too, the following text, dealing with the curse after Cain's murder of Abel:

"So now you are cursed from the earth, which has opened its mouth to receive your brother's blood from your hand. When you till the ground, it shall no longer yield its strength to you" (Genesis 4:11, 12).

This event occurred after the first curse on the ground (Genesis 3:17, 18). To whatever curse already existed, another was added. The text sounds as if this curse was limited only to Cain, but the curses in Genesis 3:14, 16–19 sound limited as well. *The* serpent would be on its belly. *The* woman would have pain in childbirth. *The* man would toil in the ground and eventually return to it. Yet in each case the change was universal, not limited only to the one upon whom it was first pronounced. So why would the curse pronounced on Cain be limited only to him? Otherwise, only the ground that *he* tilled would not yield its strength to *him*, as if the curse supernaturally went ahead of Cain, messing up only the dirt that *he* wanted to farm.

Whatever happened, and to whatever extent it happened, these texts reveal another supernatural intervention, which resulted in a change of the natural world.

"The upset of the ecological balance," wrote Richard Davidson, "is directly attributed to human's sin (Genesis 3:17, 18). The blessing of Genesis 1 and 2 has become the curse (Genesis 3:14, 17)."[25]

"God's curse," writes William VanDoodewaard, "supernaturally brings about a profound change in the created order: sin, as rebellion and disobedience, brings misery. Its end is death. The whole creation now groans with decay, disease, and disorder, while at the same time remaining sovereignly sustained, ordered and governed by God."[26]

Before the Fall, humans and beasts were, apparently, vegetarian (Genesis 1:29, 30). By chapter 9, the interaction between humans and the animal world changed (see Genesis 9:1–4), and flesh became food. By the time they started eating each other, humans and animals had no doubt developed a relationship quite different from the one they had enjoyed in Eden. It's hard to imagine the vast disconnect between an environment where neither man nor beast ate meat and our rapaciously carnivorous world now.

Nevertheless, some Christians, despite the testimony of Scripture, can't seem to break free from the evolutionary paradigm, seeing everything through it. "Perhaps you have had a wisdom tooth removed," wrote Owen Gingerich, "because you have too many teeth for the size of your mouth. That jaw is clearly not an example of intelligent design; rather, it is an imperfect adaptation that has occurred as a result of natural selection, working with the materials at hand to refashion and shorten the mammalian muzzle into a face."[27]

Is that so? Or, maybe, millennia removed from the tree of life, our DNA is slowly wearing thin.

The Flood

Finally, in the context of supernatural intervention into the earliest natural world—and the resultant discontinuity (geographically, geologically, ecologically) between then and now—comes Noah's flood.

Regarding the Flood, Scripture is as unambiguous as unambiguity can be. The Genesis flood was no more limited to a select part of the earth than the results of Adam's sin were restricted to a select part of humanity.

> Then the LORD saw that the wickedness of man was great in the earth, and that every intent of the thoughts of his heart was only evil continually. And the LORD was sorry that He had made man on the earth, and He was grieved in His heart. So the LORD said, "I will destroy man whom I have created from the face of the earth, both man and beast, creeping thing and birds of the air, for I am sorry that I have made them" (Genesis 6:5–7).

If the Flood were only local, how would this solve the problem—human corruption—that the Lord was addressing? A local deluge would not take care of this issue any more than local deluges do today, even the worst of them. The Flood makes sense only if it was global, destroying everyone who wasn't in the ark. After all, was not sin a universal problem, or was it located only in the specific area where God unleashed His cleansing and purifying fury? Theologically, a local flood doesn't do justice to the issue the texts are addressing.

> So God looked upon the earth, and indeed it was corrupt; for all flesh had corrupted their way on the earth. And God said to Noah, "The end of all flesh has come before Me, for the earth is filled with violence through them; and behold, I will destroy them with the earth" (Genesis 6:12, 13).

The end of "all flesh," or just the unfortunate flesh trapped in a local flood zone and who didn't escape to higher ground?

> For after seven more days I will cause it to rain on the earth forty days and forty nights, and I will destroy from the face of the earth all living things that I have made (Genesis 7:4).

"All living things," as on the entire planet, or just "the living things" in the flood zone?

> And the waters prevailed exceedingly on the earth, and all the high hills under the whole heaven were covered (Genesis 7:19).

All the high hills "under the whole heaven" were covered? How does one limit "the whole heaven" to a specific geographical area to the exclusion of the rest of the earth? If the text meant the Flood was confined to a local area only, why did the Word of God—which can get quite specific (see, for instance, Exodus 28:2–10)—express what happened so sloppily and inaccurately?

> And all flesh died that moved on the earth: birds and cattle and beasts and every creeping thing that creeps on the earth, and every man. All in whose nostrils was the breath of the spirit of life, all that was on the dry land, died. So He destroyed all living things which were on the face of the ground: both man and cattle, creeping thing and bird of the air. They were destroyed from the earth. Only Noah and those who were with him in the ark remained alive (Genesis 7:21–23).

How can one read this as anything but a global flood? *"Only Noah and those who were with him in the ark remained alive"*—are we to take this to mean with the exception, that is, of untold masses, millions maybe, who lived where the floodwaters didn't reach?

Then, too, what about this New Testament text?

> For this they willfully forget: that by the word of God the heavens were of old, and the earth standing out of water and in the water, by which the world that then existed perished, being flooded with water. But the heavens and the earth which are now preserved by the same word, are reserved for fire until the day of judgment and perdition of ungodly men (2 Peter 3:5–7).

Peter's words weren't just a historical statement, but a theological one about a coming universal judgment parallel to the universal judgment of the Flood. A local flood would make not just Peter's history wrong but his theology as well. The judgment that Peter is referring to here is no more localized than was Noah's flood.

Also, why tell Noah to "make yourself an ark of cypress wood; make rooms in it and coat it with pitch inside and out" (Genesis 6:14, NIV)? That is, why tell him to build a boat as opposed to just getting out of the impending flood zone?

The same with the animals. "You are to bring into the ark two of all living creatures, male and female, to keep them alive with you. Two of every kind of bird, of every kind of animal and of every kind of creature that moves along the ground will come to you to be kept alive" (Genesis 6:19, 20, NIV). Such an act makes no sense, apart from the Flood covering all the earth and killing all flesh outside the ark, as the texts say numerous times. Again, why bring animals on the boat if it were merely a local flood?

And then there's the rainbow.

I set My rainbow in the cloud, and it shall be for the sign of the covenant between Me and the earth. It shall be, when I bring a cloud over the earth, that the rainbow shall be seen in the cloud; and I will remember My covenant which is between Me and you and every living creature of all flesh; the waters shall never again become a flood to destroy all flesh. The rainbow shall be in the cloud, and I will look on it to remember the everlasting covenant between God and every living creature of all flesh that is on the earth (Genesis 9:13–16).

If the Flood were local, then every local flood makes God's Word void, because He said that the rainbow was a token of His covenant promise not to do again what He did in Genesis, which was to destroy the whole world, not a corner of Mesopotamia, by water. Every rainbow mocks God's promise if the Deluge were anything but worldwide.

Discontinuity continued cont.

With such overwhelming biblical evidence for a universal flood,[28] why do many Christians dwarf it into only a local deluge? The answer is easy. It's the lure of scientism. Many scientists claim that no scientific evidence exists for a universal flood; ergo, many Christians deny it as well. It follows almost deductively.

However, the rationale to reject the universality of the Flood is based on science, and science means induction and inductive inference, which (as we have seen) hardly guarantee accurate results. On what grounds does science base its denial, other than by inferring from the "here and now" the "done and gone"? But that's precisely the method being challenged to begin with, a method that becomes even more problematic when underpinned by an ontological naturalism that, by default, denies the supernaturalism behind the Flood itself.

How, then, could scientists possibly get it right?

The immediate concern, however, isn't the universality of the Flood, but the final—and, perhaps, most radical—layer of discontinuity that the Flood deposited between the original creation and the world today. And another layer of discontinuity—combined with the previous supernaturally wrought changes—only increases the problems that arise when scientists make inductive inferences about the original creation based on the world today.

Genesis described the Flood like this:

> In the six hundredth year of Noah's life, in the second month, the seventeenth day of the month, on that day all the fountains of the great deep were broken up, and the windows of heaven were opened. And the rain was on the earth forty days and forty nights. . . .
>
> Now the flood was on the earth forty days. The waters increased and lifted up the ark, and it rose high above the earth. The waters prevailed and greatly increased on the earth, and the ark moved about on the surface of the waters. And the waters prevailed exceedingly on the earth, and all the high hills under the whole heaven were covered. The waters prevailed fifteen cubits upward, and the mountains were covered. . . . And the waters prevailed on the earth one hundred and fifty days.
>
> Then God remembered Noah, and every living thing, and all the animals that were with him in the ark. And God made a wind to pass over the earth, and the waters subsided. The fountains of the deep and the windows of heaven were also stopped, and the rain from heaven was restrained. And the waters receded continually from the earth. At the end of the hundred and fifty days the waters decreased. . . .
>
> And it came to pass in the six hundred and first year, in the first month, the first day of the month, that the waters were dried up from the earth; and Noah removed the covering of the ark and looked, and indeed the surface of the ground was dry. And in the second month, on the twenty-seventh day of the month, the earth was dried (Genesis 7:11–8:14).

To accept at face value the scriptural depiction of the Flood is to believe in a supernatural event of catastrophic proportions unique in history. Numerous local deluges have wreaked devastating havoc in relatively confined areas, but compared with Noah's flood these were but puddles in contrast to an ocean. Much theological and scientific speculation exists about the precise meaning of "the fountains of the great deep," or the "windows of heaven," or the exact height of "fifteen cubits upward." But in the immediate concern, the discontinuity between the past world and the present one, what matters is that the Genesis flood depicts an incomprehensible change in the natural world brought about by the supernatural intervention of God. Only a power and phenomenon now unknown to us could have done to the earth what Scripture says God did through this flood.

The entire earth, including the highest peaks, covered in water? Our minds struggle to comprehend it. Nothing in human history or experience is remotely close. Our best guesses, even scientifically based guesses, are just that—guesses. Theologians have seen in the Flood, which was God's judgment upon the earth, a destruction of the old creation, in the sense of the world being cast back to the primeval state of *tohu vbohu*, "without form and void," of Genesis 1:2 before another, greatly changed existence emerged.

The claim that no scientific evidence for such a flood exists begs the question. How could scientists, working from two premises—ontological naturalism, and continuity between the past and the future—get it right about a supernatural event that has made the past radically different from the future?

What's not surprising, then, is that many scientists deny the universality of Noah's flood. Given the assumption of naturalism, and the limits of induction, they would almost have to. What's surprising is that many Christians, based on this denial, do the same, despite the stark testimony of Scripture.

The biblical record shows vast changes in the physical nature of the world occurring relatively early, changes (apparently) in the DNA of humans and plants, and a massive transformation of the planet's surface itself. That's why the inductive inferences of science, which retrodict from the "here and now," get the "done and gone" of origins wrong.

"Contemporary scientific interpretation is," wrote William VanDoodewaard, "extrapolated into the distant past with a spirit of high certainty, often equated with truth, and is typically done without any impetus to consider whether human ability, the tools of science, and the way those tools are used may be more limited than is commonly believed."[29]

The Genesis Creation—God speaking the world into existence, God breathing into a fully formed Adam "the breath of life" (Genesis 2:7)—reveals a process beyond anything that any conceivable configuration of our neurons could ever describe, much less science, given its inherent limitations. Even with six more Einsteins, science will never explain how God created the world, especially if, by default, it rules out God.

Outside the biblical account, humans are not even close to understanding Creation. On the contrary, the model of origins that science now projects blatantly contradicts the biblical account, which should provide powerful evidence to Bible-believing Christians about the limits of inductive inference in science.

The limits of induction, however, are minor compared to the greatest challenge to scientism and its pretentions, and that is the inexorable intrusion of assumption that colors, distorts, and at times upends human thought, even true thought.

1. Though not specifically the point here, it's a point worth noting, especially when it comes to many claims of scientism. One can draw valid conclusions, conclusions that are even guaranteed, logically, from the premises. But that doesn't mean the conclusion must be true. The truth or falsity of the conclusion relies on the truth or falsity of the premises, the assumptions. How, then, does one know if one's assumptions are true? That's, perhaps, the most crucial question in the entire creation-evolution controversy.

2. Peter Smith, *An Introduction to Formal Logic* (Cambridge, UK: Cambridge University Press, 2003), 2 (italics in the original).

3. Peter Lipton, *Inference to the Best Explanation*, 2nd ed., International Library of Philosophy (London: Routledge, 2004), 5.

4. David Hume, *An Enquiry Concerning Human Understanding*, Dover Philosophical Classics (Mineola, NY: Dover Publications, 2004), 17 (italics in the original).

5. Ibid., 26.

6. Bird, *Philosophy of Science*, Kindle edition, chap. 5.

7. Putnam, *Philosophy in an Age of Science*, 48.

8. Another version of this issue was introduced by Nelson Goodman in *Fact, Fiction, and Forecast* (1955). Goodman writes about a quality called "grue." An object is grue if, and only if, when observed before time *(T)* it is green, but if observed at any time later than time *(T)* it is blue. Thus, if we observe a bunch of emeralds, and all are green, then we could assume that "all emeralds are green." After all, we have empirical evidence for our position. However, if we observe those emeralds before time *(T)*, and they are green, then we have to assume that the statement "All emeralds are grue" is true too, and that if we observe them after time *(T)*, then they will be blue (not green). Thus, we have two conflicting hypotheses about the same thing, but both with strong confirming evidence. Hence the problem about drawing conclusions based on induction, which is why the grue problem has been called "the new riddle of induction."

9. David Papineau, "Philosophy of Science," in Bunnin and Tsui-James, *Companion to Philosophy*, 287.

10. Del Ratzsch, "Science and Religion," in *The Oxford Handbook of Philosophical Theology*, ed. Thomas P. Flint and Michael C. Rea, Oxford Handbooks in Religion and Theology (Oxford: Oxford University Press, 2009), 70.

11. Quoted in Putnam, *Philosophy in an Age of Science*, 47.

12. Aristotle, quoted in William Kneale and Martha Kneale, *The Development of Logic* (Oxford: Clarendon Press, 1962), 97.

13. Rosenberg, *Atheist's Guide to Reality*, Kindle edition, chap. 1.

14. John C. Lennox, *God's Undertaker: Has Science Buried God?* (Oxford: Lion, 2009), 9.

15. Richard C. Lewontin, "Billions and Billions of Demons," *New York Review of Books*, January 9, 1997, http://www.nybooks.com/articles/1997/01/09/billions-and-billions-of-demons/ (italics in the original).

16. This is the kind of admission that social-constructive theorists love. Social-constructive theorists argue that all human knowledge, including science, are social and cultural constructs as opposed to objective assertions about reality. Though their positions are overstated, that's all they are—overstated. In other words, some truth to social constructivism exists, which means even science—including the science of origins—isn't anywhere as objective as it is asserted to be.

17. Laurence BonJour, "Against Materialism," in *The Waning of Materialism*, ed. Robert C. Koons and George Bealer (Oxford: Oxford University Press, 2010), 10.

18. Carroll, *Big Picture*, 133 (italics in the original).

19. Francis S. Collins, *The Language of God* (New York: Free Press, 2006), 45.

20. Dawkins, *Selfish Gene*, 12.

21. Stuart Kauffman, *At Home in the Universe: The Search for Laws of Self-Organization and*

Complexity (New York: Oxford University Press, 1995), 31.

22. Richard Dawkins, *The Blind Watchmaker* (New York: W. W. Norton, 1996), 1.

23. Ibid.

24. Martin Heidegger, *Being and Time*, trans. John Macquarrie and Edward Robinson (New York: Harper Perennial Modern Thought, 2008).

25. Richard M. Davidson, "The Genesis Account of Origins," in Klingbeil, *Genesis Creation Account*, 124.

26. William VanDoodewaard, *The Quest for the Historical Adam: Genesis, Hermeneutics, and Human Origins* (Grand Rapids, MI: Reformation Heritage Books, 2015), Kindle edition.

27. Gingerich, *God's Universe*, 98, 99.

28. See Richard M. Davidson, "Biblical Evidence for the Universality of the Genesis Flood," in *Creation, Catastrophe, and Calvary*, ed. John Templeton Baldwin (Hagerstown, MD: Review and Herald, 2000), 79–92.

29. VanDoodewaard, *Quest for the Historical Adam*, Kindle edition.

CHAPTER 7

THE INEXORABLE
INTRUSION OF ASSUMPTION

The Passion of the Western Mind, published in 1991, was Richard Tarnas's best-selling spin on the intellectual history of Western thought from the ancient Greeks to postmodernism. In the back pages, he placed a chronology of crucial events, starting with 2000 B.C. ("Migrations of Greek-speaking Indo-European peoples into Aegean area begin") and ending with A.D. 1989, 1990 ("End of Cold War, collapse of Communism in Eastern Europe"). Amid such epochal happenings as the "Exodus of Hebrews from Egypt under Moses" (1250 B.C.), the "Birth of Jesus of Nazareth" (8–4 B.C.), the "Visigoth sack of Rome" (A.D. 410), and "Hitler comes to power in Germany" (A.D. 1933), Tarnas included "Kuhn's *The Structure of Scientific Revolutions*" (A.D. 1962).[1]

A book considered one of the most influential texts of the twentieth century, Thomas Kuhn's *The Structure of Scientific Revolutions*—though not saying anything that had not been said before[2]—plucked an intellectual nerve that's still reverberating today. The work became a philosophical phenomenon that has echoed into the succeeding generations of thinkers, who either supported Kuhn's ideas (some even taking them further than he did) or sparred against his concepts. Whether revered or reviled, *The Structure of Scientific Revolutions* has not been ignored.

What did it say? Basically what *Baptizing the Devil* is saying—that science is nowhere near as logical, rational, objective, and certain as (often) claimed or as (even more often) believed. One stream of Kuhn's thought is captured in a statement he quotes in the book, a statement by quantum physics pioneer Max Plank: "A new scientific truth does not triumph by convincing its opponents and making them see the light, but rather because its opponents eventually die, and a new generation grows up that is familiar with it."[3]

If true, even partially, what does Plank's thought say about the objectivity, much less the correctness, of scientific claims? A "scientific truth" should be accepted or rejected based on proof, on evidence, on data, right? But, certainly, not on which generation of scientists happens to be around at the time.

Unfortunately, according to Kuhn, science doesn't work nearly so rationally or objectively. Science does not allow humanity to step outside of itself, in a sense, to discover the world as it truly is. It doesn't put the scientist, or the scientific community, in an Archimedean vantage point that allows an unencumbered or unfettered view of reality. Instead, science and scientific research is, really, just another way that highly developed protoplasm with a reasoning consciousness (scientists) can view the world that it interacts with. It's often a fruitful interaction, for sure, but fruitfulness isn't synonymous with correctness or truth.

In *The Structure of Scientific Revolutions*, Kuhn wrote that human subjectivity—the values, the prejudices, the preconceptions, and the assumptions of both individual scientists and the scientific community as a whole—influence scientific endeavors and conclusions. Instead of science proceeding in a rational, logical, step-by-step "accumulation of individual discoveries and inventions,"[4] cultural, historical, and psychological factors cannot be weeded out or even purged from the scientific process and, thus, inevitably affect results. The conclusions of the scientist are, Kuhn argued, "probably determined by his prior experience in other fields, by the accidents of his investigation, and by his own individual makeup. . . . An apparently arbitrary element, compounded of personal and historical accident, is always a formative ingredient of the beliefs espoused by a given scientific community at a given time."[5]

Arbitrary elements, accidents, and individual makeup? Sounds like finger painting, not modern science.

The paradigm

Though not inventing the word *paradigm*, Kuhn made it a household term—at least in households interested in the history of science and its epistemological claims. For Kuhn, a paradigm is the background, the assumptions, the framework or model in which scientific research takes place. It is a "set of received beliefs"[6] that forms the disciplinary matrix in which the research unfolds. To do science, one must have concepts and assumptions about the nature of the world and, specifically, about the nature of the part of the world being pulled apart and parsed. The paradigm determines the questions asked, the places to look for answers, and the methods considered legitimate in looking for those answers. Paradigms are, so to speak, the supertheories or metatheories that "underline and gird an entire tradition of scientific research and theorizing."[7]

When a scientist works within a paradigm, she is doing what Kuhn famously referred to as "normal science." That is, the scientist is doing her "puzzle-solving" within this specific and (it is very important to note) limited framework. She is not going outside the paradigm; in particular, she's not challenging it, either. Rather, everything is done within the paradigm itself.

This last point is crucial. When working within a paradigm, when doing "normal science," the scientist is not questioning the paradigm; on the contrary, the paradigm is what questions everything else. The framework is not judged by what unfolds within it; instead, *the framework judges* what unfolds within it. The truth or falsity of a hypothesis is determined by how it jives with the paradigm.

"A 'system,'" wrote Norman Malcolm, "provides the boundaries within which we ask questions, carry out investigations, and make judgments. Hypotheses are put forth and challenged, *within* a system. Verification, justification, the search for evidence, occur *within* a system. The framework propositions of the system are not put to the test, not backed up by evidence."[8]

In the National Football League, when a play is challenged by an opposing team, the referees examine the play itself, but only in the context of the rules of the game. The rules are not being challenged or questioned; instead, the rules are what determine if the challenge or question is valid. That, according to Kuhn, is what a paradigm is—the rules of the game.

Scientists, wrote Leonard Brand, "do not try to test the paradigm, but assume it is true and use it to guide their exploration of new phenomena within the paradigm's domain. This process Kuhn called normal science, because that is what scientists normally do."[9]

Kuhn's paradigm is another take on the inexorable intrusion of assumption that permeates all intellectual endeavors, including science. His concept undermines the common notion of scientific neutrality and objectivity, the idea that a scientist builds his scientific theories based on neutral and objective observations of the world. According to Kuhn, that's not what happens. Neutral or objective observations are as mythical as unicorns and dragons. Scientists view the world through the lens of whatever the paradigm happens to be at a specific time in history. Different times, different paradigms; different science, different theories—and these paradigms and the theories developed within them are not, argues Kuhn, progressing on some necessarily inescapable trajectory toward truth.[10]

Which leads to the argument, valid insofar as it goes (how far it goes is an open question), that even observation is theory-laden, and that scientists have no "immaculate perception" of the world they investigate with their theories and experiments and (at times) expensive and complicated theory-laden devices. Two or three or ten scientists can look at the same thing, but each understand it differently, depending upon the paradigm through which each views it.

Or, they might not even see it at all. Medieval European astronomers, for example, working from their Aristotelean paradigm, all but ignored a supernova explosion that had been duly noted in Japan and China, because in Europe the notion of a never-changing and perfect celestial universe dominated their thinking and influenced not only how they looked at things but even what things they looked at.

"A fairly bright new star in the sky," wrote Stuart Firestein, "was apparently not considered an important enough event to record; it wasn't likely to be any more than some 'disturbance.' . . . In contrast, another supernova that could be detected by the naked eye in the night sky occurred in 1572. Now well into the Renaissance and more liberated from the tyranny of classical authority, it was recorded by astronomers throughout Europe."[11]

Theory-laden observations and interpretations might not be wrong; they're just theory-laden, that's all. The issue at hand, of course, is how one knows (if one even *can* know) whether the theory-ladenness of the observation is correct.

"The truth," wrote David Lindberg, "is that scientists, ancient or modern, begin *every* investigation with strong commitments regarding the nature of the universe and very clear ideas about which models may legitimately be employed to represent it."[12]

Along this same line, Francis Crick wrote, "The ultimate aim of the modern movement in biology is in fact to explain *all* biology in terms of physics and chemistry."[13] That's fine, even (somewhat) logical. But it is a philosophical assertion, not one dogmatically demanded by science—an assertion that, of necessity, will color whatever conclusions arise out of it.

A 2016 article in the *Guardian* covered the term *post-truth* and its being named Oxford Dictionaries' word of the year. The adjective was defined as "relating to or denoting circumstances in which objective facts are less influential in shaping public opinion than appeals to emotion and personal belief."[14] Not long afterward, another *Guardian* article appeared about post-truth and its relation to science. The title of the article? "Science Has Always Been a Bit 'Post-Truth.'"[15]

Science? Post-truth?

Haven't people been taught all their lives that science was nothing but the objective, rational, evidence-based pursuit of pure, objective truth and nothing but the truth? But now it's seen (finally!) as "a bit 'post-truth,'" that is, a situation in which emotions and personal belief, more than "objective facts," shape public opinion.

The second *Guardian* piece talked about Kuhn's book, saying, "Kuhn argued that the way that both scientists and the general public need to understand the history of science is Orwellian. He is alluding to [the George Orwell novel]

1984, in which the protagonist's job is to rewrite newspapers from the past to make it seem as though the government's current policy is where it had been heading all along. In this perpetually airbrushed version of history, the public never sees the U-turns, switches of allegiance and errors of judgement that might cause them to question the state's progressive narrative. Confidence in the status quo is maintained and new recruits are inspired to follow in its lead. Kuhn claimed that what applies to totalitarian 1984 also applies to science united under the spell of a paradigm."[16]

Interestingly enough, the article agreed with Kuhn, using an example from a recent meeting of the Royal Society and British Academy called "New Trends in Evolutionary Biology." According to the article, "Officially, the event was open to the widest possible range of criticisms of the Neo-Darwinian synthesis. Yet the invitation did not extend to proponents of intelligent design theory who have publicized most of the same criticisms of the synthesis. It would seem that the paradigm shift demanded by advocates of intelligent design would have been a step too far."[17]

It would have been a step too far, not because of science but because of the cultural assumptions that the scientific-industrial complex, dogmatically trapped in its paradigm, has imposed upon how science should be done. Meanwhile, Shawn Otto could write, "As a foundation of democracy, science is a font of tolerance. It is also a great beneficiary of diversity because it thrives on challenges from differing viewpoints to find unexpected breakthroughs and to make its conclusions stronger."[18] That is, just as long as the viewpoints aren't too differing, it seems.

The assumption of Robert Hazen

Robert M. Hazen is the Clarence J. Robinson Professor of Earth Sciences at George Mason University and a research scientist at the Geophysical Laboratory of the Carnegie Institution of Washington. He has also given lectures for The Teaching Company, including a 24-part series called "Origins of Life." The lectures present a fascinating look at how a paradigm works.

Early in the series, Hazen set out his assumptions, stating:

In this lecture series I make a basic assumption that life emerged by some kind of natural process. I propose that life arose by a sequence of events that are completely consistent with the natural laws of chemistry and physics. In this assumption I am like most other scientists. I believe in a universe that is ordered by these natural laws. Like other scientists, I rely on the power of observation and experiments and theoretical reasoning to understand how the cosmos came to be the way it is.

Using this kind of reasoning, I assume that life arose in the ancient scorched Earth from the simplest of basic raw materials: air, water, and rock. Thus, life emerged nearly four billion years ago by a series of chemical and physical processes that were completely in accord with natural laws. Though I have to confess, the nitty-gritty details of that transformation remain a deep mystery. But just because we do not know all the details does not mean it did not happen by lawful natural processes.[19]

Hazen's assumption that "life emerged by some kind of natural process" does not mean that it did actually happen that way or that it had to. His assumption is based on a philosophical, or even a metaphysical, view of reality, not a scientific one. The fact that "the natural laws of chemistry and physics" are now at work does not prove that these "natural laws of chemistry and physics," or others like (or unlike) them, started life on earth four billion years ago.

From a Christian perspective, Hazen's assumption that life arose from these laws of chemistry and physics is like assuming that the key to understanding the origins of chess can be found by studying only the physics and chemistry of the board, of the pieces, and by studying the principles behind the motion of the pieces themselves. In studying the origins of the game, one is not allowed to look, probe, or ask questions beyond the board, the pieces, and the moves themselves. That restriction would be fine if, in reality, the game of chess originated only from the board, the pieces, and the moves themselves. However, because human beings created the game, physicists, chemists, philosophers, and researchers could study the board, the pieces, and the moves deeply and carefully and for a long time, and, although they might think they had answers regarding the origins of chess, or were close to getting them, they would of necessity always be wrong.

In Hazen's paradigm, to assume that life arose "from the simplest of basic raw materials: air, water, and rock" is to make an astonishing assumption and certainly not one based on anything seen in air, rocks, and water today, or in anything that the laws of chemistry and physics now do (to the degree they are understood). After all, when was the last time anyone saw air, water, and rock—even aided by the natural laws of chemistry and physics—do anything even remotely close to what it is assumed they did billions of years ago? The conjecture that everything from phytoplankton to human consciousness arose only from "air, water, and rock," though (perhaps) not a priori impossible, requires a chasmal leap of faith regarding events of which we know little, but which we assume occurred. Or, as Hazen said it, "the nitty-gritty details of that transformation [from air, water, and rock to, say, Aristophanes] remain a deep mystery."

He also said that "I rely on the power of observation and experiments and theoretical reasoning," meaning that what he observes *today*, and the experiments that he does *today*, and the theoretical reasoning based on those present-day observations and experiments are what he uses to determine what happened "nearly four billion years ago." Working, then, not only on these assumptions, but also on the assumption that one can retrodict from the present world to the primeval one, Hazen began discussing the various theories and ideas about how, according to this paradigm, life on earth could have started.

After setting the stage with the historical background in the search for life's origins (including a lectured titled "What Is Life?" which is still an ongoing discussion), he talked about the most well-known and, at the time, potentially fruitful models for how life could have started billions of years ago from a still-unknown combination of air, water, rock, and the laws of physics and chemistry.

He began with the famous Miller-Urey experiment. In 1952, University of Chicago chemists Harold Urey and Stanley Miller (Urey's student) did experiments that showed, given the right conditions, a mixture of water and air could produce organic molecules, perhaps in some shallow, prebiotic pool on the earth's surface. The experiment created a sensation, transforming the science of life's chemical origins and prompting thousands of similar experiments for half a century. However, within a decade, difficult questions arose—such as how well did the experiment really mimic earth's supposed initial conditions—that, over time, cast a heavy shadow of just how viable a model the Miller-Urey experiment really was.

By the 1970s, alternative hypotheses to Miller-Urey were proposed, including the idea (despite Stanley Miller's fervent objections) that life, instead of arising in some shallow prebiotic pool, started in hot hydrothermal vents of the deep ocean. Scientists found some compelling theoretical and even experimental evidence for this model. However promising the idea (and some still hold to it), objections were raised, including, said Hazen, "the argument that life could not survive under such conditions."[20]

Scientists began looking in other directions. Instead of the deep ocean floor, perhaps deep space—"loaded with interesting organic molecules, which must have predated Earth by billions of years"[21]—might be where the chemical origins of life began. Cosmic debris might have had the requisite chemicals that could have spawned life here. This model, however, came with a host of unresolved problems, one reason why Stanley Miller, still defending his turf, argued, "Organics from outer space, that's garbage, that really is."[22]

Others speculated that, instead of in a shallow pool or in the deep ocean or from space, the origins of life could be found among molten rocks well above

1000°C, and even under high pressure—not an environment that would be too bio-friendly, one might think. Nevertheless, this hypothesis (and variants of it) has been, and is still being, studied. Others have resorted to another model, called the "clay-life" theory of Scottish scientist Graham Cairns-Smith. According to this idea, "fine-grained crystals of clay might, all by themselves, have been the very first life forms on earth."[23]

This back and forth—one theory, its faults; another, its faults; another, its faults—comprised a good part of Hazen's lectures. (For what it's worth, and it's worth something, he presented the intense bickering, bias, and vitriol between scientists that accompanied their science at times.) The "Origins of Life" series was well organized, logical, and fairly deep for laymen, but it presented a scientist's understanding of the current research into life's origins *within the parameters of his assumptions.*

However (and this is the fascinating part), even after Hazen presented reason after reason why model after model did not work, it never seemed to have entered his mind that none of these models provided solid answers perhaps because *the paradigm itself was wrong.*

But how could it have entered his mind? That was never the issue to begin with. These were not metamodels and metaexperiments designed to question the paradigm; the prebiotic-soup model, the 1000°C-molten-rock model, the outer-space model were all unfolded *within* the paradigm itself. The paradigm formed the outline upon which these origins-of-life models were all first projected and then, for now, rejected. The fact that no model worked never called into question the paradigm itself of how life started. They were not supposed to, any more than a flag is thrown during an NFL game in order to challenge the rules of the game.

The air-water-rock paradigm was assumed, like a plane in Euclidian geometry. The various models were being questioned, not the assumption "that life arose in the ancient scorched Earth from the simplest of basic raw materials: air, water, and rock. Thus, life emerged nearly four billion years ago by a series of chemical and physical processes that were completely in accord with natural laws." This is the starting point, the foundation upon which all that followed was premised and built.

But if that starting point happened to be wrong? What, then, could we say of all that followed from within that framework? One might be able to make accurate predictions within the framework, and one might even be able to create workable technology within it as well, but none of this makes a false paradigm true, any more than accurate predictions made with the Ptolemaic worldview meant that the earth was in the center of the universe.

Hazen's series fits snugly with *The Structure of Scientific Revolutions.* "Closely examined, whether historically or in the contemporary laboratory," Kuhn wrote, a scientific "enterprise seems an attempt to force nature into the pre-formed and relatively inflexible box that the paradigm supplies. No part of the aim of normal science is to call forth new sorts of phenomena; indeed those that will not fit the box are often not seen at all. Nor do scientists normally aim to invent new theories, and they are often intolerant of those invented by others."[24]

However, if Hazen's paradigm was wrong, then it's no wonder no model worked. The researchers were not only asking the wrong questions; they were looking for answers in places that could provide none. It's a more sophisticated, but real-life, version of the man looking for his lost keys at night in a place where he didn't lose them to begin with. Why, then, look there?

"Because," he said, "this was the only place with light."

After all, if the paradigm for life's origins forced researchers to look to mol-ten rocks well above 1000°C as a possible source of life, might not one assume that something is possibly amiss with the paradigm itself?

As happened with those who missed the supernova because it didn't fit their paradigm, maybe this paradigm has blinded origins-of-life researchers to what was right before their eyes all along. Or, as Kuhn said above, maybe their assumptions caused the phenomena not to be "seen at all."

For instance, talking about ribonucleic acid (RNA), Hazen said, "The emergence of RNA represents a crucial step in life's origins, yet no one knows where the RNA came from. Decades of frustrating chemical experiments have demonstrated repeatedly that RNA is a frustratingly difficult molecule to make. The RNA World could not possibly have emerged fully formed from random processes in the primordial soup. In spite of decades of focused study, no plausible mechanism has been found to make all the three components of RNA—the sugar ribose, a phosphate group, and a base—much less link them all together in just the right way and then string them end-to-end to make an RNA strand. There must have been some critical transition stage that bridged the prebiotic milieu and the RNA World."[25]

Perhaps. But "no plausible mechanism" has been found, because "no plau-sible mechanism" exists within the paradigm that would have allowed RNA to have "fully formed from random processes in the primordial soup." Maybe there were no "random processes" to begin with. Thus, if the paradigm assumes random processes, but none exist, it's not surprising all the models reached a dead end.

From a vantage point outside of Hazen's paradigm, his lectures reveal what happens when you make the false *necessary*. From a creationist perspective, it's like limiting a priori one's search for the origins of chess to the chessboard, the chess pieces, and the chess moves alone. No wonder scientists are finding "no plausible mechanism." *It is very difficult to find a black cat in a dark room*, warns a proverb, *especially when there is no cat.* However much design jumps out, the paradigm does not allow them to see it. In the context of how scientists interpret what they observe, Alfred Tauber wrote, "Accordingly, psychological projection, self-interest, and, most abstractly, commitments to a particular hypothesis or theory, might contaminate the sanctity of scientific facts and their proper interpretation."[26]

You think?

After World War I, for example, one reason many scientists were resistant to Einstein's special theory of relativity was that Einstein was a German, and thus it was deemed as "Hun" physics. A few decades later, his work was rejected as "Jew" physics instead.

Hazen's series shows, too, that no matter how popular or influential Karl Popper's idea of falsification is, it's not what scientists purposely do with their own theories. According to Kuhn, falsification is the opposite of the science done within a paradigm. How likely is it that scientists spend years working on a theory, publishing, promoting, researching, collaborating, writing, only to seek to falsify it once a model is established? With grants, prestige, jobs, awards, honors at stake, how many scientists openly try to undermine their own theories? Certainly not the scientists Hazen talked about, who, it seemed, vociferously defended their own theories while doing all that they could to falsify rival ones. In short, falsification is about the last thing scientists want to do to their own theories.[27]

"When one scientific theory is enshrined as the reigning paradigm," wrote John West, "dissenting views are often silenced for reasons other than lack of evidence. Dissenting views represent a threat to the ruling paradigm, and so those who have earned power and prestige from advancing it are loath to let their authority be eroded. For this and other reasons, scientists who have spent their lives working within one paradigm may have a difficult time acknowledging problems within that paradigm no matter how much contrary evidence accumulates."[28]

In the journal *Nature*, the chair of the astronomy department at Harvard warned about the danger of science trapping itself within a single worldview or paradigm. "To truly move forward," he argued, "free thought must be encouraged outside the mainstream. Multiple interpretations of existing data and alternative motivations for collecting new data must be supported."[29]

A new normal

However fundamental a paradigm may be (and here's Kuhn's most controversial idea), it is not irreplaceable. As normal science progresses, he argued, over time "anomalies"—phenomena that don't do what they are supposed to (at least according to the paradigm)—may arise. Anomalies are data that don't seem to be reading the scientific literature; they are experiments producing results that shouldn't be there. According to the paradigm, X should occur when you do Y, but Z occurs instead. And Z occurs again and again. When enough anomalies occur, persist, and can't be explained away within the paradigm, science reaches a "crisis," and the edifice that dominated that branch of science is called into question.

If unresolved, the crisis leads to a "scientific revolution." The entire paradigm is swept away, along with the assumptions, theories, formulas, and ideas that arose out of it. More radically, it's all replaced by another paradigm, which often has assumptions, theories, formulas, and ideas different from, or even contradictory to, the assumptions, theories, formulas, and ideas of the previous one. To use a political analogy, imagine decades of communism—and all the propaganda, politics, and beliefs that go with it—overthrown and replaced with the propaganda, politics, and beliefs of free-market capitalism. It's like replacing the screeds of Vladimir Lenin and Karl Marx with those of John Rockefeller and Warren Buffett.

For Kuhn, and this is important, the new paradigm isn't usually a mere modification of the old one; it's not a tweaking of this point or that. Instead, it is a rejection of the entire structure itself. It's not reshuffling the deck chairs; it's scuttling the ship and sailing a different one. "A new paradigm," wrote Leonard Brand, "is typically not just a modification of an existing one. Often it is not even compatible with the old paradigm."[30]

A new paradigm presents a new way of studying and looking at whatever you were studying and looking at before. Imagine the shift from an Aristotelean-Ptolemaic cosmos to a Copernican one. One day you see the sun moving across the sky; the next day you see, instead, how the sun appears to you as the earth spins on its axis. It's the same sun doing today the same as it did the day before, yet you see two radically different phenomena.

Objectively, nothing changed. A paradigm shift is a subjective change in the viewer, and not in what's viewed, even if in the new paradigm what's viewed appears to be different from what it appeared to be in the old one. A paradigm shift is an epistemological, not an ontological, change—regardless of how the ontology might now appear to the viewer to have changed. The point cannot be overstated: *In a scientific revolution, the only change is in the scientist and the science being done.* The world itself stays the same, no matter how differently it appears to human observers in the new paradigm. As Kuhn famously wrote, "When paradigms change, the world itself changes with them."[31] Not really, but from the human standpoint, the only standpoint we have, he's right.

Something as drastic as a scientific revolution, said Kuhn, obviously doesn't come easily. A new paradigm often faces entrenched and dogmatic opposition, especially from those who have spent their lives and built their reputations on the science they did within the old one. If scientists, contrary to Popper, aren't so ready to change a pet theory *within a paradigm*, how easily are they going to give up the paradigm itself? It would be one thing for an origins-of-life researcher to abandon the 1000°C-molten-rock theory, but drastically something else to abandon the whole air-water-rock-natural-law paradigm.

What a scientific revolution means, then, is that scientists have not only a new and different metapicture of how the world is, but new theories, a new vocabulary, new formulas, new questions, and new ways of interpreting the world, all flowing naturally from the new paradigm itself—again, even though the object of study has not changed from what it appeared to be in the old paradigm. A different paradigm can present a different view of what reality is or even a different concept of what "truth" (a slippery word in science) is.

Of course, how one can know if the new paradigm is correct begs the question. One can't, Kuhn argued; one can only hope that maybe he or she is on the right track and that, down the road, more data will help confirm it.

"The man who embraces a new paradigm at an early stage," wrote Kuhn, "must often do so in defiance of the evidence provided by problem-solving. He must, that is, have faith that the new paradigm will succeed with the many large problems that confront it, knowing only that the older paradigm has failed with a few. A decision of that kind can only be made on faith."[32]

(Faith? Did Kuhn use the word *faith* within the context of science? Apparently so, because, contrary to loud protestations to the contrary, science uses faith too; that is, if you define "faith" as belief in what you cannot "prove," a concept exceedingly sticky in general and in science in particular.)

Kuhn's point is that, contrary to popular opinion, science has not proceeded on this straight linear path of one rational and logical empirical truth—objectively pulled out of the air, water, rocks, or cells—building upon another and then upon another, like a complicated math problem, until it reaches the inevitable climax. Science is, argued Kuhn, a much more haphazard and subjective process than most people believe.

After all, if scientific "truth" changes when the paradigm changes, how "true" was the science to begin with? If the paradigm could be swept away, what about the "truths" that were hewed, hammered out, and excavated from it?

The assumptions of Charles Darwin
The Structure of Scientific Revolutions has not been without its many paladins and critics. A cottage industry arose after Kuhn's book, either for[33] or against.[34]

His work played gleefully into the hands of the postmodernists, who independently of Kuhn had launched influential critiques on the concepts of rationality and knowledge in general, including a critique of science that went far beyond where Kuhn first intended to go.

Whether normal science proceeds or crises arise or new paradigms emerge as Kuhn asserts isn't the issue here. The issue is that Kuhn brought up another manifestation of one of science's (or any epistemological endeavor's) weaknesses: the inexorable intrusion of assumption. Kuhn offered a full-frontal assault on the notion of science occurring in some überobjective vacuum that enables scientists to do science without assumptions that inevitably color the outcome. These assumptions, however assumed or whether right or wrong, affect conclusions. And though wrong assumptions do not *inevitably* lead to wrong conclusions, they likely will.

Take Darwin's theory of evolution through natural selection. Charles Darwin wasn't in an epistemological neutral zone when he proposed natural selection as the explanation for the different forms of life. On the contrary, he constructed his theory upon assumptions and presuppositions that filtered not only what he saw, but how he interpreted what he saw. Metaphysical, historical, social, personal, and even theological factors paved the road to his theory, even if he took turns that many hardcore evolutionists now believe led him astray. "Much of what Darwin said," wrote Richard Dawkins, "is, in detail, wrong."[35]

Darwin published *On the Origin of Species* (1859) less than two hundred years following Isaac Newton's monumentally influential *Principia*. Though a time of great intellectual ferment, the nineteenth century was one in which Ignaz Semmelweis (d. 1865), for instance, faced stiff resistance from the scientific establishment over his claim that if doctors washed their hands before delivering babies, the risk of infection in mothers would be reduced. It was a century in which the greatest scientific minds believed in an eternal and static cosmos, in the aether, and in a universe that worked with clocklike determinism and precision—scientific dogma now all believed to be incorrect.

Especially important was the influence that the *Principia* continued to radiate even into Darwin's time. Newton's belief not only in God, but that God worked actively in the universe, didn't keep him from writing one of the greatest scientific treatises in history. Over time, however, the mechanical nature of his laws (that is, the ability that their descriptions gave humans to predict precisely what physical objects would do, once a few numbers were plugged into the equations) pushed many thinkers toward a purely mechanistic, materialistic view of reality in which God was deemed not only superfluous but an outright drag on scientific progress.

"The astonishing success of the Newtonian theory," wrote W. C. Dampier, "in explaining the mechanisms of heaven led to an overestimation of the power of mechanical conceptions to give an ultimate account of the whole Universe."[36]

A materialist-only creation, though a concept that could be traced back to the atomists of the fifth and fourth centuries B.C., took off especially among the French, who even in the eighteenth century pushed Newton's work toward a crass materialism engulfed in natural law alone and certainly with no need of a Creator or of any divine influence. Treatises such as La Mettrie's *Man a Machine* (1747) and *The Natural History of the Soul* (1745) and Baron d'Holbach's *The System of Nature* (1770) espoused a materialist understanding of reality, one that had a great effect on Darwin. Newton's French aficionados taught that "the Newtonian system indicated reality as a great machine, in all essentials already known, so that man, body and soul, became part of an invincible mechanical necessity."[37] Carl Sagan's famous philosophical (not scientific) quote "The Cosmos is all that is or ever was or ever will be"[38] (inductive inference gone kind of berserk[39]) is another manifestation of this ancient philosophical assumption, even if Sagan's remark is an expression of epistemological humility in contrast to Richard Dawkins' cosmic inductive leap of faith: "A good case can be made that Darwinism is true," he wrote, "not just on this planet but all over the universe wherever life may be found."[40]

Many also believed, based on Enlightenment concepts of reason and progress, that humanity could uncover ultimate truth (in their thinking, the bottom-line physical nature of all reality), and do so without God, whom they didn't believe existed to begin with. Even in the eighteenth century some thought that science was on a path toward a theory of everything, a final account of the world explained through natural forces alone, a goal that some physicists are still pursuing today,[41] no matter how heavy-laden with presupposition the quest is. (After all, how could anyone know that a single theory of everything even exists?)

"The whole eighteenth century," wrote Ernst Cassirer, "is permeated by this conviction, namely, that in the history of humanity the time had now arrived to deprive nature of its carefully guarded secret, to leave it no longer in the dark to be marveled at as an incomprehensible mystery but to bring it under the bright light of reason and analyze it with all its fundamental forces."[42]

Besides the powerful influence of this materialist philosophy, Darwin was also affected by contemporary theories in geology, which—from the works of James Hutton (1795) and Charles Lyell (1830–1833)—promoted a uniformitarian view of earth's history. This is the position that the geological record can be best explained, not from any catastrophic event (such as Noah's flood), but from millions of years of the same geological processes and natural laws observed today—a view that, in recent years, has come under more criticism.[43] Nevertheless, in Darwin's time, this sentiment would have established the background in which the evolution of the species could have unfolded, thus giving him what he needed for his theory itself.

Also, Charles Darwin didn't think up the theory of evolution ex nihilo. In fact, he didn't think it up at all. The young naturalist did not venture into nature, magnifying glass in hand, and, peering intently, hit upon the idea that species evolve into other species over long ages. This idea had already been out there, millennia ago even. Old Testament scholar Ángel Rodríguez has found in ancient Near Eastern literature cosmogonic concepts that, while certainly not espousing the theory of evolution as understood today, nevertheless do "contain elements of the evolutionary ideology promoted today in some scientific circles. In that sense, the Ancient Near Eastern views should be considered part of the history of the idea of natural evolution."[44]

Perhaps one of the most incredible "scientific" treatises of antiquity was Lucretius's (c. 99–55 B.C.) *On the Nature of Things*, a tome of 7,400 lines that attempts to explain reality in terms of natural causes alone. Though written as kind of anodyne against the fear of death, or more specifically of divine retribution after death, it explained the natural world as arising out of a chance confluence of atoms, independently of the gods. Our world, Lucretius wrote, "is the creation of nature: the atoms themselves collided spontaneously and fortuitously, clashing together blindly, unsuccessfully, and ineffectually in a multitude of ways, until at last those atoms coalesced which, when suddenly dashed together, could always form the foundations of mighty fabrics, of earth, sea, and sky, and the family of living creatures."[45]

What was amazing, however, was how he argued, not just for evolution, but for a natural selection as well. Stephen Greenblatt wrote,

> The stuff of the universe, Lucretius proposed, is an infinite number of atoms moving randomly through space, like dust motes in a sunbeam, colliding, hooking together, forming complex structures, breaking apart again, in a ceaseless process of creation and destruction. There is no escape from this process. When you look up at the night sky and, feeling unaccountably moved, marvel at the numberless stars, you are not seeing the handiwork of the gods or a crystalline sphere detached from our transient world. You are seeing the same material world of which you are a part and from whose elements you are made. There is no master plan, no divine architect, no intelligent design. All things, including the species to which you belong, have evolved over vast stretches of time. The evolution

THE INEXORABLE INTRUSION OF ASSUMPTION

is random, though in the case of living organisms it involves a principle of natural selection. That is, species that are suited to survive and to reproduce successfully endure, at least for a time; those that are not so well suited die off quickly. But nothing—from our own species to the planet on which we live to the sun that lights our days—lasts forever. Only the atoms are immortal.[46]

On the Nature of Things predated *On the Origin of Species* by about 1,900 years.

Whether *On the Nature of Things* had a direct effect on Darwin, who knows, but more contemporary thinkers certainly did, including Erasmus Darwin, Charles Darwin's grandfather, who had written on the subject of evolution. Others, such as Georges-Louis Leclerc, Comte de Buffon (1707–1788), William Charles Wells (1757–1817), Jean-Baptiste Lamarck (1744–1829), and Thomas Robert Malthus (1766–1834), all had written on topics, some directly related to the supposed evolution of the species, which created the template out of which Darwin worked. Even Darwin would admit that "the only novelty in my work is the attempt to explain *how* species become modified."[47] In other words, all he did (he believed) was to explain the *how*. For Darwin, the *what*—that species had modified over long ages—was as much an assumption that he started with as it was a conclusion he arrived at.

Darwin's theodicy problem

However naturalistic Darwin's theory itself may have been, he didn't derive it from naturalistic reasons alone. He did so from *theological* reasons as well, specifically from what is known as *theodicy*. Theodicy is the question of how to reconcile a world suffused with evil and an all-powerful, all-knowing, and all-loving God—a difficulty poignantly expressed by Fyodor Dostoevsky's character Ivan Karamazov, who, after discussing a sordid litany of evil against kids, asked, "But then there are the children, and what am I to do about them?"[48] That is, how can one justify God's existence, much less His goodness, in a world in which innocent children suffer so horrifically? At one level, this theodicy problem helped form the assumptions from which Darwin worked, assumptions that even today are seen as justifications for evolution as opposed to divine creation.

In a fascinating book, *Darwin's God: Evolution and the Problem of Evil*, Cornelius Hunter argued that Darwin had an idea about what he thought a world created by God should be like, and when the creation didn't meet those theological expectations, he looked for something other than God to explain the natural world. In other words, Darwin began with his own theological views about what the world should be like if it were created by a beneficent God, and when those views didn't match up with the world, he needed a new assumption about origins. And where could he find one other than in the naturalism already suffused throughout the intellectual atmosphere of the time?

"How could divine creation," wrote Hunter, "be reconciled with such evils? It was questions like these that, for Darwin, seemed to confirm that life is formed by blind natural forces. He was motivated toward evolution not by direct evidence in favor of his new theory but by problems with the common notion of divine creation. Creation, it seemed, does not always reflect the goodness of God, so Darwin advocated a naturalistic explanation to describe how the creation came about."[49]

In short, Darwinian evolution didn't start out as science but as theology. Something other than the loving God whom he was taught about as a child had to be the explanation for the cruelty in nature, because—in Darwin's theological understanding—a loving God couldn't be it. Hence, in his mind, uncaring and amoral natural forces, not Yahweh, explained the world, especially the natural evil in it.

"There seems to me," Darwin wrote, "too much misery in the world. I cannot persuade myself that a beneficent and omnipotent God would have designedly created the . . . [parasitic wasp] with the express intention of their feeding within the living bodies of caterpillars, or that the cat should play with mice."[50] Or "What a book a devil's chaplain might write on the clumsy, wasteful, blundering, low and horribly cruel works of nature."[51]

This thinking didn't end with Darwin, either. How often today do evolutionists argue their positions from a kind of negative theology: *Why would a good God create vestigial organs? Why would a good and caring God create parasites that live off the organs of other creatures? Why would a good and loving God create animals that need to eat other animals to survive? Why would a loving God create such violence in nature?* All these questions presuppose certain traits about how God could or should have created the world.

"A great irony reveals itself here," wrote Hunter: "evolution, the theory that made God unnecessary, is itself supported by arguments containing premises about the nature of God."[52]

Of course, no Christian should shrug off the question of evil and suffering. Yet the argument that sees them as evidence for a naturalistic-only origins, as opposed to a divine Creation, is a theological or, even more broadly, a philosophical argument. It is not a scientific argument. After all, what science could possibly reveal how a loving and all-powerful God should have created the world?[53]

Though the incorrigibility of evil continues to be a common—and reasonable—concern, it does not disprove either God's existence or His love. First, nothing in Scripture hints that evil, either moral or natural, doesn't exist. Evil—its cause,[54] consequences,[55] and solution[56]—suffuses the reality that Scripture depicts. The Word never glosses over evil, even as it affirms, again and again, the goodness and love of God.[57] For the Bible writers, evil doesn't negate God or His love. Evil is difficult to understand, especially in light of the idea of God's goodness and love, but it does not disprove them.

Take, for instance, a Bible 1,175 pages long. Of those pages, only pages 1–3 and 1174, 1175 outline a paradise where the good outweighs the bad, because there is no bad. In contrast, pages 4–1173 are ravaged with every imaginable evil—violence, war, sickness, death, corruption, incest, crime, lust, greed, revenge, hate, starvation, etc. (Fortunately, too, we have the gospel promises suffusing those same pages, offering hope to us all amid the carnage.) Only a thin layer, like a coat of paint on two sides of a brick, depicts a good world; the brick itself represents this world in which evil abounds.

What's the logic, then, that argues that the God revealed in the Bible can't exist because of evil, when the Bible that reveals this God simultaneously records the evil that, supposedly, negates His existence? Bible writers who recounted all the evil, also affirmed not just God's existence but His love and goodness. They obviously saw no contradiction between evil and God's goodness.

Next, as seen in the preceding chapter, after the Fall aspects of the natural world changed, even (apparently) at the genetic level. Nature began degenerating, and nothing in Scripture indicates that this trend has stopped. The process of death and decay, which started after the Fall, has not been reversed; it could even be accelerating. A comparison of the ages of the earliest humans to those of later years shows a significant physical decline,[58] which could be indicative of a general decline in the physical world itself. Millennia ago the Lord said,

> Lift up your eyes to the heavens,
>   look at the earth beneath;
> the heavens will vanish like smoke,
>   the earth will wear out like a garment
>   and its inhabitants die like flies (Isaiah 51:6, NIV).

Hardly a picture of a physical paradise improving with age. And God alone knows what permanent changes occurred to the planet after the Flood.

Meanwhile, Paul wrote, "The creation itself will be liberated from its bondage to decay and brought into the freedom and glory of the children of God" (Romans 8:21, NIV). Paul is acknowledging a physical decay[59] that holds the world in "bondage." Whatever exactly the text means, it's certainly not presenting the world, as it is now, in a positive physical light. Scripture is not ignorant of natural evil: floods, storms, pestilence, famine, earthquakes, blight, disease—they're all depicted in the Word of God. Nor is the Word ignorant of the blind, the lame, the sick, and the diseased. And yet, even amid these harsh realities and Scripture's unvarnished admission of them, the Word still declares that "God is love" (1 John 4:8).

Then, too, what about the supernatural component of even natural evil? The first two chapters of Job show a malevolent supernatural force, Satan, who was involved not just in moral evil (Job 1:15, 17) but in natural evil as well (Job 1:19; Job 2:7). Scripture, especially the New Testament, is explicit regarding not only Satan's existence but his malevolence here on earth. "Woe to the inhabitants of the earth and the sea! For the devil has come down to you, having great wrath, because he knows that he has a short time" (Revelation 12:12).

Evangelical scholar Gregory Boyd has written on the "warfare worldview," in which he attributes evil to a cosmic conflict involving supernatural evil. "The warfare worldview," he writes, "thus presupposes the reality of relatively autonomous free creatures, human and angelic, who can and do act genuinely on their own, and who can and do sometimes go against God's will. It thus presupposes the reality of radical contingency and of genuine risk. It further presupposes that this risk has sometimes gone bad, even on a cosmic scale, and that this has turned the earth into a veritable war zone."[60]

In other words, Darwin's assumption that natural evil—from the parasitic wasp to cats tormenting mice (and, no doubt, other examples)—negates the existence of a Creator is not only a philosophical (as opposed to scientific) assumption, but a wrong one to boot. Of course, one can start with a false assumption and, still, arrive at a right conclusion; it is just less likely.

Although by 1844 Darwin had already published on his theory, some have argued that the death of his daughter Annie, in 1851, could have also influenced his thinking about the nature of life on earth. The death of a child could make anyone, especially someone already inclined toward naturalism, skeptical about God (especially a beneficent and all-powerful one) and more open to a dog-eat-dog nihilist existence that moves toward no ultimate purpose.[61]

Others see social factors at work as well.

"Each age," wrote James Moore, "fashions nature in its own image. In the nineteenth century, the English naturalist Charles Darwin (1809–82) recast the living world in the image of competitive, industrial Britain."[62]

Even Karl Marx noticed it: "It is remarkable," he wrote, "how Darwin recognizes among the beasts and plants his English society with its division of labor, competition, opening up of new markets, 'invention,' and the Malthusian 'struggle for existence.'"[63]

"It is a curious fact," wrote John C. Greene,

> that all, or nearly, all, of the men who propounded some idea of natural selection in the first half of the nineteenth century were British. Given the international character of science, it seems strange that nature should divulge one of her profoundest secrets only to inhabitants of Great Britain. Yet she did. The fact seems explicable only by assuming that British political economy, based on the idea of the survival of the fittest in the marketplace, and the British competitive ethos generally predisposed Britons to think in terms of competitive struggle in theorizing about plants and animals as well as man.[64]

How strange that nature would, indeed, divulge one of "her profoundest secrets" only to a nineteenth-century Englishman. Or, instead, maybe the competitive ethos of British society caused these Englishmen to read natural selection into nature when it was never there to begin with, at least to the degree that it could, as Darwin's theory claims, cause a proto–life-form to eventually morph into Homo sapiens. In other words, the social and political environment in which he lived could have caused Darwin to hold assumptions that he might not have held had he lived in Czarist Russia, and hence never would have arrived at his theory of evolution by natural selection to begin with. Any theory derived from subjective assumptions (as they inevitably are) doesn't automatically need to be wrong; it means only that the theory was derived from, well, subjective assumptions, which hardly guarantee the theory's veracity.

The inexorable intrusion of assumption

The origins of Darwin's assumptions are a handy, and not unimportant (considering the topic of this book), example of the bigger issue in science: the inexorable intrusion of assumption. Science does and must proceed on givens, foundations, and paradigms upon which the work rests and from which it proceeds. However, if those givens, those foundations, those paradigms are false, what's the likelihood of truth squirming out the other end? Again, technology, even accurate predictions, have been squeezed out of and milked from theories now believed incorrect. But accurate predictions and technology don't equate with truth.

For instance, a big question facing the evolutionary paradigm is altruism in beings who morphed into existence from the rough and tumble world of random mutation and natural selection. From whence did this trait arise, if looking out for number one is how we came to be? "From a Darwinian viewpoint, the existence of altruism in nature is at first sight puzzling, as Darwin himself realized."[65] Though speculations abound,[66] in one search for an explanation scientists funded with $5 million from the National Science Foundation (NSF) have tried to identify the origins of altruism by studying slime-mold amoebas.

Said the NSF website: "A slime-mold crowd of single-celled amoebas seems an unlikely place to look for the origins of complex social traits—especially altruism, where one individual risks itself for the benefit of an unrelated other. But, through an NSF Frontiers in Integrative Biological Research project, that's where David Queller and Joan Strassmann of Rice University and colleagues from the Baylor College of Medicine are looking, with good and complex reasons."[67]

No doubt, these highly educated and trained scientists do, indeed, have "good and complex reasons" for believing that their research into slime mold can shed light on the topic of human altruism, but those "good and complex reasons" sit on an array of assumptions that will affect what they see, do, and conclude. Among those assumptions are that both humans and slime-mold amoebas (to quote Robert Hazen) had their origins in the "ancient scorched Earth from the simplest of basic raw materials: air, water, and rock"; that both altruistic humans and slime-mold amoebas evolved from the earliest protolife to what they are now; that humans are linked in the evolutionary chain to slime-mold amoebas; and that the actions of slime mold can hold keys to "the origins of complex social traits—especially altruism."

Who knows what incredible insight about a whole host of things they might gain regarding the nature of slime mold? Or the technology that might come from their study? Or what brilliant projections—based on their research, along with that of other disciplines (chemistry, biophysics, evolutionary psychology)— they might make about the origins of human altruism as understood from studying slime mold? Yet the observations they make and the conclusions they draw will be seen, filtered, and interpreted through their assumptions.

And if those assumptions are wrong . . . ? What if, in fact, slime mold itself has nothing to do with the origins of human altruism, regardless of what their research uncovers?

The larger point, however, is this: Whatever these (or any) scientists see, do, and conclude, they are working from a paradigm built on a broad, deep, and vast structure of biases and assumptions, again all resting on a foundation nowhere near certain or absolute.

"We rely on experiment and observation," wrote Ronald Dworkin, "to certify our judgments in science. But experiment and observation are reliable only in virtue of the truth of basic assumptions about causation and optics that we rely on science itself, and nothing more basic, to certify. And of course our judgments about the nature of the external world all depend, even more fundamentally, on a universally shared assumption that there is an external world, an assumption that science cannot itself certify."[68]

The very idea itself, of studying slime mold to get insights into human altruism, is soaked with subjectivity from the get-go even before these researchers take their first gander through the microscope at slime mold. They can't even observe without their preconceptions affecting what they see. And, with all due respect, scientists looking at slime mold in hope of finding hints about the origins of human altruism can't be expected to see whatever they do through anything but their rather dubious assumptions to begin with.

As chapter 3 ("Mind and Cosmos") has shown, who can be sure that raw observation reveals anything but the brain's own subjective construction of what's out there (different brains, different subjective constructions) as opposed to what is really out there? The image in one's mind of a tree outside the kitchen window is not the tree outside the kitchen window; it is only a neural/hormonal configuration somewhere inside the viewer's head. (You can cut open the head, probe the gray matter, but never find the tree.) Who can be certain that anyone, including scientists, are getting *present* reality right, much less the reality that supposedly existed billions of years ago in a theorized reality that "exists" now only in hints in their heads?

Which leads, again, to the inexorable intrusion of assumption, because hints need to be interpreted, and if observation itself is theory-laden, how much more so the interpretation that follows? How does someone know what to even look for without a preconception of what they are seeking, without some theoretical assumption guiding their research, such as the assumptions of those studying slime-mold amoebas to gain insights on altruism?

Talk about preconceptual baggage!

Even scientific language can be biased toward whatever is the theory du jour. "All our language," wrote Bas van Fraassen, "is thoroughly theory-infected. . . . The way we talk, and scientists talk, is guided by the pictures provided by previously accepted theories."[69] This doesn't mean the picture guided by "previously accepted theories" is wrong, but only that it is guided by "previously accepted theories," which means it *can* be wrong, especially if the picture provided by these "previously accepted theories" is later rejected.

Right or wrong, the theory-laden picture affects not only what scientists look for but how they interpret what they find. "Modern historians of science," wrote Susan Neiman, "point out that if you start from experience without theoretical presuppositions, you are more likely to discover Aristotle's mechanics than Galileo's."[70]

"Modern science," wrote James Ladyman, "is so complex and developed it is absurd to suggest that a practicing scientist has no preconceptions when undertaking research. Scientists need specialized knowledge to calibrate instruments and design experiments. We cannot just begin with the data, we need guidance as to what data are relevant and what to observe, as well as what known causal factors to take into account and what can safely be ignored."[71]

"Seeing is not only the having of a visual experience," wrote Norwood Russell Hanson; "it is also the way in which the visual experience is had."[72]

Fine, but how does one know if the visual experience one had was had accurately? Or how does one know if that guidance is correct? What assumptions does the research presuppose before getting started, and what if those assumptions were on the wrong track? And how will those assumptions affect not only what is looked at, but how it is looked at, and how one interprets what is looked at after it is seen? All of these are questions that, to this day, have not been fully answered even amid many of the great successes of science.

Even Einstein wasn't always able to extricate himself from the current paradigm, especially as he got older (he did his best work when young).

"Enlightenment," wrote Gerald Schroeder, "is far easier when we have no preconceived notions of what must be true. The social and professional pressure to conform to accepted ideas can be monumental even whenever mounting data contradict their validity. It's called cognitive dissonance. As great a mind as Einstein's bowed to convention when his cosmological equation of the universe showed that the universe might be in a state of violent expansion, that the galaxies might be flying out from some moment of creation. Rather than publish this astonishing prediction he changed his data to match the popular, though erroneous idea that our universe was static."[73]

Changed data to match the popular notion? Einstein?

Finding the Higgs boson

Though (as with everything else in the philosophy of science) debate exists regarding the extent that the theory-ladenness of observation affects research, or even if it does, or what the limits of sense perception bring to even the rawest observation, one argument commonly brought up is this: Don't scientists create instruments to help them better understand the world beyond sense perception? Of course they do, and these instruments can be very helpful, but that's probably not a move someone should take who wants to defend empiricist epistemology as giving an accurate view of the world. On the contrary, scientific devices can make the inexorable intrusion of assumption even more problematic.

"Believing as I do," wrote David Berlinski, "that neutrinos have mass—it is one of my oldest and most deeply held convictions—I believe what I do on the basis of the fundamental laws of physics and a congeries of computational schemes, algorithms, specialized programming languages, techniques for numerical integration, huge canned programs, computer graphics, interpolation methods, nifty shortcuts, and the best efforts by mathematicians and physicists to convert the data of various experiments into coherent patterns, artfully revealing symmetries and continuous narratives. The neutrino has nothing to do with it."[74]

Berlinski's point, and Ladyman's above, move in the same direction: scientific instruments can't be built without the one building the instrument building into the instrument his presuppositions and assumptions. Of course, the scientist might have brilliant and well-founded reasons for his assumptions; not only that, those assumptions might even be dead-on right. But they might be dead-on wrong, too, and thus the instrument gives a distorted view of whatever is being looked at, measured, parsed, or analyzed. Or how does one know that the instrument works correctly? Or suppose unknown factors modify what the instrument is supposed to reveal? Or does the instrument itself affect what is to be objectively viewed, a question that has become exceedingly problematic for scientists probing quantum reality.

Perhaps the greatest scientific instrument to date is the Large Hadron Collider (LHC), built by CERN in Europe to study aspects of reality frighteningly too subtle for our blunt biological sensors. The LHC is one of a complex array of powerful machines that, basically, smash protons, whose remains are then painstakingly analyzed.

Here's a bit of what happens:

The proton source is a simple bottle of hydrogen gas. An electric field is used to strip hydrogen atoms of their electrons to yield protons. Linac 2, the first accelerator in the chain, accelerates the protons to the energy of 50 MeV. The beam is then injected into the Proton Synchrotron Booster (PSB), which accelerates the protons to 1.4 GeV, followed by the Proton Synchrotron (PS), which pushes the beam to 25 GeV. Protons are then sent to the Super Proton Synchrotron (SPS) where they are accelerated to 450 GeV.

The protons are finally transferred to the two beam pipes of the LHC. The beam in one pipe circulates clockwise while the beam in the other pipe circulates anticlockwise. It takes 4 minutes and 20 seconds to fill each LHC ring, and 20 minutes for the protons to reach their maximum energy of 6.5 TeV. Beams circulate for many hours inside the LHC beam pipes under normal operating conditions. The two beams are brought into collision inside four detectors—ALICE, ATLAS, CMS and LHCb— where the total energy at the collision point is equal to 13 TeV.

The accelerator complex includes the Antiproton Decelerator and the

Online Isotope Mass Separator (ISOLDE) facility, and feeds the CERN Neutrinos to Gran Sasso (CNGS) project and the Compact Linear Collider test area, as well as the neutron time-of-flight facility (nTOF).[75]

The point is, they don't just smash atoms and, then, grasp a subatomic particle with tweezers and declare, "Eureka!"

Take the recent "discovery" of the Higgs boson, a manifestation of an energy field that supposedly suffuses all space and that gives matter mass as it moves through the Higgs field. At CERN, protons were smashed into each other at speeds close to c, the speed of light. In the collision, a Higgs boson supposedly was created. However, the Higgs boson decays after a zeptosecond ($10^{-21\text{th}}$ of a second), and no device now created could come close to detecting it. Instead, researchers go through the difficult, theory-laden, and painstaking task of detecting the particles the Higgs boson decays into—work that requires an astonishing amount of computer software, hardware, and analysis. And even then, questions exist about whether the detected particles were really coming from the Higgs or from something else, because every Higgs decay can also be created by non-Higgs mechanisms as well.

Again, from CERN itself: "Each collision generates particles that often decay in complex ways into even more particles. Electronic circuits record the passage of each particle through a detector as a series of electronic signals, and send the data to the CERN Data Centre (DC) for digital reconstruction. The digitized summary is recorded as a 'collision event.' Physicists must sift through the 30 petabytes or so of data produced annually to determine if the collisions have thrown up any interesting physics."[76] In short, they have to measure trillions of collisions.

The colliders, the detectors, and then the computers analyzing what the detectors detect after the protons race through the colliders reflect billions of dollars' worth of assumption, presupposition, and theory. No question, it's fantastically complicated; no question, either, these researchers know what they are doing. But it's important not to forget *what* they are doing, and that is probing unseen and hypothetical realities, but doing so within a massive and complicated theoretical framework, a paradigm built upon layers and layers of assumptions, some of which (if not all), over time, will likely be revamped, revised, or maybe superseded. And whatever they did in discovering the Higgs boson, *one thing that they did not do is actually see one.*

Instead, working from a web of assumptions, they analyzed data that they interpreted to indicate the existence of a Higgs boson, which was represented on their computer screens by a "bump in the data from the detector."[77] What caused the bump on the computer screens, it is believed, was the Higgs.

Which is fine. The "bump in the data" was explained by the zeptosecond existence of the Higgs. Yet this leads to another question, perhaps even more fundamental than the one of assumptions (but inseparably tied to it), and that is—What is a scientific explanation, anyway, and how is it justified?

Contrary to popular notions about science, this basic issue remains controversial, and unanswered. And if questions exist about the meaning of explanation itself and what it means to explain regarding what we can study here and now with the LHC and the like, how much more problematic are such questions when scientists make claims about events hidden by the veil of time? What this issue (and others we have looked at so far) should do, if nothing else, is help us step back and look more critically at the claims emerging from the scientific-industrial complex, especially when those claims at times so clearly conflict with the Word of God.

1. Tarnas, *Western Mind*, 446–467.

2. About sixteen years before Kuhn's *Structure*, chemist Michael Polanyi wrote *Science, Faith and Society* (London: Oxford University Press, 1946), in which he talked about the subjectivity of science, not quite as Kuhn did but in ways that echoed what Kuhn would later say: "The part played by new observations and experiment in the process of discovery in science is usually over-estimated. The popular conception of the scientist patiently collecting observations, unprejudiced by any theory, until finally he succeeds in establishing a great new generalization, is quite false. . . . All this new knowledge of nature was acquired merely by the reconsideration of known phenomena in a new context which was felt to be more rational and more real." 14.

3. Quoted in Kuhn, *The Structure of Scientific Revolutions*, 2nd ed., International Encyclopedia of Unified Science (Chicago: University of Chicago Press, 1970), 151.

4. Kuhn, *Structure*, 2.

5. Ibid., 4.

6. Ibid.

7. Curd and Cover, *Philosophy of Science*, 1304. Notice their use of the word "tradition" in the quote. Not a word generally thought of as belonging to science though it has been used and, given the context of what's being discussed here, it's appropriate.

8. Norman Malcolm, "The Groundlessness of Belief," in *Readings in the Philosophy of Religion*, 2nd ed., ed. Kelly James Clark (Ontario: Broadview Press, 2008), 216 (italics in the original).

9. Leonard R. Brand, "A Biblical Perspective on the Philosophy of Science," *Origins*, no. 59 (2006): 9.

10. This whole question brings up the issue of peer review. Peer review is kind of the semiofficial imprimatur of scientific work. Yet the question remains: What are the peers reviewing—the paradigm itself or just the research in the paradigm? In most cases, of course, it's the latter, with anything challenging the paradigm itself likely not to pass peer-review muster. In short, peer review might (or might not) say a lot about how well some research project functions within a paradigm. But it says little, or maybe even nothing, about whether the paradigm itself is valid. In most cases that's not what is even being questioned.

11. Stuart Firestein, *Ignorance: How It Drives Science* (Oxford: Oxford University Press, 2012), 114, 115.

12. Lindberg, *Beginnings of Western Science*, 102 (italics in the original).

13. Francis Crick, *Of Molecules and Men*, Great Minds Series (New York: Prometheus Books, 2004), 10 (italics in the original).

14. Quoted in Alison Flood, " 'Post-Truth' Named Word of the Year by Oxford Dictionaries," *Guardian*, November 15, 2016, https://www.theguardian.com/books/2016/nov/15/post-truth-named-word-of-the-year-by-oxford-dictionaries.

15. Steve Fuller, "Science Has Always Been a Bit 'Post-Truth,' " *Guardian*, December 15, 2016, https://www.theguardian.com/science/political-science/2016/dec/15/science-has-always-been-a-bit-post-truth.

16. Ibid.

17. Ibid.

18. Shawn Otto, *The War on Science: Who's Waging It, Why It Matters, What We Can Do About It* (Minneapolis: Milkweed Editions, 2016), 189.

19. Robert M. Hazen, "Origins of Life" (Chantilly, VA: Teaching Company, 2005), part 1, p. 14.

20. Ibid., part 2, p. 15.

21. Ibid., 25.

22. Quoted in ibid., 37.

23. Ibid., 103.

24. Kuhn, *Structure*, 24.

25. Hazen, "Origins of Life," part 2, p. 189.

26. Alfred I. Tauber, *Science and the Quest for Meaning* (Waco, TX: Baylor University Press, 2009), 61.

27. One of the greatest examples of this idea, of attempting to break out of the old paradigm, occurred in the work of Francis Bacon (1561–1626) and his *Novum Organum,* in which in response to the trouble he was getting into by challenging the Aristotelian worldview he penned the famous line, "I cannot be called on to abide by the sentence of a tribunal which is itself on its trial." *The Philosophical Works of Francis Bacon*, trans. Ellis and Spedding, ed. John M. Robertson (London: George Routledge and Sons, 1905), 262.

28. John G. West, *Darwin Day in America: How Our Politics and Culture Have Been Dehumanized in the Name of Science* (Wilmington, DE: ISI Books, 2007), 241.

29. Avi Loeb, "Good Data Are Not Enough," *Nature News*, November 2, 2016, http://www.nature.com/news/good-data-are-not-enough-1.20906.

30. Leonard R. Brand, *Faith, Reason, and Earth History* (Berrien Springs, MI: Andrews University Press, 1997), 52.

31. Kuhn, *Structure*, 111.

32. Ibid., 158.

33. See, for instance, Paul Feyerabend, *Farewell to Reason* (London: Verso, 1987), and *Against Method*.

34. See, for instance, Israel Scheffler, *Science and Subjectivity* (Indianapolis: Bobbs-Merrill, 1967).

35. Dawkins, *Selfish Gene*, 195.

36. W. C. Dampier, *A History of Science and Its Relations With Philosophy and Religion* (New York: Cambridge University Press, 1989), 196.

37. Ibid., 197.

38. Carl Sagan, *Cosmos* (New York: Ballantine Books, 2013), 1.

39. "Those who say that science can answer all questions are themselves standing outside science to make that claim. That is why naturalism—the modern version of materialism, seeing reality as defined by what is within reach of the sciences—becomes a metaphysical theory when

it strays beyond methodology to talk of what can exist. Denying metaphysics and upholding materialism must itself be a move within metaphysics. It involves standing outside the practice of science and talking of its scope. The assertion that science can explain everything can never come from within science. It is always a statement about science." Roger Trigg, "Why Science Needs Metaphysics," *Nautilus*, October 1, 2015, http://nautil.us/issue/29/scaling/why-science-needs-metaphysics.

40. Dawkins, *The Blind Watchmaker*, xiv.

41. See Paul Davies, *The Mind of God: The Scientific Basis for a Rational World* (New York: Touchstone, 1992).

42. Ernst Cassirer, *The Philosophy of the Enlightenment*, trans. Fritz C. A. Koelln and James P. Pettegrove (Princeton, NJ: Princeton University Press, 1951), 47.

43. See Brand, *Faith, Reason, and Earth History*, 62.

44. Ángel M. Rodríguez, "Biblical Creationism and Ancient Near Eastern Evolutionary Ideas," in Klingbeil, *Genesis Creation Account*, 328.

45. Lucretius, *On the Nature of Things*, trans. Martin Ferguson Smith (Indianapolis: Hackett, 2001), 62.

46. Stephen Greenblatt, *The Swerve: How the World Became Modern* (New York: W. W. Norton, 2011), 5, 6.

47. Frederick Burkhardt et al., eds., *The Correspondence of Charles Darwin: Volume 8, 1860* (Cambridge, UK: Cambridge University Press, 1993), 39 (italics in the original).

48. Fyodor Dostoevsky, *The Brothers Karamazov*, trans. Constance Garnett (New York: Macmillan, 1922), 257.

49. Cornelius G. Hunter, *Darwin's God: Evolution and the Problem of Evil* (Grand Rapids, MI: Brazos Press, 2001), 10.

50. Quoted in ibid., 12.

51. Quoted in ibid., 10.

52. Ibid., 11.

53. Some Christians think that theistic evolution helps solve the problem of natural evil. It doesn't; it makes it only worse. Even an antireligionist such as Jerry Coyne sees the theodicy problem that theistic evolution creates: "There is no obvious explanation, for instance," he writes, "why an omnipotent and loving God who directed evolution would lead it into so many dead ends. After all, over 99 percent of the species that ever lived went extinct without leaving descendants. The cruelty of natural selection, which involves endless wastage and pain, also demands explanation. Wouldn't a loving and all-powerful God simply have produced all existing species de novo, as described in Genesis?" Jerry A. Coyne, *Faith Versus Fact: Why Science and Religion Are Incompatible* (New York: Viking, 2015), 147. Coyne has a good point.

54. Genesis 3:1–7; Ezekiel 28:15; Revelation 12:7.

55. Romans 6:23; Romans 8:22; Job 1, 2.

56. 1 Corinthians 15; Revelation 21:1.

57. Jeremiah 31:3; John 3:16; 2 Corinthians 13:11; 1 John 4:16.

58. According to the Bible, some of the earliest humans lived for seven hundred to nine hundred years (see Genesis 5). By Genesis 11, life spans had greatly decreased. By Genesis 25, they got even lower. Scripture talks about the life span of people being between seventy and eighty years of age (Psalm 90:10). In previous centuries, the average life span was, and in some places still is, lower. The fact that in recent years advances in medical science have increased life spans from what they were a hundred years ago is still only a minuscule advance over what they were originally. Hence, compared to nine hundred years, the extra ten to twenty years science has afforded us, while precious, hardly negate the argument.

59. The Greek word, *ftheiro*, means destruction, perishing, a state of decomposition.

60. Gregory A. Boyd, *God at War: The Bible and Spiritual Conflict* (Downers Grove, IL: IVP Academic, 1997), 58. See also Ellen G. White, *The Great Controversy Between Christ and Satan* (Mountain View, CA: Pacific Press®, 1950). It's interesting to note, too, that one of the things that bothered Darwin about nature was how a parasitic wasp would actually live inside the body of a caterpillar and eat it from within, while at the same time seeking to keep the caterpillar alive as long as it could. The ichneumon wasp will insert a toxin in the caterpillar that will paralyze but not kill it. That way, the ichneumon larvae deposited inside the caterpillar can eat the inner organs and tissue but in a way that will keep the host alive for as long as possible. Commenting on this horrific practice, Stephen Jay Gould used language that sounded very much as if coming from Gregory Boyd's warfare worldview of the cosmos. Wrote Gould, "We seem to be caught in the mythic structures of our own cultural sagas, quite unable, even in our basic descriptions, to use any other language than the metaphors of battle and conquest." Stephen Jay Gould, *Hen's Teeth and Horse's Toes* (New York: W. W. Norton, 1994), 35.

61. "But Annie's death changed things between Charles and Emma, says historian Deborah Heiligman. Darwin became more willing to proclaim his theories—and his religious doubts." Robert Krulwich, "Death of Child May Have Influenced Darwin's Work," *Morning Edition*, NPR, February 12, 2009, http://www.npr.org/templates/story/story.php?storyId=100597929.

62. Ferngren, *Science and Religion*, 208.

63. Quoted in Tom Bethell, *Darwin's House of Cards: A Journalist's Odyssey Through the Darwin Debates* (Seattle: Discovery Institute, 2017), 68.

64. Quoted in Ronald L. Numbers and Kostas Kampourakis, eds., *Newton's Apple and Other Myths About Science* (Cambridge, MA: Harvard University Press, 2015), 108.

65. Samir Okasha, "Biological Altruism," *Stanford Encyclopedia of Philosophy* (Fall 2013 Edition), ed. Edward N. Zalta, https://plato.stanford.edu/archives/fall2013/entries/altruism-biological/.

66. Paul Bloom, "Moral Design Is the Latest Form of Intelligent Design. It's Wrong," *New Republic*, January 15, 2014.

67. "The Evolution of Biological Social Systems," September 2003, http://www.nsf.gov/od/lpa/news/03/pr03106_slimemold.htm.

68. Ronald Dworkin, *Religion Without God* (Cambridge, MA: Harvard University Press, 2013), 16.

69. Van Fraassen, *Scientific Image*, 14.

70. Susan Neiman, *Evil in Modern Thought* (Princeton, NJ: Princeton University Press, 2015), 137.

71. Ladyman, *Understanding Philosophy of Science*, 57.

72. Norwood Russell Hanson, *Patterns of Discovery* (Cambridge, UK: Cambridge University Press, 1972), 15.

73. Gerald L. Schroeder, *The Hidden Face of God: How Science Reveals the Ultimate Truth* (New York: Free Press, 2001), 185, 186.

74. David Berlinski, *The Devil's Delusion* (New York: Basic Books, 2009), 49. Bas van Fraassen expressed it like this: "A look through a telescope at the moons of Jupiter seems to me a clear case of observation, since astronauts will no doubt be able to see them as well from close up. But the purported observation of micro-particles in a cloud chamber seems to me a clearly different case—if our theory about what happens there is right. The theory says that if a charged particle traverses a chamber filled with saturated vapour, some atoms in the neighbourhood of its path are ionized. If this vapour is decompressed, and hence becomes super-saturated, it condenses in droplets on the ions, thus marking the path of the particle. The resulting silver-grey line is similar (physically as well as in appearance) to the vapour trail left in the sky when a jet passes. Suppose I point to such a trail and say: 'Look, there is a jet!'; might you not say: 'I see the vapour

trail, but where is the jet?' Then I would answer: 'Look just a bit ahead of the trail . . . there! Do you see it?' Now, in the case of the cloud chamber this response is not possible. So while the particle is detected by means of the cloud chamber, and the detection is based on observation, it is clearly not a case of the particle's being observed." Van Fraassen, *Scientific Image*, 16, 17.

75. "The Accelerator Complex," CERN, https://home.cern/about/accelerators.

76. "Computing," CERN, https://home.cern/about/computing.

77. Ben Allanach, "Particle Hunting at the LHC: The Higgs Boson," *Plus*, December 11, 2015, https://plus.maths.org/content/particle-hunting-lhc-higgs-boson.

CHAPTER 8

THE WHY QUESTION

M ihi a docto doctore
Domandatur causam et rationem quare
Opium facit dormire.
A quoi respondeo,
Quia est in eo
Vertus dormitiva,
Cujus eat natura
Sensus assoupire.[1]

These words, verbal flummery of a mock Latin sort, appeared in a 1673 musical drama by Molière, *The Imaginary Invalid*. A spoof and satire on seventeenth-century Parisian life, the story also mocked the medical profession's dubious practices and assumptions, with which Molière himself was personally acquainted. In the drama, the above words were uttered during a ceremony in which learned medical professionals were giving a student his final exam before proffering upon him honors. Loosely translated, the verbiage goes something like this: " 'What is the cause and reason why opium makes one sleep?' He answered, 'The reason is that there is a dormitive virtue *(vertus dormitiva)* in it, whose nature is to cause the senses to become drowsy.' "
The learned doctors respond:

Bene, bene, bene, bene respondere.
Dignus, dignus est intrare
In nostro docto corpore.
Bene, bene respondere.[2]

Translation? "Well, well, well, well he has answered. Worthy, worthy is he to enter into our learned body. Well, well he has answered."
Despite their premeditated preposterousness, these lines were among the skit's most famous, particularly the phrase *dormitive virtue*, which has become

a popular example of circular reasoning, in which something is explained by something else, perhaps more abstractly, but without revealing anything new.

To say that opium puts one to sleep because of its dormitive virtue, however unsatisfying it may be as an explanation, is still an explanation of sorts. Dormitive virtue is not, technically, a synonym of opium, so the phrase does some explanatory work. The next question, then, would have to be: Why does its dormitive virtue put one to sleep? Dormitive things, by definition, put people to sleep. Thus, in this case, to ask why is like asking, *Why is a circle round?*

The medical student's answer, then, wasn't as inane as Molière meant it to be. It points, rather, to a fundamental issue regarding what scientists can or cannot do, especially if one sees scientists as doing more than just making predictions, creating technology, or simply *describing* either how the world is or simply how it appears to our limited senses. If one views scientists as in a quest for truth, for causes, for explanations about what happens in reality itself, then the answer "dormitive virtue" might be closer to what the scientist does than one might comfortably think.

This question of scientific explanations isn't as obvious or simple as is commonly believed. Numerous unanswered issues remain. What are scientific explanations, as opposed to theological or literary or historical ones? How far down, so to speak, do scientists have to go (to chemicals, atoms, quarks, quantum fields) before they are truly explaining something? What is an explanation? What does it mean to say that *X* explains *Y*? How are explanations justified? And what happens when there are various explanations for the same phenomena?

Some scientists, at least those who think science teaches us about the real world, argue for what has been called *Inference to the Best Explanation* (IBE). This view claims that when several different theories seem to explain a phenomenon, scientists should pick the best one. Yet that's almost as circular as dormitive virtue. Of course they should pick the best one. But how do they know which *is* the best one? What criteria, assumptions, parameters, rules, tests, and standards lead scientists to the "best" explanation?

These are difficult questions. So difficult that nonrealists believe it's a waste of time, an intrusion of metaphysics and philosophy into a discipline, science, that has no room for them. Even so, whether or not nonrealists like to admit it (and they don't), science can no more be done without philosophy and metaphysics than math can be done without symbols.[3]

These contested issues, like many others, present more reasons why people can respect science, acknowledge what it has revealed and described, and enjoy its technological fruits, but without groveling before its every authoritative proclamation—especially when those proclamations often change or when they are highly speculative assertions based on assumptions about hypothetical events that occurred millions or even billions of hypothetical years ago. This is all the more true (for Christians, anyway) when those hypothetical events in a hypothetical time contradict God's Word.

The *why* question

Hundreds of years after Newton, the question of scientific explanation or causation remains thorny. Some philosophers argue that the very concept of explanation or causation "is hopelessly subjective, so subjective even that it should have no part in proper science."[4] Causation deals with what caused an event, what made it happen, what can be seen as the explanation for it. And although explanation and causation aren't necessarily synonymous, they are related. This relationship, called the *causal model*, asserts that to explain an event or a fact is to provide information about its causes. *Y* explains *X* because *Y* caused *X*. *Y* (the rain) caused *X* (the wet ground).

In short, *Y* is the answer to the *why* question for *X*.

"To explain the phenomena in the world of our experience," wrote philosopher of science Carl Hempel, "to answer the question 'why?' rather than only the question 'what?' is one of the foremost objectives of all rational inquiry; and especially, scientific research in its various branches strives to go beyond a mere description of its subject matter by providing an explanation of the phenomena it investigates. While there is rather general agreement about this chief objective of science, there exists considerable difference of opinion as to the function and the essential characteristics of scientific explanation."[5]

Indeed, in any area, the answer to the *why* question can be cunningly elusive. When asked, "Why do you rob banks?" American bank robber John Dillinger answered, "Because that's where the money is."

Like Molière's *vertus dormitiva*, this answer doesn't explain much, but it's not circular, either. It just doesn't go deep enough, perhaps. What would be deep enough? John Dillinger's upbringing? His relationship with his mother? The economics of the country at the time of his robberies? Peer pressure? Or maybe the true explanation for Dillinger robbing banks, at least a scientific one, is to be found only in the molecular structure of his brain.

Adolph Hitler, as a young man in Austria before World War I, was twice (in 1907 and in 1908) rejected by the Academy of Fine Arts Vienna. Suppose he had been accepted and had become a successful artist instead of being appointed, in 1933, Reich Chancellor of Germany? According to the causal model, could not World War II be explained by Hitler's rejection from the Academy of Fine Arts Vienna? And because World War II led to the Cold War, couldn't the Cold War also be explained by Hitler's rejection

THE WHY QUESTION 143

from the Academy of Fine Arts Vienna in 1907 and 1908?

It's hard to argue against these explanations; yet, like "dormitive virtue" and "that's where the money is," they seem highly problematic, not real answers to the *why* question.

When Isaac Newton penned the *Principia*, he described how the law of gravity worked, or at least how it appears, to us, to work. But he had no explanation why it did what it appeared to do. It was like someone describing, in detail, a cat chasing its tail but not knowing why the cat does it.

Centuries after Newton, Albert Einstein developed the general theory of relativity (GR), which went deeper than Newton's theory of gravity. According to GR, gravity is not a force, but the curvature of space and time by mass. What, then, explains gravity? It is mass bending space and time.

A common analogy is a bowling ball on a mattress. The weight of the ball presses on the mattress. A marble will roll along the indentation in the fabric toward the bowling ball. According to GR, this is what mass does to space and time; it curves them, as the bowling ball does the mattress. Gravity is nothing, then, but objects moving in a straight line in curved space and time, like the marble on the mattress.

Did Einstein explain what Newton only described? Matter curves space and time. But isn't this merely a deeper description of gravity, as opposed to an explanation? Wouldn't an explanation reveal *why* matter bends space and time? One could reply that the answer is, *Because space, time, and matter follow Einstein's field equations*. But that answer, too, only describes *what*, not *why*. Why do space, time, and matter follow those equations? At present, scientists can say only that they do, because—well, because they do!

"The great delusion of modernity," said philosopher Ludwig Wittgenstein, "is that the laws of nature explain the universe for us. The laws of nature describe the universe, they describe the regularities. But they explain nothing."[6]

According to Aristotle, objects fall to earth because it is their nature to fall to earth. They just do. It's like asking why a circle is round. According to Newton, objects fall to earth because any two bodies in the universe attract each other with a force that is directly proportional to the product of their masses and inversely proportional to the square of the distance between them. But why do any two bodies in the universe attract each other with a force that is directly proportional to the product of their masses and inversely proportional to the square of the distance between them? Because, according to Einstein, mass bends space and time. But why does mass bend space and time? Because space and time follow Einstein's field equations. Why? At this point, no deeper theory has been accepted, so for now all that can be said is that space and time and mass follow Einstein's field equations, because—well, because they do.

Scientists might one day explain GR at a deeper level. But they will do so only by another theory, one more fundamental than GR, using other equations, ideally simpler ones.[7] Meanwhile the new and deeper theory may allow scientists to make more accurate predictions than they could with GR alone. And scientists may even create innovative, life-changing technology from the new theory as well. Yet even this deeper theory will need an explanation itself, something deeper than it. How far down the descriptive chain must scientists go until, as opposed to just another (even if deeper) description, they arrive at a scientific "explanation"? At what point, if ever, does the *why* question stop? And if it does, *where* (other than to say something like, "*X* does *Y* because *X* does *Y*")?

However much progress physicists have made in explaining gravity (as opposed to merely describing it), they sometimes quip, "Gravity attracts me to the earth because gravity attracts me to the earth"—a contemporary expression of Aristotle's twenty-three-hundred-year-old argument that objects fall to the earth because it's just the nature of objects to fall to the earth.

Sounds like a physics version of dormitive virtue.

Which is why dormitive virtue might not be that far off as an explanation. In centuries past, it might have been theorized that opium puts people to sleep because "the great goddess, Snoozer of south Albania, puts you to sleep when you take opium." That's a prescientific answer.

Today, however, science says that the polynuclear aromatic hydrocarbons in opium get into the central nervous system, and that causes sleep. But why do polynuclear aromatic hydrocarbons cause sleep? It's because they attach to opioid receptors in the brain, and that induces sleep. But why do polynuclear aromatic hydrocarbons attached to opioid receptors in the brain induce sleep? Because of the chemical reactions in the opioid receptors. But why do these chemical reactions in the opioid receptors cause sleep? Maybe the only way to explain *why* is at the molecular and atomic level. But whatever answer comes, even at that level or deeper, the *why* question remains. Thus, maybe opium does induce sleep because of its dormitive virtue after all.

In science, as with any epistemological endeavor, descriptions, causes, explanations (whatever one calls them) stop at some point.

"Any theory," wrote Martin Curd and J. A. Cover, "will eventually bottom out, having to posit some regularities as basic or primitive, without receiving any further explanation at a deeper level."[8]

"To be sure there is justification," wrote Wittgenstein; "but justification comes to an end."[9]

"We must," wrote David Hume, "stop somewhere in our examination of causes; and there are, in every science, some general principles, beyond which we cannot hope to find any principle more general."[10]

Science, ideally the crème de la crème of the search for truth, eventually becomes recursive, self-referential; theories ultimately end up explaining themselves by referring back to themselves. GR, perhaps the greatest intellectual and scientific achievement of history, comes down to "Gravity attracts me to the earth because gravity attracts me to the earth."

Sooner or later, the *why* question simply doesn't get answered.

Wrote Jim Holt: "But the final theory of physics would still leave a residue of mystery—why *this* force, why *this* law? It would not contain within itself an answer to the question of *why* it was the final theory. So it would not live up to the principle that every fact must have an explanation—the Principle of Sufficient Reason."[11]

Justification stops, or just keeps circling itself.

"The intertwining of theory and experiment," wrote John Polkinghorne, "inextricably linked by the need to interpret experimental data, does indeed imply that there is an unavoidable degree of circularity involved in scientific reasoning. This means that the nature of science is something more subtle and rationally delicate than simply ineluctable deduction from unquestionable fact. A degree of intellectual daring is required, which means that ultimately the aspiration to write about the *logic* of scientific discovery proves to be a misplaced ambition."[12]

The self-referential paradox

This bottoming out of scientific explanation is crucial in grasping the limits of where scientists can go in describing (explaining?) reality, or at least how reality appears to humans. An interesting parallel unfolds in the self-referential paradox, which exemplifies a similar limitation on human knowledge.

John creates on his computer desktop a folder, named SR, for "Self-Referential" (though the name doesn't matter). John opens the folder, and a dropdown menu box appears on the desktop near the SR icon. John grabs the SR icon and moves it into the dropdown menu box for the SR folder. The icon doesn't go in, no matter how many tries.

It can't. The only way the SR icon can go into its own folder would be if the software on the computer were corrupted. If the logic and reasoning behind the processes were working correctly, then the folder SR could never go into itself, because it's impossible to put one thing into another when what you want to put *in it* is the same thing that you want to put *it in.*

Another analogy: can a scale weigh itself? The same with language. How do you define the concept of "words" when you need words themselves to define the concept? You're assuming a priori the validity of what you are questioning.

How do we get past language to understand language? Metalinguistics has been an attempt to create some sort of linguistic field in which one could step out of language and examine it. The only problem, though, is that whatever metalanguage was created would still be a language, so one is back, if not in the same place he started, close enough. It's kind of like answering that opium puts you to sleep because of its dormitive virtue.

This conundrum extends to logic and reason, the foundation upon which science works. After all, science itself could not be done without logic and reason, the tools used to analyze and, hopefully, explain whatever is seen, found, and revealed. All the empirical evidence in the world is useless if not analyzed, and what is analysis other than the application of logic and reason to the data, regardless of how subjective, contingent, psychological, cultural, or even wrong the premises?

How, though, does one study logic and reason when these are the very things we use to study them—the things that we are questioning to begin with? How can we step back from logic and reason and view them objectively, outside of the very logic and reason that is being questioned?

"Similarly," wrote Michael Lynch, "with the basic principles of deductive logic: I can't prove basic logical principles without relying on them. In each case, I seem to have hit rock bottom: I can't argue for a basic epistemic principle without presupposing my commitment to it."[13]

In other words, whatever conclusions we would draw about logic and reason would, of necessity, entail logic and reason, which puts us back where we started, kind of like with GR. And if logic and reason can't be fully justified, what about the science that arises from them?

This question of self-referential paradox, of things bottoming out, leads to the mind-boggling and foundation-shattering work of Kurt Gödel and his Incompleteness Theorem,[14] which proved that formal mathematical proof comes to an end, and does so without absolute "closure." With his revolutionary paper, Kurt Gödel proved that within any given mathematical system, certain propositions or statements can't be proved or disproved using the rules of that system. One might be able to prove all the propositions and axioms in the system by going outside, to a new and larger system. But then that new and larger system will have its own statements that can be proved only by a new and larger system outside of that one, and on and on.

Knowledge, then, of even simple mathematics remains incomplete, and so one can never be certain that the axioms of arithmetic will not contradict each other. Thus, in something as rigid and logical as math, some aspects just can't be "proven." Even cold hard math—the supposed foundation of objective certainty—comes with intrinsic, inescapable contingencies.

Before Gödel, mathematician and philosopher Bertrand Russell expressed his frustration with the limits of putting mathematics on a firm logical basis:

I wanted certainty in the kind of way in which people want religious faith. I thought that certainty is more likely to be found in mathematics than elsewhere. But I discovered that many mathematical demonstrations, which my teachers expected me to accept, were full of fallacies, and that, if certainty were indeed discoverable in mathematics, it would be in a new kind of mathematics, with more solid foundations than those that had hitherto been thought secure. But as the work proceeded, I was continually reminded of the fable about the elephant and the tortoise. Having constructed an elephant upon which the mathematical world could rest, I found the elephant tottering, and proceeded to construct a tortoise to keep the elephant from falling. But the tortoise was no more secure than the elephant, and after some twenty years of very arduous toil, I came to the conclusion that there was nothing more that *I* could do in the way of making mathematical knowledge indubitable.[15]

"The one distinguishing feature of mathematics," wrote Morris Kline on the results of Gödel's work, "that it might have claimed in this century, the absolute certainty or validity of its results, could no longer be claimed."[16]

"In effect, then," Douglas Hofstadter commented, "Gödel destroyed the hopes of those who believed that mathematical thinking is capturable by the rigidity of axiomatic systems, and he thereby forced mathematicians, logicians, and philosophers to explore the mysterious newly found chasm irrevocably separating provability from truth."[17]

Separating provability from truth, *irrevocably*? And in something as cold, rigid, and formal as mathematics?

Which points to a conundrum regarding the outer limits of all human knowledge, however acquired. "One possibility," wrote Thomas Nagel, "is that some things can't be explained because they have to enter into every explanation."[18] That is, you can't explain logic and reason because logic and reason are needed in every explanation.

The icon experiment, and what it implies, is an object lesson on the limits of knowledge, including the tools and methods used to arrive at whatever we know, or think we know, about anything, including (and maybe especially) science. If justification bottoms out in mathematics, or logic and reason, how much more so in empirical endeavors such as science, which is built initially upon a web of belief, a host of subjective assumptions (a paradigm) that, sooner or later, bottoms out as well?

This problem isn't limited to theories within a paradigm, or even to paradigms themselves. It's more fundamental; it gets to the limits of knowledge itself. Which means that however broad, foundational, and grand the paradigm; however "empirically verified" or "mathematically worked out" the reasons for it; however many esteemed scientists and Nobel laureates believe it; or however much technology comes from it—sooner or later justification for it stops. To use another analogy: you can never get to the bottom of the swamp. No matter how far down one goes, or how great the predictions and widgets that arise from the descriptions (explanations?) made on the way down, sooner or later it will curve around in a self-referential circle: "Gravity attracts me to the earth because gravity attracts me to the earth."

And, thus, the *why* question remains unanswered.

Bottoming out

And, if this limitation of knowledge is problematic for things that exist now—like the Higgs boson, which, ideally, can be created in the Large Hadron Collider and then "detected"—what about science when it makes bold proclamations regarding (for instance) the supposed evolution of whale brains fifty million years ago or about the origins of life 3.8 billion years ago, possibly in molten rocks above 1000°C? Historians disagree about the cause of events in the twentieth century, and yet how many people intellectually genuflect before the latest scientific declaration about dinosaurs evolving feathers hundreds of millions of years ago or how the gills of *Panderichthys* provided the transitional form that led to the evolution of the human ear—both of them?

Working within the neo-Darwinian paradigm, scientists make claims about events that occurred, supposedly, millions and billions of years gone by. Yet none of the scientists were there, none of the hypothesized events now exist, and none of the claims about the evolutionary past can be studied the same way that the Higgs boson is (and even that's filled with a host of assumptions too) or the same way polar bears' mating habits are. Whatever bold conjectures are made about the evolution of the human chin[19] or of banana skins or of the sea turtle's digestive system, they're always speculation based upon a vast web of assumptions, which include (1) that the dating is correct, (2) that the understanding of the natural world millions and billions of years ago is correct, and (3) that these events happened.

Scientists might have what they think are good reasons for these assumptions; they might even be good reasons. But good reasons for something don't make something so. Scientists at one time had good reasons for believing in astrology, alchemy, phrenology, the phlogiston theory of heat, the indivisibility of atoms, and an eternally existing geocentric universe.

As Mary Hesse expressed it, due to radical changes in even the most entrenched scientific ideas, "at any given stage of science it is never possible to know *which* of the currently entrenched predicates and laws may have to give way in the future."[20]

Jonathan Sacks wrote,

> The sheer improbability of the scientific discoveries of the twentieth and twenty-first centuries is overwhelming. In 1894, Albert A. Michelson, the German-born American physicist, said, "The more important fundamental laws and facts of physical science have all been discovered, and these are now so firmly established that the possibility of their ever being supplanted in consequence of new discoveries is exceedingly remote." In 1900, speaking to the British Association for the Advancement of Science, Lord Kelvin said, "There is nothing new to be discovered in physics now. All that remains is more and more precise measurement." The long list of failed predictions should tell us to expect the unexpected. We are the unpredictable animal navigating our way through a universe that, from quantum physics to black holes to the Higgs boson, is stranger than any nineteenth-century scientist could have dreamed.[21]

Hilary Putman wrote about his favorite Woody Allen movie, *Sleeper*, in which Miles Monroe, the owner of a health-food store, is unfrozen after centuries in cryogenic suspended animation, only to discover that science had now "established" that cigarette smoking was beneficial to one's health. "Medical science," Putman continued, "has not, of course, changed its mind about the badness of smoking, but it has changed its mind about many things. And if science constantly changes its mind, then why should one be a 'realist' of any kind about its findings? And if one says that most scientific 'findings' are *approximately true*, then where are the criteria by which we can determine how good the approximation is?"[22]

There's more, a lot more.

Stuart Firestein wrote,

> Phrenology, the investigation of brain function through an analysis of cranial bumps, functioned as a legitimate science for nearly 50 years. Although it contained a germ of truth, certain mental faculties are indeed localized to regions of the brain, and many attested to its accuracy in describing personality traits, it is now clear that a large bump on the right side of your head just behind your ear has nothing to do with your being an especially combative person. Nonetheless, hundreds of scientific papers appeared in the literature, and several highly respected scien-

tific names of the 19th century were attached to it. Charles Darwin, not himself a subscriber, was reckoned by an examination of a picture of his head to have "enough spirituality for ten priests"! In these, and many other cases (the magical *phlogiston* to explain combustion and rust, or the heat fluid *caloric*), apparent knowledge hid our ignorance and retarded progress. We may look at these quaint ideas smugly now, but is there any reason, really, to think that our modern science may not suffer from similar blunders? In fact, the more successful the fact, the more worrisome it may be. Really successful facts have a tendency to become impregnable to revision.[23]

The "luminiferous aether," for instance, was a substance thought to permeate all space, the medium through which light, gravity, and electromagnetism moves, just as the ocean carries water waves and the air sound waves. Despite its elusiveness, few doubted the aether's existence because, according to the greatest scientific minds, *it had to exist*. As it turned out, these thinkers had scientific, philosophical, and rational justification for believing the false to be true.

"One can have a false belief," wrote Alexander Bird, "that is nonetheless justified (for instance we may allow that Maxwell's belief in the electromagnetic aether was justified, even though we take it to be a false belief)."[24]

"A reality," wrote Daniel Robinson, "that once seemed readily expressed in the language of the science of Newton and Galileo would now be closer to mythology than to reality. My own father was alive and well when the best minds in physics regarded nothing as more certain than the *aether*. The same term today seems as if it were taken from astrology."[25]

Whatever the justification for believing in the accuracy of their dating mechanisms, however many and solid (within the paradigm) are the steps in building those justifications, and no matter how deep the steps go, sooner or later justification stops. Whatever the reasons for believing that scientists can extrapolate from nature today to nature three billion years ago, somewhere along the way those reasons bottom out. Whatever the vast web of belief from which evolutionary theory is derived, eventually it stops with *"X does Y because X does Y."*

"It is intellectually troubling for us to conceive," wrote Norman Malcom, "that a whole system of thought might be groundless, might have no rational justification. We realize easily enough, however, that grounds soon give out— that we cannot go on giving reasons for our reasons."[26]

Of course, because explanations bottom out, because the ultimate *why* question remains unsolved, doesn't prove them wrong, but only that they cannot be proven right, which means that *they could be wrong*—and at the foundational level too.[27] That's bad epistemological mojo because, the further down the error, the greater the epistemological carnage that follows. In a complex math problem, an early error often means that each subsequent step, no matter how flawlessly executed, will be corrupted all the way to the conclusion.

Robert Hazen's assumption "that life arose in the ancient scorched Earth from the simplest of basic raw materials: air, water, and rock"[28] was, basically, where his line of reasoning bottomed out, where the justification stopped. He didn't defend this position; he assumed it. But to assume that life, as complicated as it is, began fortuitously from air, water, and rock requires an immense philosophical leap of faith. And because that leap was in the wrong direction (one could argue), it's no wonder that none of the scenarios arising from it have so far been accepted. Even if one were, such as that life arose in molten rocks above 1000°C, what would that mean other than that a majority of the scientific establishment—their worldview defined and limited by this entrenched paradigm—has accepted, for now, that theory as the best explanation or description? And yet no matter how many steps there are in justifying the theory, it will become circular once it reaches the bottom assumption. "Life arose in the ancient scorched Earth from the simplest of basic raw materials: air, water, and rock, because life arose in the ancient scorched Earth from the simplest of basic raw materials: air, water, and rock."

Like "dormitive virtue" and "gravity attracts me to the earth," it's an explanation, of sorts, but not a very satisfying one; and it certainly doesn't answer the *why* question, especially when it's also incorrect from a biblical Creation perspective.

It's like the chessboard analogy, with the unproven philosophical assumption that only within the chessboard, the chess pieces, and the rules of the game can the origins and purposes for the game be found. Thus, what's left? "The game of chess arose out of the game of chess because the game of chess arose out of the game of chess."

It explains little and, in this case, even the little is wrong.

Other models

We have seen that the justification for scientific theories bottoms out, having to assume certain regularities as primitive, as brute fact (X does Y because X does Y), without any deeper explanation. This adds to the epistemological dissonance over scientific explanation as a whole. Even to this day, "debates about the nature of explanation are also at the heart of long-standing controversies in science."[29] (The question of what constitutes a scientific "theory" is, also, unresolved.) Most people are aware of the controversy about what killed the dinosaurs or about the health benefits of red wine. But hypnotized by the illusion of science as a cold, hard, objective search for truth, few realize that conflict over *scientific explanation* itself even exists. The popular myth that science has fully explained such and such—from the origins of the universe, to the evolution of dung beetles—is just that, a popular myth, especially because explanation, the *why* question, inevitably bottoms out.

Over the years, different models have been proposed in an attempt to find an overarching principle that captures the essence of scientific explanation and solves some of the epistemological problems involved. No consensus exists. Some argue that the idea of science *explaining* reality is itself misguided, an unwarranted intrusion of metaphysics into what should be nothing more than descriptions of what appears to our senses, descriptions that enable us to measure, modify, or even control nature to our own technological advantage. Anything beyond is speculative metaphysics, which degenerates into logical circularity (X does Y because X does Y). Who cares why X does Y; it just does, and whatever technology we can get from X doing Y, whatever predictions we can make from it—that's all that matters.

Nevertheless, one popular attempt at explaining explanation is the deductive-nomological (D-N) model ("nomo," from the Greek *nomos*, which means "law"), proposed by Carl Hempel. Despite its foreboding name, the D-N model states that a scientific explanation involves an event that needs to be explained (the *explanandum*) and at least one physical law (the *explanans*) that does the explaining. According to this model, if the law is true, the event *must* follow (hence the word *deductive* in the name).

Let's take, for example, "the apple fell" as the explanandum (the event that needs explaining). The explanans (the law explaining why it fell) would be "the law of universal gravitation." Because of that law, the apple had to fall. Or take this example: Explanandum: "Why does the pressure in a container increase when the air in the container is heated?" Explanans: "Because of the universal law that when a fluid is heated it expands." Because of this law, the air had to expand when heated.

However reasonable, this D-N model (as do the others) has faced a barrage of criticism. Johns Hopkins professor Peter Achinstein argued, for instance,

The following explanation . . . satisfies all of Hempel's conditions for being a correct D-N explanation:

At time *T*, Ann ate a pound of arsenic

Anyone who eats a pound of arsenic dies within 24 hours

Therefore,

Ann died within 24 hours of T.[30]

But suppose Ann were killed three hours later, not by arsenic but by ISIS? If so, the above explanation would be false. It does not explain why Ann died within 24 hours of T, even if the explanandum ("Ann died within 24 hours") was correct; even if the explanans ("Anyone who eats a pound of arsenic dies within 24 hours") contained a true law; and even if the explanans deductively implies the explanandum. However logical and verified by myriad examples, Hempel's model has weaknesses that critics have gleefully exploited, like a virus on a damaged organ. Meanwhile, even in examples that follow the D-N model, the circularity remains: why does the explanandum (whatever it is) follow the explanans (whatever it is)? Eventually, the answer comes down to—it just does.

Other attempts to explain scientific explanation include the inductive-statistical model, the statistical relevance model, the causal mechanical model, unificationist accounts, and pragmatic theories of explanation, most of which have subsets as well. Each, though, comes heavy-laden with critics who vociferously parade about examples of "bona fide" scientific explanations that don't fit under these models or examples of discarded scientific explanations (or even nonscientific explanations) that do.

How does one fit evolution, for example, under the D-M model? Darwin's theory is based on two assumptions: (1) all organisms on earth, from turnips to human beings, share a single common biological ancestor; (2) natural selection is an important cause for the characteristics of all life-forms on earth. Whatever the evidence interpreted to support them, neither assumption is a natural law. Instead, both are historical hypotheses about the earth's distant past. "It is difficult to find," wrote Elliott Sober, "a law of evolution in Darwin's writings."[31]

The point isn't to debate various models of scientific explanation; the point is to show that when controversy exists regarding something as basic as what constitutes a scientific explanation, people need to be more cautious, more critical, before zombie-like accepting the latest scientific explanation about anything—especially when those explanations concern hypothetical prehistorical events. When scientific explanations about present reality—about that which can be handled, heard, and seen; about that which can be tested and retested; about what can be parsed, prodded, and analyzed by expensive and complicated machines—have been modified and even reversed (such as when a pharmaceutical is recalled for safety concerns or ineffectiveness by the same scientific establishment that at one time paraded the scientific evidence for both the drug's safety and the drug's effectiveness[32]), why do so many people still unquestionably accept every scientific proclamation explaining supposed events occurring millions or billions of years ago?

The six-hundred-million-year-old mutation

For example, a 2016 headline from the University of Oregon read, "A Mutation, a Protein Combo, and Life Went Multicellular."[33] The article began: "All it took was one genetic mutation more than 600 million years ago. With that random act, a new protein function was born that helped our single-celled ancestor transition into an organized multicellular organism."[34] Their minds saturated by the presuppositions and assumptions of the evolutionary worldview, most people don't appreciate the intellectual chutzpah of this claim, the highly imaginative and speculative leap from what is observed to what is not observed, from what is now to what has long been gone (or what wasn't even there to begin with).

For starters, what is seen, the observation, especially in cases such as this, came heavy-laded with assumption upon assumption, which Peter Achinstein describes as "those propositions of the theory that are not treated as being derived from others in the theory."[35] In other words, they assumed things about what they saw, assumptions that came from a source other than, and prior to, the specific explanation that they were proposing. It was what they needed beforehand to even come up with the theory or explanation. In this case, the broad meta-assumption (out of which a host of smaller assumptions arose) was naturalism, the unproved philosophical contention that life arose from natural forces alone. This was the grand underpinning and template through which they interpreted what they observed.

Next, they extrapolated backward, from the seen in the present to the unseen in the past, a past that, *today*, "exists" only in their minds. Even if this hypothetical event, the genetic mutation that led to multicellularity, occurred just as they claim, the mutation and the block of time in which it occurred don't exist now. Unlike rocks, protons, and gravity, this six-hundred-million-year-old genetic mutation "exists" now only in the minds of the scientists who make the claim. Sure, one could argue similarly about an event yesterday or even two thousand years ago. But the epistemic leap from the present moment to yesterday or to two thousand years ago is a qualitatively different leap from the present moment to six hundred million years in the past.[36]

Of course, this is what evolutionary biologists do. They speculate about genetic events millions, even billions of years ago. Which is fine if one accepts the paradigm to begin with, but it's still important to remember *what* they are doing. In this case, subjective, fallible, and intellectually biased human beings—educated for years to see the world through a specific, culturally influenced paradigm, working *today* in a laboratory built around those assumptions, and studying only what exists *today*—claim to explain an event at the genetic level at an unknown place on the planet in some hypothetical life-form supposedly existing at a time so far out of our reach that they can only speculate about it.

But when biologists face an endless array of unanswered questions about what exists *in the here and now*, in what can be tested, analyzed, prodded, and poked again and again from numerous angles and with various devices—these researchers claim to have an explanation about *a single genetic event six hundred million years ago*? Or more specifically, the claim is that research in a lab today, aided by "some molecular time travel,"[37] has enabled them to explain how a genetic mutation more than half a billion years ago paved the way for our single-celled ancestor to become multicellular.

However well their research might have worked within the confines, parameters, and presuppositions of the paradigm, the proposed explanation arises from a host of unproven claims—from the accuracy of the dating (and all the assumptions behind it, which, eventually, bottom out), from the claim that we can tell from the present what happened six hundred million years ago (including all the assumptions that here, too, bottom out), and from the assertion that the proposed event actually occurred (an idea built upon assumptions that, sooner or later, end in circularity).

In a summary prepared for the original research article, we read, "For billions of years, life on Earth was made up of single cells. In the lineage that led to animals—and independently in those that led to plants and to fungi—multicellular organisms evolved as cells began to specialize and arrange themselves into tissues and organs. Although the evolution of multicellularity is one of the most important events in the history of animal life, very little is known about the molecular mechanisms by which it took place."[38]

Though nearly every concept in those sentences emerges from a swamp of assumption, the authors admit that little is known about how this transition to multicellularity happened more than half a billion years ago. Note that the assumption that it did happen isn't being questioned—only *how* it happened. Right out of the gate, then, the edifice upon which they did their research is assumed, not proven. The claim is that, though our ancestors were only single-celled entities for billions of years (one would be fascinated to see what assumptions that assumption rests on!), a genetic mutation allowed a single-celled entity to start becoming multicellular, a process that over hundreds of millions of years led to, among other things, Dvorak's Ninth Symphony.

The paper itself expressed the findings like this:

To form and maintain organized tissues, multicellular organisms orient their mitotic spindles relative to neighboring cells. A molecular complex scaffolded by the GK protein-interaction domain (GK_{PID}) mediates spindle orientation in diverse animal taxa by linking microtubule motor proteins to a marker protein on the cell cortex localized by external cues. Here we illuminate how this complex evolved and commandeered control of spindle orientation from a more ancient mechanism. The complex was assembled through a series of molecular exploitation events, one of which—the evolution of GK_{PID}'s capacity to bind the cortical marker protein—can be recapitulated by reintroducing a single historical substitution into the reconstructed ancestral GK_{PID}. This change revealed and repurposed an ancient molecular surface that previously had a radically different function. We show how the physical simplicity of this binding interface enabled the evolution of a new protein function now essential to the biological complexity of many animals.[39]

Their explanation about how, through a series of ancient "molecular exploitation events," the "physical simplicity of this binding interface enabled the evolution of a new protein function" has, however, come under considerable criticism[40]; in fact, the researchers were forced to backtrack on their initial claims:

We have modified the text in numerous ways to be more cautious on this point and to base our claims more solidly on what is known in the literature. . . .

More generally, we have gone through the text and have changed our wording to dispel the impression that GK_{PID} complex is the sole driver of spindle orientation in all animals and all cell types and to avoid the implication that the evolution of the GK_{PID} complex explains all instances of spindle orientation in all animals.[41]

So it turns out that their explanation is more speculative than their paper first claimed. Also, they revamped their claims to make them based more "solidly on what is known in the literature." What literature? Of course, the literature written by other scientists, working from the same presuppositions, the same paradigm, and the same limits and biases. Which proves only that their revised theory fits more closely with "what is known in the literature," but it proves nothing about how well their theory fits with what really happened. And, with all due respect, extrapolating back from a lab today to an incident at the genetic level of a hypothetical life-form a hypothetical six hundred million years ago in regard to a "GK_{PID} complex" has to be exceedingly speculative—whatever the justifications for their reasoning.

Nevertheless, the finding was heralded as another astounding explanation of our evolutionary origins. A *Washington Post* headline proclaimed, "Startling New Finding: 600 Million Years Ago, a Biological Mishap Changed Everything."[42] The *Post* then told its readers,

> In a paper published in the open-access journal eLife this week, researchers say they have pinpointed what may well be one of evolution's greatest copy mess-ups yet: the mutation that allowed our ancient protozoa predecessors to evolve into complex, multi-cellular organisms. Thanks to this mutation—which was not solely responsible for the leap out of single-cellular life, but without which you, your dog and every creature large enough to be seen without a microscope might not be around—cells were able to communicate with one another and work together.
>
> Incredibly, in the world of evolutionary biology, all it took was one tiny tweak, one gene, and complex life as we know it was born.[43]

Scientific research, said the *Post*, "and a cool bit of evolutionary time travel known as ancestral protein reconstruction"[44] led to this astonishing explanation about how this one mutation more than half a billion years ago changed the course of history. (One wonders how a "cool bit of evolutionary time travel" fits in with the much vaunted "scientific method," but that's another story.) The article continues: "In this case, the reconstruction took Prehoda and his colleagues back about 600 million years, when ancient beings no bigger than a single cell swam through vast shallow seas covering what are now continents. There's pretty much no fossil record from this period—what kind of fossil could be left by something smaller than a pinhead?—so insights into life at that time rely on researchers' imaginations and intense scrutiny of modern DNA."[45]

Thus, anyone reading the article will come away with the understanding that a "cool bit of evolutionary time travel," added to the "researchers' imaginations and intense scrutiny of modern DNA," has given the world more proof about how humanity's evolutionary origins unfolded, this time through a single genetic event six hundred million years ago, at a time when our direct ancestors ("ancient beings no bigger than a single cell") "swam through vast shallow seas covering what are now continents," regardless of the layers of speculation upon speculation upon speculation upon which the claim rests.

The evolutionary-industrial-cultural complex

Despite the imaginative pole vault over the time and space separating a lab in twenty-first-century Oregon from a single cell's genetic mutation more than half a billion years ago somewhere in the sea, many people will accept this claim about a six-hundred-million-year-old gene muck-up that led to our multicellularity. After all, *It's science*; and the paper ("Evolution of an Ancient Protein Function Involved in Organized Multicellularity in Animals") had been peer-reviewed, and then published by the intellectual hegemons of the scientific-industrial complex.

What could be more oracular than that?

Besides, the evolutionary paradigm and the assumptions that underlie it like a Russian nesting doll have dominated Western culture since the early twentieth century. This paradigm is so entrenched, so hardwired into the collective cultural consciousness, that most don't question it any more than their ancestors questioned the geocentric universe, the luminiferous aether, the absolute nature of space and time, and spontaneous generation—all of which have been tossed into the wreckage-strewn landfill of rejected scientific dogma and paradigms (with the notable exception of spontaneous generation, which has been recycled by the prevailing theory of origins and its assumption that "life arose in the ancient scorched Earth from the simplest of basic raw materials: air, water, and rock"). Meanwhile, from kindergarten to graduate school, the curriculum is suffused with the evolutionary paradigm, and popular culture assumes it the way that it has now assumed gay rights. The press mouths platitudes about assumed evolutionary events billions of years ago with the same mundaneness with which it reports the temperature in Cleveland. So it's no wonder that a great many people accept it, including Christians (who should be more skeptical, to say the least).

When scholarly paper after paper in geology, paleontology, psychology, biology, genetics, sociology,[46] and medicine assume the paradigm, why should anyone do otherwise? When an issue of the *Journal of Evolutionary Biology*[47] (the name itself reveals the assumptions) sports such titles as "Repeated Evolution of Exaggerated Dewlaps and Other Throat Morphology in Lizards," "Colour Pattern Homology and Evolution in *Vanessa* Butterflies (Nymphalidae: Nymphalini): Eyespot Characters," and "Connecting Proximate Mechanisms and Evolutionary Patterns: Pituitary Gland Size and Mammalian Life History," what plebe dare challenge, not just the specific claims about "connecting proximate mechanism" but the paradigm itself, from which these and thousands of other scholarly papers draw their theoretical nourishment?

And when the cognoscenti—with the passion of a Rosa Luxemburg espousing Marxist dogma—assert the certainty of Darwinian dogma, why should anyone question it? Richard Dawkins, named the world's top "thinker,"[48] declared, "Evolution is a fact in the same sense as it is a fact that Paris is in the Northern Hemisphere."[49] Daniel Dennett, a fellow-traveler in Darwinism, claimed, "The fundamental core of contemporary Darwinism . . . is now beyond dispute among scientists. . . . The hope that it will be 'refuted' by some shattering breakthrough is about as reasonable as the hope that we will return to a geocentric vision and discard Copernicus."[50] The National Academies of Science assured readers, "Many scientific theories are so well-established that no new evidence is likely to alter them substantially. For example, no new evidence will demonstrate that the Earth does not orbit around the sun (heliocentric theory), or that living things are not made of cells (cell theory), that matter is not composed of atoms, or that the surface of the Earth is not divided into solid plates that have moved over geological timescales (the theory of plate tectonics). Like these other foundational scientific theories, the theory of evolution is supported by so many observations and confirming experiments that scientists are confident that the basic components of the theory will not be overturned by new evidence."[51]

A steady drone of statements like these over the airwaves, digitalized and disseminated through cyberspace, etched in print, and asserted again and again in every venue (from graduate seminar to truck stop) are bound to become cultural hardware, despite the warning of Imre Lakatos that "the hallmark of scientific behavior is a certain scepticism even towards one's most cherished theories. Blind commitment to a theory is not an intellectual virtue: it is an intellectual crime."[52] Lakatos aside, the evolutionary paradigm is now assumed, taken for granted, and what's assumed and taken for granted is not easily uprooted, especially when knighted with the gravitas that the adjective *scientific* bestows upon whatever it modifies. If blind commitment to a theory is an intellectual crime, then Darwinists are intellectual first-degree felons.

Despite the certitude of expression, it took a lot of Botoxed logic to equate the epistemic status of evolution with that of Paris being in the Northern Hemisphere or with heliocentrism. The knowledge of Paris' location on the planet and the sun's in the solar system differs from the knowledge that arises from looking at the selective breeding of animals and speculating that life evolved from natural selection. Whatever the debate about the distinction between *observational science* and *historical science*—to equate knowledge about the location of Paris today with the knowledge of a genetic mutation six hundred million years ago, or even with the macroevolutionary Darwinian evolutionary paradigm itself, is to assume not just the ignorance of the masses but their gullibility as well.

Sure (so the argument goes), no one ever saw a dinosaur evolve feathers millions of years ago, but no one has ever seen an electron either. Thus (so the argument goes), because both are accepted scientific teaching, dinosaurs evolved feathers just as surely as electrons exist. This is like equating the existence of Julius Caesar to that of unicorns, as neither has been seen by anyone

alive today. The distinction between knowledge of the neo-Darwinian synthesis and knowledge of Paris's latitude and longitude involves much more than
the difference between what images sculpted in light enter human pupils and
what don't.

Others have seen this problem. John Lennox, in dealing with the argument
about how macroevolution is as proven as, for instance, the orbit of the earth
around the sun, wrote:

> We now have two important reasons why macroevolution does not have
> the same status as the fact that the earth orbits the sun. Firstly, the claim
> that the earth orbits the sun is a matter established by observation. That
> is manifestly not the case for Lewontin's claim that "birds arose out of
> 'non-birds'" (whatever the latter might have been). That process has never
> been observed. Secondly, the fact that the earth orbits the sun is not only
> a matter of observation, it is also a matter of repeated observation. Le-
> wontin's claim about the origin of birds concerns an unrepeatable, unob-
> served, past event. To put an unobservable and unrepeatable phenome-
> non in the same category as an observable and repeatable one would seem
> to be such an elementary blunder, that one cannot help wondering if his
> aforementioned fear of a divine footprint is playing a key role, and that
> materialistic prejudice is overriding common (scientific) sense.[53]

Challenging the hegemonic paradigm

It's ironic, too, how vociferously and dogmatically the scientific-industrial
complex systematically squashes any dissent from the inflexible aplomb with
which the "hegemonic paradigm" of evolution is promulgated. Ironic, because
science was, originally, a break with the status quo, a revolution against the
hegemonic paradigm of the time. One of the most crucial lines in intellectual
history came from Francis Bacon (1561–1626), considered the father of modern science. When castigated by the intellectual authorities for challenging the
Ptolemaic-Aristotelian worldview, he replied, "I cannot be called on to abide
by the sentence of a tribunal which is itself on its trial."[54]

*Don't condemn me by your paradigm when your paradigm is precisely what I am
challenging to begin with.* And though entrenched 1,300 years longer than the
Darwinian one has been now, the entire Ptolemaic-Aristotelian paradigm (and
not just some of the theories arising from it) turned out to be dead wrong even
after centuries of the best and brightest assuming it.

Anyone today who, like Galileo, dares deviate from the "tribunal" (now the
scientific-industrial complex) and its reigning paradigm (the neo-Darwinian
synthesis) is intellectually tarred and feathered. Even those who believe in evolution, in life on earth evolving from a common ancestor millions of years ago,

but who reject the Darwinian methodology of random mutation and natural selection as the sole dynamic forces behind these changes, are pilloried as the intellectual equivalents of flat-earthers, astrologers, Holocaust deniers, and, worst of all, creationists. Even though, as shown earlier, Richard Dawkins can assert, with impunity, that "nothing and nothing in some strange way cancels itself out to produce something. And quantum theory allows that to happen."[55] But woe to the scientist who implies that random mutation and natural selection alone might not fully explain (for instance) the numerous and complicated steps needed in human blood coagulation.

The late Francis Crick (of Crick-and-Watson fame) believed that life was way too complicated to have arisen on earth by chance, as science now insists that it did. Instead, the Nobel laureate proposed *panspermia,* "the theory that organisms were deliberately transmitted to the earth by intelligent beings on another planet."[56] Thus, one of the last century's greatest scientific minds proposed that aliens in spaceships might have seeded life here, and yet *he* gets a fair hearing by the scientific community. But those who hint at purposeful design or forethought in the formation of that same life face the intellectual equivalent of what Rome did to Galileo when he disputed the hegemonic paradigm of his time. The bigotry and unfairness of a discipline that prides itself on objectivity and intellectual freedom (as long as one doesn't deviate from the paradigm) has not gone unnoticed, either.

Atheist and evolutionist Thomas Nagel wrote,

> Even though writers like Michael Behe and Stephen Meyer are motivated at least in part by their religious beliefs, the empirical arguments they offer against the likelihood that the origin of life and its evolutionary history can be fully explained by physics and chemistry are of great interest in themselves. Another skeptic, David Berlinski, has brought out these problems vividly without reference to the design inference. Even if one is not drawn to the alternative of an explanation by the actions of a designer, the problems that these iconoclasts pose for the orthodox scientific consensus should be taken seriously. They do not deserve the scorn with which they are commonly met. It is manifestly unfair.[57]

Nagel, though highly respected, faced a barrage of criticism when he dared to question, not the overall paradigm of evolution itself, but the idea that, as currently formulated, the paradigm could explain human consciousness.

Humans, even those with PhDs in evolutionary biology, are an ever-changing mosaic of their past, the sum of all the complex subjective and conditional social, cultural, emotional, and intellectual instances of their lives.

Armed with a Large Hadron Collider in Europe or with methods of "molecular time travel" from a lab in Oregon or a Laser Interferometer Gravitational-Wave Observatory detector in Livingston, Louisiana, and Hanford, Washington, people (even scientists) are still packets of flesh and bone carrying around their own fecal matter and (not far away) their own brains—a few pounds of carbon-based organic material (about 75 percent water) closer in composition to Colonel Sanders' fried chicken than to a hard drive. How can these beings, individually or collectively, transcend the reality that they are immersed in and composed of and observe that reality from any perspective other than through the theory-infected lens of their own subjectivity, which, besides being wired in them at conception, is continuously refashioned, adjusted, and reformatted by the endless stream of contingencies in which humans exist? Even with their devices, human views are limited to their individual consciousness, each one private, personal, and inscrutably formed by, and locked within, a clump of meat so small, isolated, and subjective against the reality that it inhabits and seeks to explore. As Nietzsche said, "In the final analysis, one experiences only oneself,"[58] and oneself is always highly subjective.

A thousand great minds are still only a thousand great minds, not one mind a thousand times greater than any single mind, and if all these great minds are looking for the lost keys in the wrong place because that's where the light is, then none are going to find them. Neil Turok, director of the Perimeter Institute for Theoretical Physics, was credited with the following statement in a blog referring to challenges in current physics: "This led people to the realisation, he [Turok] says, that even though hundreds or thousands of people are working on an idea, it may still be wrong."[59] And if that's true about physics dealing with things that exist today—such things as are observed in telescopes and particle accelerators—how much more so is it true about things that supposedly happened millions or billions of years out of our reach?

Also, if human knowledge results only from evolutionary processes, what is our certitude but a contingent configuration of chemicals and neurons, anyway? Life that arose, by chance, "in the ancient scorched Earth from the simplest of basic raw materials: air, water, and rock," even after it becomes multicellular enough to evolve a consciousness, is still at the core just life that arose by chance from air, water, and rock, which, molded by survival and not by the search for epistemic truth, has no reason to assume certainty about anything other than what presumably fitted it for survival. As one scientist quipped, *Cousin to the amoeba, how can we be sure?*[60] On a more serious note, physicist Percy Bridgman, of Harvard, wrote that "the structure of nature may eventually be such that our processes of thought do not correspond to it sufficiently to permit us to think about it at all. . . . The world fades out and eludes us. . . . We are confronted with something truly ineffable. We have reached the limit of the vision of the great pioneers of science, the vision, namely, that we live in a sympathetic world in that it is comprehensible by our minds."[61]

No question, the reality that's in our face every day remains complicated. "If you fill a kettle with water," wrote David Deutsch, "and switch it on, all the supercomputers on Earth working for the age of the universe could not solve the equations that predict what all those water molecules will do—even if we could somehow determine their initial state and that of all the outside influences on them, which is itself an intractable task."[62]

That, for a kettle of water, which is nomological (law-like) in nature and existing in the present? Thus, it takes a mass of intellectual chutzpah to make bold statements about the certainty of *biological* (not nomological) events millions and even billions of years in the past, especially when justification for scientific explanation always ends and becomes self-referential. It's the old dormitive virtue problem expressed so eloquently by Molière centuries ago.

"If justification does come to an end," asked Michael Lynch, "what fills the void? One answer goes like this: the central lesson is that when justification comes to an end, *tradition* takes over. All belief is framed by tradition—by historic, meaning-laden practices embedded within the fabric of one's culture."[63]

Tradition? Culture? Meaning-laden practices? Maybe for other things, but not for science, because doesn't science, after all, transcend all these contingencies with that archetypical conduit to epistemic certainty—the scientific method?

---

1. Molière, *The Imaginary Invalid* (Project Gutenberg, 2003), under "Third Interlude," http://www.gutenberg.org/files/9070/9070-h/9070-h.htm.

2. Ibid.

3. Though the question of interpretation as opposed to explanation includes the whole spectrum of science, it's especially strong in the baffling world of quantum mechanics, where centuries of human concepts of logic and reason and cause and effect seem painfully inefficient. "There are some researchers who would like to brush away this entire subject of interpreting quantum mechanics. They have a very pragmatic outlook and only care that the results on the measuring instruments are correct. These *instrumentalists* are only concerned that the equations work and make the correct predictions. They see no reason to pay any attention to *why* the equations work or what the underlying reality of the physical universe is. Their motto is 'Shut up and calculate!' They believe that one should not waste time pondering what is going on 'under the hood' and question whether a deeper reality even exists. To them, the underlying nature of the real world is either beyond us or is not worthy of thought. They think that the study of the interpretation of quantum mechanics is 'only' metaphysics and hence should be thrown into the garbage heap of bad ideas." Yanofsky, *Outer Limits of Reason*, 212.

4. Bird, *Philosophy of Science*, 64.

5. Carl G. Hempel and Paul Oppenheim, "Studies in the Logic of Explanation," *Philosophy of Science* 15, no. 2 (April 1948): 135.

6. Quoted in John C. Lennox, *Gunning for God* (Oxford: Lion, 2011), 228.

7. This leads to another popular, but not uncontested, assumption in science: the idea that the best theories, the deepest theories, are the simplest. It is sometimes referred to as *Occam's razor* (a phrase that William of Occam, for whom it was named, himself never used). This is a philosophical assumption, not a scientific one. However, in the subject immediately at hand, Newton's theory of gravity in contrast to Einstein's, who's going to assert that Einstein's field equations, a deeper theory than Newton's law of gravity, are the simpler of the two, even if they are now believed to be the better of the two?

8. Curd and Cover, *Philosophy of Science*, 1238.

9. Ludwig Wittgenstein, *On Certainty*, eds. G. E. M. Anscombe and G. H. von Wright, trans. Denis Paul and G. E. M. Anscombe (New York: Harper Torchbooks, 1972), 27e.

10. David Hume, *An Enquiry Concerning the Principles of Morals* (1912 reprint of 1777 edition; Project Gutenberg, 2010), sec. 5, pt. 2, http://www.gutenberg.org/files/4320/4320-h/4320-h.htm.

11. Jim Holt, *Why Does the World Exist? An Existential Detective Story* (London: Profile Books, 2012), 78 (italics in the original).

12. John Polkinghorne, *Quantum Physics and Theology: An Unexpected Kinship* (New Haven, CT: Yale University Press, 2007), 5 (italics in the original).

13. Michael P. Lynch, *In Praise of Reason* (Cambridge, MA: MIT Press, 2012), 52, 53.

14. Kurt Gödel, *On Formally Undecidable Propositions of Principia Mathematica and Related Systems*, trans. B. Meltzer (New York: Dover Publications, 1992).

15. Bertrand Russell, *Portraits From Memory and Other Essays* (New York: Simon and Schuster, 1956), 54, 55 (italics in the original).

16. Morris Kline, *Mathematics: The Loss of Certainty* (Oxford: Oxford University Press, 1980), 263, 264.

17. Douglas R. Hofstadter, foreword to *Gödel's Proof*, rev. ed., by Ernest Nagel and James R. Newman, ed. Douglas R. Hofstadter (New York: New York University Press, 2001), xiv.

18. Thomas Nagel, *The Last Word* (New York: Oxford University Press, 1997), 76.

19. Ann Gauger, "On the Origin of Chins," Evolution News, February 11, 2016, http://www.evolutionnews.org/2016/02/on_the_origin_o_8102606.html.

20. Mary Hesse, *The Structure of Scientific Inference* (Berkeley: University of California Press, 1974), 20, 21 (italics in the original).

21. Jonathan Sacks, *The Great Partnership: Science, Religion, and the Search for Meaning* (New York: Schocken Books, 2012), 272, 273.

22. Putnam, *Philosophy in an Age of Science*, 105.

23. Firestein, *Ignorance*, 23, 24 (italics in the original).

24. Bird, *Philosophy of Science*, 231, 232.

25. Williams and Robinson, *Scientism: The New Orthodoxy*, 30 (italics in the original).

26. Malcolm, "Groundlessness of Belief," in Clark, *Readings in the Philosophy of Religion*, 218.

27. "Science does not tell us 'why'; it only answers questions concerning what happens, not 'why' it happens. This longing to find out 'why' is nothing more than the longing to derive scientific statements from general principles that are plausible and intelligible. Such a longing stems from the belief that there are such principles. There have been, of course, a great many opinions about the criteria for what is plausible and intelligible." Frank, *Philosophy of Science*, 23.

28. Hazen, "Origins of Life," part 1, p. 14.

29. Klemke, Hollinger, and Rudge, with Kline, *Introductory Readings*, 198.

30. Achinstein, *Evidence, Explanation, and Realism*, 30 (italics in the original).

31. Elliott Sober, "Philosophy of Biology," in Bunnin and Tsui-James, *Blackwell Companion to Philosophy*, 321.

32. For instance, "Fourteen years ago, a leading drug maker published a study showing that the antidepressant Paxil was safe and effective for teenagers. On Wednesday, a major medical journal posted a new analysis of the same data concluding that the opposite is true." Benedict Carey, "Antidepressant Paxil Is Unsafe for Teenagers, New Analysis Says," *New York Times*, September 16, 2015, https://www.nytimes.com/2015/09/17/health/antidepressant-paxil-is-unsafe-for-teenagers-new-analysis-says.html?mcubz=0.

33. Jim Barlow, "A Mutation, a Protein Combo, and Life Went Multicellular," Around the O, January 7, 2016, http://around.uoregon.edu/content/mutation-protein-combo-and-life-went-multicellular.

34. Ibid.

35. Peter Achinstein, *Concepts of Science: A Philosophical Analysis* (Baltimore: Johns Hopkins University Press, 1968), 125.

36. Though this is not the time and place to delve into the ponderous question of the ontological status of the past (or the future), there is an *epistemological* difference between what one can believe about events days, weeks, or thousands of years ago, and what supposedly happened millions or billions of years ago. More recent events can be remembered, recorded, and testified to by sources that events millions and billions of years ago don't have. Much more conjecture, speculation, and assumptions are needed when one seeks to reconstruct the supposed evolutionary history of dinosaurs than to reconstruct the history of the Peloponnesian War.

37. Barlow, "Life Went Multicellular."

38. Douglas P. Anderson et al., "Evolution of an Ancient Protein Function Involved in Organized Multicellularity in Animals," eLife, January 7, 2016, http://elifesciences.org/content/5/e10147v1.

39. Ibid.

40. "Researchers Proclaim: Instant Animals by Chance," Evolution News, February 16, 2016, http://www.evolutionnews.org/2016/02/researchers_pro102612.html.

41. Quoted in ibid.

42. Sarah Kaplan, "Startling New Finding: 600 Million Years Ago, a Biological Mishap Changed Everything," *Washington Post*, January 11, 2016, https://www.washingtonpost.com/news/morning-mix/wp/2016/01/11/startling-new-discovery-600-million-years-ago-a-single-biological-mistake-changed-everything/.

43. Ibid.

44. Ibid.

45. Ibid.

46. Even political science is now being seen through the evolutionary model.

Support for the application of Darwinism to human affairs spans the political spectrum. Writing for the conservative *National Review*, law professor John McGinnis has urged conservatives to jump on the bandwagon of sociobiology and its Darwinian framework. According to McGinnis, discoveries during the last two decades have led to a convincing revival of Darwinism, and "any political movement that hopes to be successful must come to terms with the second rise of Darwinism." McGinnis is not alone among intellectuals in championing a rapprochement between conservatism and modern Darwinism. More nuanced versions of this view can be found in the writings of James Q. Wilson and in political theorist Larry Arnhart's provocative book, *Darwinian Conservatism*. Arnhart declares that "conservatives need Charles Darwin. They need him because a Darwinian science of human nature supports conservatives in their realist view of human imperfectibility and their commitment to ordered liberty." Arnhart goes so far as to suggest that conservatism is doomed unless it embraces Darwinian theory. "The intellectual vitality of conservatism in the twenty-first century will depend on the success of conservatives in appealing to advances in the biology of human nature as confirming conservative thought." Notably, conservative theorists like Arnhart who defend Darwinian theory try to avoid the virulent reductionism championed by many in the scientific community.

On the other side of the political divide, Princeton professor Peter Singer has declared that "it is time to develop a Darwinian left." Of course, there always has been a Darwinian left . . . , but Singer has called for the Left to integrate the findings of modern Darwinism into its agenda. "It is time for the left to take seriously the fact that we have evolved from other animals; we bear the evidence of this inheritance, not only in our anatomy and our DNA, but in what we want and how we are likely to try to get it." West, *Darwin Day in America*, xv.

47. *Journal of Evolutionary Biology* 28, no. 11 (November 2015).

48. "World Thinkers 2013," *Prospect*, April 24, 2013, http://www.prospectmagazine.co.uk /features/world-thinkers-2013.

49. Dawkins, *Greatest Show on Earth*, 10.

50. Daniel C. Dennett, *Darwin's Dangerous Idea: Evolution and the Meanings of Life* (New York: Simon and Schuster), Kindle edition, chap. 1.

51. "Is Evolution a Theory or a Fact?" National Academy of Sciences, http://www.nas.edu /evolution/TheoryOrFact.html.

52. Imre Lakatos, *The Methodology of Scientific Research Programmes*, Philosophical Papers, vol. 1 (Cambridge, UK: Cambridge University Press, 1978), 1.

53. Lennox, *God's Undertaker*, 117.

54. Bacon, *Philosophical Works*, 262.

55. Dawkins, interview by Quinn, *After Words*.

56. F. H. C. Crick and L. E. Orgel, "Directed Panspermia," *Icarus* 19 (1973): 341, http:// profiles.nlm.nih.gov/ps/access/SCBCCP.pdf.

57. Thomas Nagel, *Mind and Cosmos: Why the Materialist Neo-Darwinian Conception of Nature Is Almost Certainly False* (Oxford: Oxford University Press, 2012), 10.

58. Friedrich Nietzsche, *Thus Spake Zarathustra* (New York: Penguin Books, 1969), 173.

59. Louise Mayor, "Why Converge?" *Physics World* blog, June 22, 2015, http://blog .physicsworld.com/2015/06/22/why-converge/.

60. Goldman, "Science Wars," part 2, p. 151.

61. Quoted in Huston Smith, *Beyond the Postmodern Mind: The Place of Meaning in a Global Civilization*, 3rd. ed. (Wheaton, IL: Quest Books, 2003), 7, 8.

62. David Deutsch, *The Beginning of Infinity: Explanations That Transform the World* (New York: Viking, 2011), 107.

63. Lynch, *In Praise of Reason*, 61 (italics in the original).

CHAPTER 9

THE MYTH OF THE METHOD

In the quixotic quest for perfect love (or a reasonable facsimile thereof), some dating websites have applied the scientific method to digital matchmaking. The logic is flawless—kind of.

Our brains are vibrant hives of such chemicals as 3-(2-aminoethyl)-1H-indol-5-ol for serotonin; or 4-(2-aminoethyl)benzene-1,2-diol for dopamine; or (2S)-1-[(4R,7S,10S,13S,16S,19R)-19-amino-7-(2-amino-2-oxoethyl)-10-(3-amino-3-oxopropyl)-13-[(2S)-butan-2-yl]-16-[(4-hydroxyphenyl)methyl]-6,9,12,15,18-pentaoxo-1,2-dithia-5,8,11,14,17-pentazacycloicosane-4-carbonyl]-N-[(2S)-1-[(2-amino-2-oxoethyl)amino]-4-methyl-1-oxopentan-2-yl] pyrrolidine-2-carboxamide for oxytocin. Dubbed "the love hormones," these compounds have been discovered, analyzed, and synthesized only through the scientific method.

Why not use the scientific method, then, to study the big picture, the end result of these hormones—love itself? Are not people primarily physical, subject to the same physical laws that everything is, from the orbits of planets to the "orbits" of electrons? If so, and if love is what we do as physical creatures subordinate to physical laws, shouldn't science and the scientific method help us do it?

For instance, if the scientific method has shown that hundreds of millions of years ago whale ancestors transitioned from land to the sea (as Richard Dawkins wrote, whales "ceased to be land creatures altogether and reverted to the full marine habits of their remote ancestors"[1]), certainly the scientific method should be capable of helping lonely Jane or frisky Peter find the perfect mate. If love is *at least* serotonin, dopamine, and oxytocin, then, when seeking to make a match, along with finding out whether one's love prospect prefers Mozart's "Der Schauspieldirektor" to Led Zeppelin's "Living Loving Maid," why not include what science reveals about his or her inner nuts and bolts, something only science and the scientific method could possibly do?

"A handful of dating Web sites," said the *New York Times*, "are competing to impose some science, or at least some structure, on the quest for love by using different kinds of tests to winnow the selection process."[2] That is, along with the usual questions about favorite movies or "Do you like dogs?" some sites want to add things such as DNA swabs "to test for genetic markers in your immune system that may indicate compatibility."[3]

The myth of the method

Using the scientific method to find love? If this approach ultimately turns out to be a boondoggle, the boondoggling would arise, not from the method but from its application—like using Larousse's French dictionary to translate Ovid's *Metamorphoses* to English. (This probably wouldn't get one line, much less all fifteen books, translated, but the problem would not be with Larousse but with the application.) After all, isn't the scientific method the time-honored means of exhuming truth, of discerning reality, but without the foibles, contingencies, and mushiness of shadowy disciplines such as philosophy, theology, literary criticism, history, ethics, and aesthetics? The scientific method is designed to separate fluffy sentiment from hard reality; it eliminates the inherent intellectual prejudices that taint and distort objectivity—what Francis Bacon (1561–1626) called the "four classes of Idols which beset men's minds."[4] The scientific method, deemed the apogee of epistemological pursuit, makes other pursuits the intellectual equivalent of reading goat livers or studying astrology charts on table mats in Chinese restaurants.

And what kid, educated in the West, hasn't been taught all about the intellectual certitudes of "the scientific method," which consists of a few simple steps, often depicted like this: (1) ask a question, (2) do research on the question, (3) construct a theory, (4) test the theory by experiment, (5) draw conclusion. Unfortunately, each step is crunched and distorted by layers of subjectivity that make the process ridiculously simplistic, like depicting Christmas as nothing but the voyage of Santa and Rudolph on the evening of December 25.

Besides, the epistemic status that "the scientific method" claims for itself is self-referentially self-refuting. Nothing is scientific about the scientific method. The scientific method does not lead to the scientific method. The scientific method is not a scientific discovery, like nuclear fission or RNA transcription; nor is it the result of scientific research and induction about the natural world (or at least how that world appears to us). It comes, instead, from philosophy, the B- or C-team of epistemological inquiry, at least in contrast to the much ballyhooed scientific method itself. Why should anyone who believes that the scientific method is the best means of finding truth believe that the scientific method is the best method for finding truth? To do so is to contradict oneself.

Despite all the grade-school hype, and despite how often the phrase "the scientific method" has been reverently repeated, bandied about, and etched in popular consciousness, most scientists know that it's not so simple. Daniel Thurs wrote,

> The so-called scientific method is a myth. That is not to say that scientists don't do things that can be described and are unique to their fields of study. But to squeeze a diverse set of practices that span cultural anthropology, paleobotany, and theoretical physics into a handful of steps is an inevitable distortion and, to be blunt, displays a serious poverty of imagination. Easy to grasp, pocket-guide versions of the scientific method usually reduce to critical thinking, checking facts, or letting "nature speak for itself," none of which is really all that uniquely scientific. If typical formulations were accurate, the only location true science would be taking place in would be grade-school classrooms.[5]

Philosopher of science Paul Feyerabend wrote about a lecture by Karl Popper at the London School of Economics in the 1950s. Popper began with a line eventually etched into the intellectual canon: "I am a Professor of Scientific Method—but I have a problem: there is no scientific method."[6]

Decades of grade-school texts and tabloid-level hype have codified the notion that when the scientific method is applied to anything,[7] especially (but not only) science, the result is mystically, magically assumed to have been carefully and rationally and thoroughly worked through and critically examined—the surest path to truth available to us. Yet, far from a rigid path of procedure and process, "the scientific method" is a rhetorical device, a mere confluence of words that ill fit the reality it purports to describe. Instead of this earthly manifestation of metaphysical principles exhumed from überreality and translated into laboratory and field procedures, the scientific method is a myth.

No one method defines how science is done in any one branch, much less in them all, as if some metaprocesses synchronize the procedures for doing everything from paleobotany to quantum chromodynamics. A gargantuan gap divides the nonexistent scientific method that calculates the mass of the earth from the same nonexistent scientific method that claims bats and dolphins both evolved sonar from a common gene millions of years ago (even if the bat's ancestral precursor took to the air and the dolphin's to the sea). Whatever method the scientists used to reach each conclusion, it certainly was not the same one.

In *Against Method*, in *Farewell to Reason*, and in other writings, Paul Feyerabend argued that science is "an essentially anarchic enterprise,"[8] not that it leads to anarchy but that its methods are not as systematic, established, and universal as the myth trumpets. There is no useful and exceptionless method-ological rule to govern the progress of science, he argued, except for the useful and exceptionless methodological rule that *anything goes*. "There is no one 'sci-entific method,'" Feyerabend wrote, "but there is a great deal of opportunism; anything goes—anything, that is, that is liable to advance knowledge as under-stood by a particular researcher or research tradition."[9] For Feyerabend, "given any rule, however 'fundamental' or 'rational,' there are always circumstances when it is advisable not only to ignore the rule, but to adopt its opposite."[10]

This "anarchy" isn't bad; on the contrary it's how knowledge of any kind, including science, progresses. Science is as much an art as, well, a science, and often is done with the same tenor of chance, imagination, and genius that inspires art. This subjectivity doesn't make various and multifaceted steps in science irrational, just not as formal and rigid as the myths of the method project.

"Scratch the surface of the scientific method," wrote Daniel Thurs, "and the messiness spills out."[11] But what does it matter? Does the theory "work," in that it enables the scientist to make accurate or even unexpected predictions? Or to build a faster computer chip? Or to measure how much weaker gravity is than other fundamental forces? As we saw in another context, if it "works," who cares if it's true or not? In this context, if it "works," who cares what methods the scientist used to get there, even if he were influenced by a dream, experimental data, or the Bhagavad Gita?

Of course, for a method that supposedly doesn't exist or that is a mere rhetorical device, the fruit derived from it—from gene therapy to the space station, from the germ theory to general relativity—is amazingly rich. Even if the scientific method itself is a myth, it doesn't mean that science and the procedures of science are not powerful means of extracting from the world an understanding of the world, however limited and contingent that under-standing remains. (*How* limited and contingent, of course, begs the question.) The immediate purpose here is, simply, to detox people from the opium of scientism and the intellectual stupor caused by belief in "the scientific method" as the ultimate arbiter of truth, especially when the method, or at least any one single method, doesn't even exist (which makes its epistemological tyranny that much more problematic and deceptive). This is especially crucial when millions of Christians will, in the twinkling of an eye, stretch, bend, twist, or chuck (if need be) the most basic beliefs the moment the scientific method is invoked in a way that contradicts those beliefs.

Just because science has done astonishing things (such as revealing details about cell membrane permeability or building the Large Hadron Collider) doesn't mean it's correct when it says that birds and crocodiles evolved from the same common ancestor 240 million years ago, or even that evolution itself is true. The success of one (the Large Hadron Collider) does not in any way imply the truth of the other (evolution), even if both claims boast their origins in "the scientific method." Equating the two would be like equating "Jim Morrison lives!" scribbled on a DC subway wall with Andrew Marvell's "To His Coy Mistress" simply because both come under the rubric of the English language.

The demarcation problem

And the question of the scientific method isn't the only thing unresolved. An even broader question remains: What is science itself? Or more specifically: What is the difference between science and pseudoscience? Even now, despite all the incredible achievements of science, no specific answer has been found.

Amazing—because when something is labeled "science" or is said to have been "proved" by science, then by default all dissent is deemed suspect, substandard, and foolish, the ravings of ignoramuses and uninformed hillbillies, especially when it comes to questioning the Aristotelianism of our era, Darwinian evolution. Besides the unanswered question of what it even means when science "proves" something, if no universally agreed on line of demarcation between science and pseudoscience has yet been articulated, then why shouldn't all knees bow before the claims of pseudoscience just as they do before science?

"The problem," wrote Michael Gordin, "of separating science from pseudoscience is devilishly difficult. One essential characteristic of all those doctrines, labeled as 'pseudosciences,' is that they very much resemble sciences, and so superficial characteristics fail to identify them."[12] Nor can pseudoscience be dissed simply as wrong science, because many scientific theories now believed wrong—phlogiston theory, the aether, circular orbits of planets—were once derived by bona fide science using "the scientific method."

The question of what constitutes science isn't new; the topic received great attention by Karl Popper in the last century. Popper talked about the theories of Sigmund Freud, Alfred Adler, and Karl Marx, whose views were greatly admired, at least by some, for their grand explanatory power. For Popper, though, this expansive explanatory power was precisely the reason why they were suspect, not as necessarily being wrong but as being not "scientific." The issue in the demarcation problem is not whether something is necessarily true or false, but whether it is science or pseudoscience. After all, something could be called science and be wrong, as has often been the case, while something could be labeled pseudoscience and be correct. Popper wrote that we know "very well that science often errs, and that pseudo-science may happen to stumble on the truth."[13]

According to Popper, the problem with these theories, what made them more like "primitive myths"[14] than like science, and more like "astrology . . . than astronomy,"[15] was that any outcome, even contradictory ones, could be explained by the theory. A Marxist, he said (Popper wrote when communism was still a force to be reckoned with), could not open a newspaper without seeing verification for his theory, regardless of the events. The Freudian, Popper argued, constantly found verification for his views, as well as the Adlerian (a form of psychology) for his, no matter the results.

"I may illustrate this," he wrote, "by two very different examples of human behaviour: that of a man who pushes a child into the water with the intention of drowning it; and that of a man who sacrifices his life in an attempt to save the child. Each of these two cases can be explained with equal ease in Freudian and in Adlerian terms."[16] Popper then explains how each action, though opposite, could still be explained by either theory. In short, to repeat a term from an earlier chapter, neither of the theories could be "falsifiable" based on experimental evidence.

For Popper, for something to be science, as opposed to pseudoscience, it had to be falsifiable; ideally, some experiments or empirical data could show the theory was wrong (if you remember, for Popper, no theory, in principle, could ever be shown to be correct, only to be wrong).

"One can sum up all this," he wrote, "by saying that *the criterion of the scientific status of a theory is its falsifiability, or refutability, or testability.*"[17] He's not making falsifiability *the* defining characteristic of science as if there were nothing else; he is saying only that it is a necessary condition. After all, the statement "Spiders from Mars will kill you before you finish reading this sentence" is clearly falsifiable, but the result does not mean that the reason behind your claim arose from scientific inquiry.

However influential and popular, Popper's theory doesn't work, at least not as *the* demarcation criterion, because at times it excludes what's definitely deemed science or includes what's definitely deemed not. A cottage industry has arisen around the demarcation problem (distinguishing science from pseudoscience), and most discussions inevitably deal, directly or indirectly, with Popper's falsification benchmark.

According to Larry Laudan, for instance, Popper's falsification criterion means countenancing as "scientific" every falsifiable fruitcake claim. "Thus," he wrote, "flat Earthers, biblical creationists,[18] proponents of laetrile or orgone boxes, Uri Geller devotees, Bermuda Triangulators, circle squarers, Lysenkoists, charioteers of the gods, *perpetuum mobile* builders, Big Foot searchers, Loch Nessians, faith healers, polywater dabblers, Rosicrucians, the-world-is-about-to-enders, primal screamers, water diviners, magicians, and astrologers all turn out to be scientific on Popper's criterion—just so long as they are prepared to indicate some observation, however improbable, which (if it came to pass) would cause them to change their minds."[19]

Take astrology, for instance, from among Laudan's list of execrable epistemological endeavors—a favorite example used in demarcating the difference between science and pseudoscience. Though once a time-honored profession (practiced by such scientific nephilim as Claudius Ptolemy, Johannes Kepler, and Tycho Brahe), today it's considered in the same class as Loch Nessians, polywater dabblers, and the like. Who, with the exception of astrologers or astrology buffs, *doesn't* believe that it is at best a pseudoscience and at worst the intellectual equivalent of palm reading?

Unfortunately, it's not so simple.

"Most philosophers and historians of science agree," wrote Paul Thagard, "that astrology is a pseudoscience, but there is little agreement on *why* it is a pseudoscience."[20] After all, falsification (as just one criterion) doesn't work with astrology, because many of its predictions have categorically failed, as even its most vehement aficionados admit. However, as with those things that are deemed bona fide science, mere occurrences of events not fitting the theory, or of even failed predictions according to the theory, don't necessarily make the whole caboodle wrong. Astrologers, like astronomers, physicists, and evolutionary biologists make mistakes; more often than not, they don't fully understand everything they are doing. As already seen, *justification ends* and—when it does (and even before it does)—mistakes, failed predictions, and anomalies arise.

Few scientific theories, if any, don't have incongruities, glitches, failed predictions—phenomena that don't do what the theory says they should do or that do what the theory says they shouldn't do. But (as with astrology) arguments can be given to explain why the incongruity, glitch, failed prediction, and unexpected phenomenon don't nullify the theory. Scientists (like astrologers) often come up with all sorts of auxiliary hypotheses and qualifications and special conditions introduced to save the phenomena, to keep the theory intact despite these problems.

"Scientists," wrote Imre Lakatos, "have thick skins. They do not abandon a theory merely because facts contradict it. They normally either invent some rescue hypothesis to explain what they then call a mere anomaly or, if they cannot explain the anomaly, they ignore it, and direct their attention to other problems."[21] (Not exactly the ideal of science proposed by Popper, who argued that scientists should always be looking for ways to falsify their pet theory.)

As seen earlier, two of the most "successful" theories of the present age (in terms of predictive power), general relativity and quantum theory, when put together give impossible results, and yet no one is talking about dumping either (at least not yet, and probably not in our lifetimes). In other words, just as it's not always easy to prove a theory true, it's not always easy to prove a theory false, either—which makes Popper's falsification somewhat problematic, at least in terms of showing a clear distinction between science and pseudoscience. If every theory in science were discarded the moment that an anomaly arose, little science would be left.

Besides falsification, other attempts at demarcation murmur out there—vagueness (pseudoscience) versus precision (science); lack of progression (pseudoscience) in contrast to progress (science); no discernable mechanism (pseudoscience) versus known mechanisms (science); not accepted by established authorities (pseudoscience), accepted by established authorities (science); and so forth. The problem is that in many cases any one of these criteria alone, or several together, would have labeled what is now deemed as science to be pseudoscience, or vice versa. (Remember, Newton had no discernable mechanism for gravity, yet who calls the *Philosophiæ Naturalis Principia Mathematica* pseudoscience?)

It's one thing when a United States Supreme Court justice in arguing over whether or not something is obscenity could say, "I know it when I see it."[22] Maybe that's fine for a jurisprudential definition of "smut," but it seems inordinately subjective for something as consequential as the difference between science and pseudoscience. Considering the unrivaled epistemological status science has wrapped itself in, wouldn't it be nice if quantum physics could be differentiated from astrology or the like?

The demarcation problem, along with problems regarding the scientific method or the nature of scientific explanation or justification of a scientific theory or the legitimacy of scientific assumptions, is a philosophical, not scientific, problem. It can't be answered by science, but only by something outside of science, and what else could that be but philosophy, specifically epistemology? How do we know what we know or think that we know about the demarcation problem or the nature of a scientific explanation or the validity of our assumptions? What scientific experiment, what scientific theory, could reveal *how we can prove* that our assumptions are correct? Not necessarily that the assumptions *are* correct (which begs the question), but how we can "prove" that they are? How can that be done scientifically?

And even if one could come up with a scientific experiment that shows *how to prove* assumptions correct, what assumptions would that experiment be based on, and how can one know if those assumptions themselves are correct? What science can finally and definitively reveal what constitutes a true scientific explanation? After all, one doesn't use the nonexistent scientific method to demarcate science from pseudoscience (or even bad science) the way that Richard Dawkins used the same nonexistent scientific method to conclude that we are the "distant cousins of bananas and turnips."[23] What is scientific about what determines how science should be done or about what science does or even about what constitutes science itself? These are all philosophical questions with only philosophical answers. Science is supposed to be this great definer of truth (at least that is how it is portrayed to the public), and yet the processes, assumptions, methods, and practices of science are themselves construed from processes outside of science itself.

Which means, for instance, that the endless and unrelenting and dogmatic attacks on "creation science" as pseudoscience are philosophical in nature, not scientific. Nothing in science itself, nothing inherent in reality itself (or at least as it appears to us through the processes of science) a priori demands ontological naturalism, the denial of any "divine foot in the door." Rather, the assumptions of naturalism are philosophical, based on a *philosophy* of science, which for many reasons (none scientific) proclaims that the moment anything divine is hinted at, alluded to, or hypothesized as possible, then "science" is no longer being done.

The naturalist assumption, naturally

The ancient Greeks, those whom we might loosely call the world's first "scientists," sought natural phenomena to explain other natural phenomena. Even when admitting that he had no clue how gravity worked (calling the idea that two bodies influenced each other across the expanse of space "an absurdity"), Isaac Newton never evoked God to explain this gap in his knowledge scientifically, despite being a creationist. In the twelfth century, Adelard of Bath argued that in doing "natural philosophy" (the contemporary term for "science") one should use only natural explanations in seeking to explain natural phenomena. The causes of phenomena may be invisible or immaterial (such as fields), but nothing supernatural should be invoked as the mechanisms, the causes, the explanations, or the descriptions of them.

"As science advanced in the late nineteenth century," wrote Stephen C. Meyer, "it increasingly excluded appeals to divine action or divine ideas as a way of explaining phenomena in the natural world. This practice came to be codified in a principle known as methodological naturalism. According to this principle, scientists should accept as a working assumption that all features of the natural world can be explained by material causes without recourse to purposive intelligence, mind, or conscious agency."[24]

Though just another philosophical assumption about how science should be done, methodological naturalism (MN) is accepted by most scientists, even those who believe in a Creator God, at least in terms of studying ongoing law-bound processes (though the idea of a physical "law" is exceedingly problematic as well[25]).

"If you are a scientist doing these experimental studies," wrote geologist and Christian Leonard Brand, "are you tempted to use supernatural explanations? Do you have to remind yourself not to do that? Do you know of any active scientist who is tempted to think that God is tinkering with the chemicals in his/her experiments, or a physiologist who is tempted to think that their routine observations have a supernatural cause?"[26]

Brand's questions were rhetorical, his point being that the concept of MN is now superfluous, "a relic of history,"[27] from a time when some scientists might have invoked the supernatural to explain the natural. It's certainly not representative of how most science is done today or how it has mostly been done in the past, even when done by creationists or believers in a Creator.

The problem with MN is that this concept has been expanded, illogically, to include ontological naturalism as well. Scientists rely on natural explanations only because all reality (rumor has it) is only naturalistic. Yet just because one doesn't appeal to the supernatural in doing science doesn't mean that the supernatural does not exist, any more than just as one doesn't appeal to God as the immediate cause of a forest fire or a sunny day means that God doesn't exist. The scientific authorities, however, aren't content to limit the methods of science to naturalism. Instead, they argue, without any scientific basis, that all reality itself must be that way and that any deviation *toward* the divine is as heretical to scientific authorities today as deviation *from* it was to the theological authorities centuries ago.

Phillip E. Johnson wrote,

> Darwinists assume that naturalistic principles fully explain the history of the cosmos and its life forms. This reflects a philosophical doctrine called scientific naturalism. Said to be a necessary consequence of the inherent limitations of science, scientific naturalism transforms the limitations of science into limitations upon reality in order to maximize the explanatory power of science and its practitioners. It is, of course, entirely possible to study organisms scientifically on the premise that they were all created by God, just as scientists study airplanes and even works of art without denying that these objects are intelligently designed.[28]

Nevertheless, this kind of thinking has led directly to the popular sentiment that the deeper science probes into the structure of endoplasmic reticulum, or the better it understands why bumblebees buzz, or why the strong nuclear force binds quarks, or the farther astronomy probes the NGC 5128 galaxy, then the more evidence is uncovered that God does not exist, an absurd conclusion that follows only if one has already presupposed that nonexistence.

Look, for instance, at the rainbow. Scripture teaches that it is the sign of God's promise never again to destroy all flesh with a flood.

> And God said: "This is the sign of the covenant which I make between Me and you, and every living creature that is with you, for perpetual generations: I set My rainbow in the cloud, and it shall be for the sign of the covenant between Me and the earth. It shall be, when I bring a cloud over the earth, that the rainbow shall be seen in the cloud; and I will remember My covenant which is between Me and you and every living creature of all flesh; the waters shall never again become a flood to destroy all flesh." (Genesis 9:12–15)

Is not this another example of how science disputes faith, and how the progress of science turns the theological certitudes of antiquity into debunked superstitions instead?

Not quite.

Sure, thanks to science (physics and optics), we now know that a rainbow occurs when sunlight is both refracted and reflected in drops of water that disperse the light at various angles (with the most intense light at 40° to 42°). Light enters a raindrop at one point, is reflected off the back of that drop at another, and leaves at another, creating the colors that we see (and a host of others that we don't). Yet even if we could parse, measure, predict, and quantify everything about a rainbow down to the innards of each photon and the underbelly of every quark, what would that prove other than we better understand the natural laws God used to create this sign of His covenant promise? Science no more removes God from the equation than understanding the action of hormones in the limbic system reduces human love to something akin to the liver secreting bile. Accurate, but narrow and crudely beside the point.

"In philosophical terms," wrote John Lennox, "they make a very elementary category mistake when they argue that, because we understand a mechanism that accounts for a particular phenomenon, there is no agent that designed the mechanism."[29]

Far from disproving the Genesis account, science has simply shown that God created our world in such a way that when sunlight and mist are in a specific relationships to each other, the mist breaks up the light by refracting and reflecting it at different angles that create bands of electromagnetic waves that appear to us as the colors of the rainbow. And He did it to remind us of His covenant promise to never again destroy the world by water. Thus, instead of voiding the Flood story or the origin of the rainbow, science (one could argue) has simply given us deeper insights into God's creative power.

Nevertheless, the late Christopher Hitchens could write, "Religion has run out of justifications. Thanks to the telescope and the microscope, it no longer offers an explanation of anything important."[30]

One wonders just what Christopher Hitchens saw in telescopes or microscopes that makes religion—or more specifically, God—antiquated or no longer "an explanation of anything important." One could just as easily argue that the billions of galaxies hurling across the cosmos in fantastically large pinwheels of fire and light (as revealed by the telescope), as well as the fantastically ordered and complicated universe of a single cell (as revealed by a microscope), point logically to a Creator of immense and intricate power, the source of all that is. Yet Hitchens' flapdoodle is indicative of another canard that, unfortunately, too many Christians have bought into as well, indicative of their devastating tendency to surrender whenever science, or something wrapped in the veneer of science, is invoked.

What else could explain, for instance, Rudolf Bultmann's famous but fantastically erroneous quote? "We cannot use electric lights and radios and, in the event of illness, avail ourselves of modern medical and clinical means and at the same time believe in the spirit and wonder world of the New Testament."[31] Why? What is it about electric lights, radio, or modern medicine that, by default, denudes reality of a supernatural dimension? Modern technology doesn't. All it does, at most, is show that humans have learned to better harness nature, a fact irrelevant to the existence of God or to a transcendent supernatural realm. Bultmann's quote is just another example of Christians throwing up a white flag of surrender before an enemy who, frankly, poses no real threat except in the Christian's own compromised mind.

The nonexistent God of the gaps

A popular cartoon shows two scientists looking at a complicated formula on a blackboard. Amid the numbers, letters, and symbols are the words *And then a miracle occurs.* One scientist points to that sentence on the blackboard and says to the other, "I think you should be a bit more explicit here in step two."

The cartoon makes fun of a notion known as "the God of the gaps." Though understood in variegated and nuanced ways, this idea is that when scientists confront a phenomenon they cannot "explain," then God's mysterious working must be the answer. "Creationists eagerly seek a gap in present-day knowledge or understanding," wrote Richard Dawkins. "If an apparent gap is found, it is *assumed* that God, by default, must fill it."[32] Of course, once science comes up with an explanation, God (the thinking goes) is by default pushed out until, thanks to microscopes, telescopes, atom-smashers, and the like, He is all but relegated to the attic, unneeded and unheeded, because science (the thinking goes) can explain everything that was once attributed to a Creator.

Yet what serious scientist, creationist or evolutionist, involved in research does what was mocked in that cartoon? And just because science hypothesizes an "explanation" for a phenomenon doesn't mean that God is automatically excluded. What is it about science uncovering a level of reality previously not understood that, by default, voids even the notion of a Creator? That's about as logical as arguing that once science can explain the chemistry of the paint in Van Gogh's *The Potato Eaters*, then there's no need to posit a Van Gogh. The painting has been explicated as far down as any conceivable explication can go, at least for now. But it's a metaphysical notion, not a scientific one, that divinity is by default voided the moment science makes a new "discovery" or devises a new formula or comes up with a description of a phenomenon at what is considered to be the most foundational level—the turtle at the bottom of the pile.

Sure, hundreds of years ago some unfortunate old woman selling herbs in the marketplace might have been burned at the stake as a witch, blamed for causing a drought that today could be better explained by a change in the surface temperature of the ocean. And, sure, the Incas feared that jaguars attacking the moon were the cause of a change in the night sky that can now be scientifically explained as a lunar eclipse. But these incidents, and thousands of years of others like them, are indicative only of human ignorance. They have nothing to do with the existence of God. If someone from two hundred years ago were suddenly transported into our time and attributed the "miracles" of an iPhone to the machinations of demons, would this mean that silicon chips, radio waves, and cell-phone towers don't exist?

Contrary to the "God of the gaps" fallacy, it's what we know about the world, not what we don't know (the gaps), that reveals God to us. Our better grasp, for instance, of the complicated enzyme cascade that forms blood clots doesn't mean God has nothing to do with it, even if centuries ago someone might have attributed clotting to the intervention of elves or imps. If anything, our deeper scientific understanding of natural phenomena, in all their complexity and mystery, reveals more about how God works in our world than had been previously understood. One could just as easily argue, from the metaphysical position, that God does exist (as opposed to the metaphysical one that He doesn't), that the more science reveals about nature the more it reveals about the God who created that nature to begin with.

But now ask the beasts, and they will teach you;
And the birds of the air, and they will tell you;
Or speak to the earth, and it will teach you;
And the fish of the sea will explain to you.
Who among all these does not know
That the hand of the LORD has done this,
In whose hand is the life of every living thing,
And the breath of all mankind? (Job 12:7–10)

However, because (thanks to science) we understand better the cardiovascular, muscular, and respiratory systems of pigeons in flight; or because (thanks to science) we better understand CO_2 excretion in catfish, is God, their Creator, therefore deductively removed from the equation? Why? This spontaneous rejection of God is a nonscientific conclusion, nowhere necessitated by the facts, and certainly not deductively reached from anything that science has discovered in fish, birds, or any "living thing." The spontaneous rejection of God arises only from the metaphysical assumption of ontological naturalism, itself an exceedingly broad generalization about reality that nothing in science, at least to this point, justifies or even hints at. This dogmatic petrifying of scientific atheism is a great example (to quote Nietzsche) of ideas elevated to the status of "truth" only because they "have been enhanced, transposed, and embellished poetically and rhetorically, and which after long use seem firm, canonical, and obligatory."[33]

According to Scripture, God is not only the Creator of the physical world, but also its Sustainer. That is, He is actively, even now, keeping the universe in existence. Talking about the Lord, Scripture says that He is *upholding all things by the word of His power*" (Hebrews 1:3; italics mine). Paul told the Athenians that in the Lord "we live and move and have our being" (Acts 17:28). Psalm 104 says of God that "He causes the grass to grow for the cattle, and vegetation for the service of man, that he may bring forth food from the earth" (v. 14). The theme of God not just as Creator but also as Sustainer permeates both Testaments.

In an article about the reduction of Kepler's three laws of planetary motion to Newton's law of gravity, Paul and Patricia Churchland wrote, "Kepler's account thus turned out to be just a special case or a special application of Newton's more encompassing account. And astronomical motions turned out to be just a special instance of inertial and force-governed motions of massive bodies in general. The divine or the supernatural character of the heavens were thereby lost forever."[34]

The divine character of the heavens were thereby lost forever? The statement reveals nothing about science but everything about the inherent materialist bias of the Churchlands, who applied their own metaphysical presuppositions to the data, regardless of how warrantless that application was. What in the reduction of Kepler's law to Newtonian mechanics forever dislodged God from having created the cosmos or, for that matter, from using Newton's law of gravity to sustain it as well? That scientists don't see gods pushing the planets through their orbits (as Aristotle taught) does not prove materialistic atheism true. This quote is an example of scientists making nonscientific statements about science not justified by the facts.

When Newton described the laws of gravity and used mathematical formulas to do so, how did those laws and formulas make the idea of God superfluous? When Einstein, with his theory of general relativity, theorized that gravity is the effect of mass curving space and time, and used complicated non-Euclidean geometry to describe the effect, what in the theory excluded the existence of God or even God's role in any of it? If Scripture unequivocally teaches that God Himself sustains all existence, then the deeper science delves into the physical processes of existence, the more it reveals about Him—without necessarily proving or disproving His existence. When someone, a scientist or not, attributes the actions of nature to God (whether those actions are scientifically understood or not), from a biblical standpoint that person is correct, regardless of how far back science peels the onion on whatever the process in nature happens to be.

Meanwhile, a scientific explanation is only that, a "scientific" one, and thus remains limited within its own man-made confines about what it can claim, regardless of what lies beyond those confines. Given the limits of what nature reveals to us, added to the self-imposed and often philosophically based presuppositions of science, it's hard to imagine how science could ever "prove" the workings of God, no matter how obvious those workings are. Neither can science ever "disprove" that those working are from God, no matter how many layers of reality it peels away and uncovers, even down to the "zeros and ones" of all reality. One wonders what the Churchlands, or anyone for that matter, would expect to find in nature that would prove God created and sustains it? Far from being a logical conclusion of science, atheistic materialism is a philosophical assumption unnecessarily, and dogmatically, imposed on reality by the hegemons of the scientific-industrial complex and their willing minions.

Everything from nothing

In the cartoon mocking the "God of the gaps" fallacy, it's important to remember that "step two," not step one, was mocked. After all, how can a scientific formula account for step one without that step first being explained by something prior to it, which means that step one isn't the first step, after all? For it to be the ultimate step one, to fill that first gap, it would have to be uncaused and eternal, and what else likely could that be but an uncreated Creator, such as the One depicted in Scripture?

Not unaware of the conundrum, some cosmologists argue that the universe arose out of "nothing." What else? With the exception of an eternally existing God, only "nothing" needs no explanation—and if your science demands the exclusion of the divine anywhere along the line, then "nothing" is the only logical option.[35] Here is the epistemological background to Dawkins's quote that "nothing and nothing in some strange way cancels itself out to produce something."[36]

In his book *The Grand Design*, England's Stephen Hawking wrote, "Because there is a law like gravity, the universe can and will create itself from nothing. . . . Spontaneous creation is the reason there is something rather than nothing, why the universe exists, why we exist."[37]

Just because a scientist, even a famous one such as Hawking, makes a statement doesn't by default make the words a scientific statement or even an intelligent one. What Hawking wrote here was not physics but metaphysics, abstract philosophizing about what can be only abstractly philosophized about, nothing more.

His sentence begins with the words "Because there is," implying that "there is" something. The first part of the sentence, which points to something, contradicts the last part, which points to nothing. Whatever "there is" might be fleeting, imperceptible, inaccessible, and even incomprehensible, but it is not "nothing."

Hawking, in fact, tells us what "there is" actually is. He said, "Because there is a law like gravity." No doubt, the science here is heavy, and maybe only someone with a PhD in theoretical physics can grasp what might seem to be missing to everyone else. But what is not missing in that sentence are the two nouns "law" and "gravity." A "law," in this case a law of nature, is *something*, not nothing. And, sure, gravity might be weak (raise your arm and you've just pushed against the gravitational pull of the entire earth), but it's not nothing. Isn't gravity what holds the moon in orbit around the earth and the earth in orbit around the sun? Thus it is obviously *something*. So how does one argue that "because there is a law like gravity, the universe can and will create itself from nothing"?

People are looking for something, anything, even nothing (that which, by definition, does not exist) as the creative force behind our origins—in order to avoid admitting God as the Creator. For some, God—the foundation of all existence—is replaced by "nothing," the negation of all existence.

"It seems impossible," wrote best-selling author Bill Bryson, "that you could get something from nothing, but the fact that once there was nothing and now there is a universe is evident proof that you can."[38]

"If we are to be honest," wrote Peter Atkins, "then we have to accept that science will be able to claim complete success only if it achieves what many might think impossible: accounting for the emergence of everything from absolutely nothing. Not almost nothing, not a subatomic dust-like speck, but absolutely nothing. Nothing at all. Not even empty space."[39]

If tempted to think that these statements about the universe being created from "nothing" originated, not in cold hard science but from philosophical assumptions, cultural presuppositions, and personal prejudices, one would likely be correct. (Of course, as we should know by now, science is influenced by such factors much more than the hoi polloi are told.) And precisely because of these subjective elements, scientists have got it completely wrong regarding the origins of our universe.

Though chronologically preceding the theory of a universe arising from nothing, the theory of life evolving through random mutation and natural selection is still the logical outgrowth of the same assumptions, leading to the notion of a universe from nothing. Both concepts are fueled by similar atheistic, materialistic presuppositions. Christians recoil, and rightly so, at the idea of the universe originating from nothing. But its logical cousin, the formation of life through chemical evolution, doesn't ignite a similar reaction in them, even if both theories arise from the same metaphysical toxicity, and even if both are contrary to Scripture.

The same fossilized dogmatism that refuses to acknowledge anything supernatural in the origins of the world is the same fossilized thinking that excludes anything supernatural in the formation of life through chemical evolution or even spontaneous generation. The phrase "*natural* selection" specifically disallows the supernatural, a fact that theistic evolutionists somehow seem to ignore or try to work around. When Richard Dawkins writes, "Biology is the study of complicated things that give the appearance of having been designed for a purpose,"[40] this nonscientific statement reveals his materialist prejudices, his militant rejection of any hint of divinity or intelligent design. Unfortunately, theistic evolutionists, merely by being theistic evolutionists, reinforce those same prejudices. The cloak of theism that these Christians throw over evolution does a sorry job of covering up the crass materialism underpinning the whole caboodle.

Christianity was always, ideally, to have been countercultural. "If the world hates you, you know that it hated Me before it hated you" (John 15:18). Unfortunately, and to faith's embarrassment, history has proven Christians often far too willing to acclimate to their political, social, and cultural environment, whatever it happened to be. In the past two centuries alone, be it slavery in the Confederacy, the racism of the Jim Crow south, or the policies of Nazi Germany, Christians (with some individual exceptions) have had a dismal record of compromise and acquiescence.

After all, are the great-great-grandchildren of antebellum slave owners so much better people than their great-great-slave-owning-grandparents? If not, then why are they appalled and disgusted by the practices of their Christian ancestors? Why would they (even the secular versions) never consider doing what their churchgoing, Jesus-loving predecessors did with such fervor that it took a war to stop them? Or why seventy-five years ago were many church-going southern Christians such evil racists that they acquiesced in, or even openly supported, practices that, today, only evil racists would acquiesce in or support? If these Christians weren't evil racists, then why did they acquiesce in or support such evil and racist practices?

The answer is that Christians too easily acclimate to culture instead of transcending it—or more important, countering it. (This was also a big problem for ancient Israel, the spiritual ancestors of Christianity.) Could, then, the continual attempts of Christians to incorporate the neo-Darwinian synthesis, the Aristotelianism of our era, into the Christian faith be just another example, a contemporary one, of the same principle, that of Christians surrendering to the culture rather than standing firm against it?

But it's science! This argument presupposes one of the most pervasive cultural trends of our time: the myth of scientism. The claim that it's not culture but science answers nothing, especially when the point of this book is to show that science is hardly the fount of objective rational truth that it's often seen to be. Instead, science is tainted and colored by many of the same subjective philosophical forces that taint and color culture.

Sure, one could argue that science is more objective than are trends in fashion, music, or food. But being more objective than the influences behind chic, hip-hop, or Tex-Mex food hardly makes something true. After all, alchemy is more objective than haute couture, but that hardly makes the assumptions, beliefs, or theories of alchemy true or even nearly true. And who knows what well-accepted, experimentally verified scientific beliefs of today will one day be rejected with the same disdain that alchemy is now? Error is error, even if that error is harder to detect, especially when "enhanced, transposed, and embellished poetically and rhetorically" and promulgated by a host of objective justifications, all expressed with passion and sincerity by true believers whose views have been peer-reviewed in the most prestigious scientific journals in the history of humanity. Or to put it in simpler terms, chemist John Ashton wrote,

"Most scientists and educators believe that evolution is true—simply because that is what they have been taught when they went through school, college, and university. Most science textbooks, science academies, science museums, and popular biology authors echo the view that evolution is a proven fact of science."[41]

The muck of the mire

A painful irony manifests itself in how readily and easily Christians have accepted evolutionary theory because, after all, *It's science!* And not only science, but science that many learned, scholarly, prize-winning scientists, educators, and philosophers have declared ex cathedra is true.

Stephen Meyer wrote,

> Today modern neo-Darwinism seems to enjoy almost universal acclaim among science journalists and bloggers, biology textbook writers, and other popular spokespersons for science as the great unifying theory of all biology. High-school and college textbooks present its tenets without qualification and do not acknowledge the existence of any significant scientific criticism of it. At the same time, official scientific organizations—such as the National Academy of Sciences (NAS), the American Association for the Advancement of Sciences (AAAS), and the National Association of Biology Teachers (NABT)—routinely assure the public that the contemporary version of Darwinian theory enjoys unequivocal support among qualified scientists and that the evidence of biology overwhelmingly supports the theory. For example, in 2006 the AAAS declared, "There is no significant controversy within the scientific community about the validity of the theory of evolution." The media dutifully echo these pronouncements.[42]

What Christian, then, wants to be against science, especially against a branch of science we're assured is as certain as the existence of Paris in the northern hemisphere? And even worse, what Christian wants to be a "biblical creationist"—and, thus, bundled with the intellectual lumpenproletariat of flat-earthers, astrologers, and Holocaust-deniers?

It's ironic, because even as more Christians were succumbing to the lure of scientism, many secular thinkers in the twentieth century, both within and without science itself, were starting to question the assumptions, the processes, and the claims of science, arguing that scientific "knowledge" often incorporated judgments and assertions that were not necessarily logical or factual or even scientific, and that science might not be this überobjective explication of the world that science's Ministry of Truth has promulgated. The entire postmodern project, though an assault on claims of intellectual objectivity in general, also took strong shots at science itself, helping expose some of the same issues looked at in *Baptizing the Devil.* The question isn't so much whether these postmodern attacks were correct, or fruitful;[43] what's fascinating is the self-proclaimed sacred domain of science and scientific knowledge, the Holies of Holies in terms of epistemological pursuit, suddenly facing assault, not from a bunch of Bible-thumping hayseeds who believe in Adam and Eve and Noah's ark, but from the ultrasophisticated secular cognoscenti of the academy.

Kuhn's *The Structure of Scientific Revolutions*, though not the first work to question the veracity of scientific knowledge, certainly rattled the scientific regime's claims of epistemological supremacy. Chemist Michael Polanyi also questioned the objectivity of science and even the possibility of objectivity in science, arguing that any scientific theory is like a pair of spectacles. The theory itself is the lens through which you look at whatever you are examining, the means (the assumptions, procedures, rules, and expectations) by which one does whatever one does in science. He wrote,

> There is no mystery about this. You cannot use your spectacles to scrutinize your spectacles. A theory is like a pair of spectacles; you examine things by it, and your knowledge of it lies in this very use of it. You dwell in it as you dwell in your own body and in the tools by which you amplify the powers of your body. It should be clear that someone who is said to be "testing" a theory is in fact relying, in this subsidiary and very uncritical way, upon other tacitly accepted theories and assumptions of which he cannot *in this action* be focally aware.[44]

In other words, the scientist is, at least to some degree, assuming what he sets out to prove, a cardinal logical fallacy. This limit doesn't mean that science can't progress or discover new things or make accurate and novel predictions, as science obviously does. It means only that one can't be as dogmatic about the truth of whatever science claims to have found, especially when the claims are about a complex biological function that we're told happened eight hundred million years ago.

As we have already seen, Paul Feyerabend was another critic of the scientific establishment's dogmatism. For him, it's not that science was irrational, or even wrong; it just doesn't possess any sacred and privileged method for finding truth (if finding truth is what science is even about). Nor does science progress from an Archimedean perspective that transcends the mucky mire of human subjectivity enabling it to study, judge, or even understand the world free from the muck in the mire. On the contrary, science proceeds directly out of that mucky mire, with much of the muck influencing its assumptions, procedures, methods, and conclusions every step of the way. Scientism's epistemological arrogance is just a mask covering an internal cosmos of doubt, assumption, and bluff. Science, said Feyerabend, comes with holes, inconsistencies, contradictions, errors, false starts, and is influenced by culture, faith, and politics. All these contingencies are not necessarily bad. It's just, he insists, how science is done.

Feyerabend's claim about science proceeding out of culture is interesting in light of Freeman Dyson's assertion that the common element of all science is "rebellion against the restrictions imposed by the locally prevailing culture, Western or Eastern as the case may be."[45] *The scientist as rebel?* Maybe in the 1700s, but not today. That idea is more outdated than the phlogiston theory of heat. Far from rebelling against culture, science helps shape it and even proceeds from it. Meanwhile, woe to anyone who dares question, much less rebel against the scientific culture's dogma, especially when it comes to the regime's metaphysical assumptions regarding origins. Once the in-your-face rebel against dogmatic authority, science has now become that dogmatic authority.

Talking about one claim of quantum physics, called complementarity (as a symbol for scientific claims in general), Feyerabend argued that once that aspect of the theory was accepted by the scientific establishment, the following scenario unfolds:

> By now the success of the theory has become public news. Popular science books (and this includes a good many book on the philosophy of science) will spread the basic postulates of the theory: applications will be made in distant fields. More than ever the theory will appear to possess tremendous empirical support. The chances for the consideration of alternatives are now very slight, indeed. The final success and fundamental assumptions of the quantum theory and of the idea of complementarity will seem to be assured . . . [even if] this appearance of success *cannot in the least be regarded as a sign of truth and correspondence with nature.* Quite the contrary, the suspicion arises that the absence of major difficulties is a result of the decrease of empirical content brought about by the elimination of alternatives, and of facts that can be discovered by the help of these alternatives. In other words, *the suspicion arises that this alleged success is due to the fact that in the process of application to the new domains the theory has been turned into a metaphysical system.* Such a system will of course be very "successful" not, however, because it agrees so well with the facts, but because no facts have been specified that would constitute a test and because some such facts have even been removed. Its "success" *is entirely manmade.*[46]

Feyerabend is talking here about physics, which can be tested again and again *now*, which exists in the here and *now*, and which is accessible to research *now*—in contrast to macroevolution, which supposedly occurred in the long inaccessible past and, thus, can only be postulated about. And even then, those postulations arise only by retrodiction from the present to the past, something quite different from doing physics or chemistry on things that exist today.

Yet his sequence of the acculturation of complementarity is astonishingly similar to what has happened with the acculturation of evolutionary theory as well. From the ability to do advanced mathematics to the love of music, what today isn't given a Darwinian explanation? None of these factors, Feyerabend argues, means that this particular theory is true or that it even closely aligns with the facts.

Feyerabend wouldn't claim that science isn't useful or that it can't make "good" theories. It's just that, as we have seen, being good isn't the same thing as being true, which for some people is an irrelevant distinction, because finding truth isn't (they believe) what science is or can be or even should be about.

Feyerabend, though considered radical, wasn't *that* radical, at least in his basic assertions. A more radical critique against science came from postmodern critics like Jacques Derrida, Michel Foucault, and others, who challenged the whole question of knowledge in general, which included science and, in some ways, *especially* science. For them, the inherent subjectivity of human experience and, hence, the knowledge that arises from it, became the defining characteristic of all experience and knowledge. Though contingency exists in all that we could possibly know, that contingency itself became (for these thinkers) the dominant "metaphysic" (a word they would hate but, nevertheless, still applies to them) regarding every knowledge claim, including scientific ones. Truth, far from existing "out there" or in some transcendent or Platonic realm, is something etched out of the tools, methods, language, and fabric of a particular culture in a specific time and place. Different culture, different time, different place, then different tools, different methods, different languages, different fabrics, and thus different truth. Truth concocted, not discovered; it's like cakewalk jazz, not the Higgs field.

Frenchman Michel Foucault (1926–1984) argued, rationally enough, that we don't view reality outside of or apart from a social, political, cultural, or historical context. What we see, study, experience, and believe are, he said, to a great degree socially constructed. Concepts such as madness, sexuality, illness, and crime change over time and through history; worse, it's the political or cultural powers who decide what these things are, and then use their man-made definitions as a means of political, social, and cultural oppression.

Foucault created what he called a "genealogical" method for looking at what we believe, which purports to show that any given system of thought comes from the contingent, artificial, and changing trends of history, as opposed to being cold, hard facts rooted in cold, hard reality. This contingent and changing subjectivism applies to science as well, which he labeled as another means of oppression. (And though his use of the word *scientific* is often broader than is commonly understood, it certainly includes the common use of the term as well.) The genealogical method, he wrote, is "an insurrection against the centralizing power-effects that are bound up with the institutionalization and workings of any scientific discourse organized in a society such as ours. . . . Genealogy has to fight the power-effects characteristic of any discourse that is regarded as scientific."[47]

Algerian Jacques Derrida (1930–2004) took things even further than Foucault, arguing the inherent limitations in language itself breeds subjectivity in all our knowledge, including scientific knowledge. Words are mere arbitrary signs that, at their core, have little relationship to the reality they point to. Texts, including scientific texts, are open-ended; their meanings depend, not upon external reality, but on a host of complicated interdependence with other signs, whose meaning depend upon other signs, and on and on. Everything, including science, is a text only; and as such, it is open to myriad interpretations, none of which can, with justification, claim epistemological supremacy.

"The 'privileged' status of scientific discourse," wrote Paul Gross and Norman Levitt (deriding Derrida's views), "is yet another illusion deriving from the conceits of Western metaphysics, and must therefore be rejected."[48]

American Richard Rorty (1931–2007) was another who, intuiting the inherent limits of human knowledge, became obsessed with those limits to the point of arguing the whole attempt to understand the natural world is misguided, because we just can't do it. In, perhaps, his most famous tome, *Philosophy and the Mirror of Nature*, he wrote that we need to "abandon the Platonic notions of Truth and Reality and Goodness as entities which may not be even dimly mirrored by present practices and beliefs, and to settle back into the 'relativism' which assumes that our only useful notions of 'true' and 'real' and 'good' are extrapolations from those practices and beliefs."[49] Rorty argued that true wisdom "is to see human beings as generators of new descriptions rather than beings one hopes to be able to describe accurately."[50] In other words, science doesn't even describe; all it does is generate description, as do all human epistemological pursuits. Whatever exactly it means to "generate description," it's certainly not discovering truth, which for Rorty is a waste of time anyway. *Come on, after 2,500 years of trying and failing, it's time* (he argues) *to move on.*

Of course, these postmodern critiques of science, and other even more radical ones, have themselves come under considerable criticism, and rightly so. And one of the most widely publicized attacks, called "Sokal's Hoax," will go down into intellectual immortality.[51] Postmodernism is just a sophisticated version of the philosophical battles Plato waged 2,300 years ago. It's an obsession with the limits of knowledge, to the point of arguing not just against objective knowledge per se (which, as "knowledge," that is, as "human knowledge," is by nature contingent, subjective, and to some degree fuzzy to begin with), but against the very notion of objective truth itself—*even independent of any human awareness of it*. This is a position against not only the concept of science itself (after all, what's the purpose of doing science if one doesn't assume that an objective reality exists out there?), but against Christianity, too, which certainly posits an objective reality. Besides, postmodernism is essentially self-refuting. If everything is relative, contingent, culturally biased, and so forth, then postmodernism itself must be as well.

The use here of the postmodern critique of science is hardly to argue in its favor. As with many things, some validity exists, even if it's taken at times to the more ludicrous extremes of Rorty or Derrida. Instead, this section simply shows that others have not fallen under the spell of scientism, as so many Christians have, and to such a detriment of the faith as well.

How much of a detriment? The next chapter explores that question.

1. Dawkins, *Greatest Show on Earth*, 169, 170.

2. Natasha Singer, "Better Loving Through Chemistry," *New York Times*, February 6, 2010, http://www.nytimes.com/2010/02/07/business/07stream.html?src=tptw.

3. Brian Barrett, "Online Dating Meets the Scientific Method," Gizmodo, February 10, 2010, http://gizmodo.com/5468928/online-dating-meets-the-scientific-method.

4. Francis Bacon, *The New Organon, and Related Writings* (Indianapolis: Bobbs-Merrill, 1960), 47.

5. Daniel P. Thurs, "That the Scientific Method Accurately Reflects What Scientists Actually Do," in Numbers and Kampourakis, *Newton's Apple*, 210.

6. Quoted in Paul Feyerabend, *Killing Time* (Chicago: University of Chicago Press, 1995), 88.

7. Hence, some books have been titled with names such as *Complete Scientific Method for Saxophone* (1922) and *Scientific Method of Raising Jumbo Bullfrogs* (1932). There's even a DVD touting a "PROVEN Scientific Method for Potty Training" (*Babies on Potties*, 2008).

8. Feyerabend, *Against Method*, 5.

9. Feyerabend, *Farewell to Reason*, 36.

10. Feyerabend, *Against Method*, 14.

11. Thurs, "Scientific Method," in Numbers and Kampourakis, *Newton's Apple*, 210.

12. Michael D. Gordin, "That a Clear Line of Demarcation Has Separated Science From Pseudoscience," in Numbers and Kampourakis, *Newton's Apple*, 221.

13. Popper, *Conjectures and Refutations*, 44.

14. Ibid., 45.

15. Ibid.

16. Ibid., 46.

17. Ibid., 48 (italics in the original).

18. How fascinating that Laudan puts "biblical creationists" in with flat-earthers and bigfoot searchers. It shouldn't be surprising, but it shows the power that scientific paradigms exert even among the greatest philosophers of science of the last century.

19. Larry Laudan, "The Demise of the Demarcation Problem," in Michael Ruse, ed., *But Is It Science? The Philosophical Question in the Creation/Evolution Controversy*, Frontiers of Philosophy (Amherst, NY: Prometheus Books, 1996), 346 (italics in the original).

20. Paul Thagard, "Why Astrology Is a Pseudoscience," in Curd and Cover, *Philosophy of Science*, 27.

21. Lakatos, *Scientific Research Programmes*, 4.

22. Jacobellis v. Ohio, 378 U.S. 184 (1964).

23. Dawkins, *Greatest Show on Earth*, 8.

24. Stephen C. Meyer, *Darwin's Doubt: The Explosive Origin of Animal Life and the Case for Intelligent Design* (New York: HarperOne, 2013), 19.

25. Most people assume that science studies natural laws and that to find laws is the summum bonum of science. The concept of a natural law, though, is highly controversial. What defines a law in nature? How are laws differentiated from accidental generalizations? Numerous answers have been given to these and other questions, none without contrary examples and responses. Some, meanwhile, argue that the idea of a law in nature shows a bias toward physics, and that nature itself doesn't of necessity have to follow laws as such. The science of economics, for instance, follows some strict laws; but are those the same as "laws" in astronomy, or even psychology or chemistry? Newton's law of gravity is called a "law," even if it gets corrected, refined, or superseded by general relativity. Laws are often deemed to be what occurs with regularity, but that's a grossly inadequate depiction. If every day, year after year, Joe comes home, eats a TV dinner, and plops on the sofa with a case of beer, is that a law, even if it happens with unceasing regularity? Others have argued that laws in science are metaphysical holdovers from theology of some sort, because wouldn't the existence of a law imply some sort of "superior being" who issued that law? Even to this day, even with all the talk of scientific laws and the mathematical equations that describe them, no agreement exists on a definition of them. See, for instance, Nancy Cartwright, "Do the Laws of Physics State the Facts?" *Pacific Philosophical Quarterly* 61 (1980): 75–84.

26. Leonard Brand, "Naturalism: Its Role in Science," *Origins*, no. 64 (2015): 26.

27. Ibid., 27.

28. Phillip Johnson, "What Is Darwinism?" in *Man and Creation: Perspectives on Science and Theology*, ed. Michael Bauman (Hillsdale, MI: Hillsdale College Press, 1993), 181.

29. Lennox, *God's Undertaker*, 45.

30. Christopher Hitchens, *God Is Not Great: How Religion Poisons Everything* (New York: Twelve, 2007), 282.

31. Rudolf Bultmann, *New Testament and Mythology, and Other Basic Writings*, ed. and trans. Schubert M. Ogden (Philadelphia: Fortress Press, 1984), 4.

32. Richard Dawkins, *The God Delusion* (Boston: Mariner Books, 2008), 125 (italics in the original).

33. Quoted in Walter Kaufmann, ed. and trans., *The Portable Nietzsche* (New York: Penguin Books, 1976), 47.

34. Paul M. Churchland and Patricia S. Churchland, "Intertheoretic Reduction: A Neuroscientist's Field Guide," in John Cornwell, ed., *Nature's Imagination: The Frontiers of Scientific Vision* (Oxford: Oxford University Press, 1995), 66.

35. Despite Richard Dawkins's argument that a Creator God only pushes the problem of existence one step back (After all, he asks: Who created God?), that argument is wrong. An eternally existing God needs no explanation for His origins, because He has no origins. He has always existed, hence, by default, nothing explains Him. In contrast to the famous question "Why is there something instead of nothing?" which begs an answer, "nothing" itself needs no explanation, because, after all, it is nothing. Hence, only two things don't need something prior to explain them—an eternally existing God and nothing. And if God is automatically excluded, you are left with "nothing" as the only logical explanation of the universe. How "logical" is that answer? Well, the reader can decide.

36. Dawkins, interview by Quinn, *After Words*.

37. Stephen Hawking and Leonard Mlodinow, *The Grand Design* (New York: Bantam Books, 2010), 180.

38. Bill Bryson, *A Short History of Nearly Everything* (New York: Broadway Books, 2003), 13.

39. Peter Atkins, "The Limitless Power of Science," in Cornwell, *Nature's Imagination*, 131.

40. Dawkins, *The Blind Watchmaker*, 1.

41. John F. Ashton, *Evolution Impossible: 12 Reasons Why Evolution Cannot Explain the Origin of Life on Earth* (Green Forest, AR: Master Books, 2012), 19.

42. Meyer, *Darwin's Doubt*, x, xi.

43. As with most intellectual endeavors, there's usually some truth to it, just not as much as proponents claim, which itself is a bit ironic—a project that claims itself to be true when the whole point of the project is to question the very idea of truth itself.

44. Polanyi and Prosch, *Meaning*, 37 (italics in the original).

45. Freeman Dyson, "The Scientist as Rebel," in Cornwell, *Nature's Imagination*, 1.

46. Paul Feyerabend, "Explanations, Predictions, Theories," in Bernard Baumrin, ed., *Philosophy of Science: The Delaware Seminar*, vol. 2, *1962–1963*, p. 27 (italics in the original).

47. Michel Foucault, *"Society Must Be Defended,"* Lectures at the Collège de France, 1975–1976, trans. David Macey (New York: Picador, 2003), 9.

48. Paul R. Gross and Norman Levitt, *Higher Superstition: The Academic Left and Its Quarrels With Science* (Baltimore: Johns Hopkins University Press, 1998), 78.

49. Richard Rorty, *Philosophy and the Mirror of Nature* (Princeton, NJ: Princeton University Press, 1980), 377.

50. Ibid., 378.

51. Alan Sokal, a respected physicist from New York University, submitted a paper to a journal called *Social Text*, the flagship journal of social-construction-of-reality folks, the postmoderns, those who see science, as they do all reality, as relativistic, contingent, and so forth. The article was titled "Transgressing the Boundaries: Toward a Transformative Hermeneutics of Quantum Gravity." In it, Sokal wrote this:

> As Althusser rightly commented, "Lacan finally gives Freud's thinking the scientific concepts that it requires." More recently, Lacan's *topologie du sujet* has been applied fruitfully to cinema criticism and to the psychoanalysis of AIDS. In mathematical terms, Lacan is here pointing out that the first homology group of the sphere is trivial, while those of the other surfaces are profound; and this homology is linked with the connectedness or disconnectedness of the surface after one or more cuts. *Social Text*, no. 46/47 (Spring/Summer 1996): 224, 225.

And this:

> Furthermore, as Lacan suspected, there is an intimate connection between the external structure of the physical world and its inner psychological representation qua

knot theory: this hypothesis has recently been confirmed by Witten's derivation of knot invariants (in particular the Jones polynomial) from three-dimensional Chern-Simons quantum field theory. Ibid, 225.

And this:

> Analogous topological structures arise in quantum gravity, but inasmuch as the manifolds involved are multidimensional rather than two-dimensional, higher homology groups play a role as well. These multidimensional manifolds are no longer amenable to visualization in conventional three-dimensional Cartesian space: for example, the projective space *RP3*, which arises from the ordinary 3-sphere by identification of antipodes, would require a Euclidean embedding space of dimension at least 5. Nevertheless, the higher homology groups can be perceived, at least approximately, via a suitable multidimensional (nonlinear) logic. Ibid.; italics in the original.

The problem is everything written here, as in the whole scholarly article, was abject nonsense. Sokal spent time studying the language and jargon of postmodernism, and then he wrote the article in that jargon. The piece was composed of such utter silliness that any physicist, had he or she reviewed it, would have seen instantly that it was nonsense.

But Sokal took a gamble: he bet that the editors of the magazine would not have his paper vetted in a peer review. He thought that the editors, some of the leading postmodern thinkers in the whole movement, would be so happy to have an eminent physicist from the other side, from the realist side, write a paper for their publication that pretty much takes their position, that they wouldn't even bother to get it checked for the science.

And he was right. They didn't. Thus, *one of the premier intellectual journals of postmodernism published as a serious intellectual text an article that a scientist purposely concocted of sheer silliness.* While the relativists cried foul, those who took a more realist view of science saw the hoax as a powerful revelation of just how wrong the whole postmodern critique of science really was. See Alan Sokal, *Beyond the Hoax* (Oxford: Oxford University Press, 2008).

CHAPTER 10

BEGINNINGS AND ENDINGS

Poet Anne Sexton, in a metric of words, wrote, "She prayed in all the churches of the world and learned a great deal about culture."[1] How naïve, of course, to assume that one gets culture only through the bijou or the boob tube. Churches are created by people, Christian people even, and even Christian people are hewed and hued by their culture. And when their culture is dominated by the ethos of scientism, and when scientists—backed up by laboratory studies, mathematical formulas, and peer reviews—herald their latest findings, especially about human origins, only intellectual troglodytes (it seems) dare question them. Everyone else (it seems), Christians too, follow along in step like the Hamelin children with the Pied Piper.

Take, for instance, Michael Dowd's *Thank God for Evolution*,[2] a book "celebrated by" various Nobel laureates, including John Mather, a 2006 Nobel Prize winner in physics, who wrote, "The universe took 13.7 billion years to produce this amazing book. I heartily recommend it. I am often asked how science and religion can coexist. This is a wonderful answer."[3] And though not a Nobel Prize winner, author and columnist Lisa Earle McLeod was equally effusive: "This book will transform your life and worldview. Read it, read it to your children, take it to church and have your preacher read it from the pulpit. Dowd unlocks the secrets of the universe's most powerful pairing (science and spirituality) and helps you discover your own calling—God's purpose for your life—in the process."[4]

Whether *Thank God for Evolution* accomplishes all of the above, discerning readers can decide for themselves. But what Dowd, a self-described "exuberantly born-again evolutionary evangelist,"[5] does is to argue not only that evolution fits with the Bible but that it also provides the key to understanding the Scriptures and, indeed, the mysteries of human life in general. That is, science, particularly the science of evolution, is the lens through which we should view Scripture, theology, and life itself.

Dowd, not given to subtlety, does however supply the following caveat:

Jesus as "the way, the truth, and the life" will still be central in an evolutionary form of Christianity, just as the backbone of our common ancestor who swam in the sea more than 400 million years ago is still within us, providing vital support. . . .

Of necessity, this evolutionary effort will also mean that some of the teachings will be translated almost beyond recognition, just as our skin is so unlike that of our scaly reptilian ancestors. Then, too, some passages will have so little utility that they will disappear, just as the primate tail was lost within our lineage of apes.[6]

In other words, the incorporation of evolution into Christianity can work only if certain biblical teachings are transformed "almost beyond recognition"; that is, only if these biblical teachings are greatly changed. (Notice what's changed. Not science to fit biblical teaching, but biblical teaching to fit science.) In fact, says Dowd, some texts will have "so little utility" that they will disappear—another way of saying that they will need to be discarded.

What biblical teachings might be changed "almost beyond recognition," or what biblical texts will be of so "little utility" that they will have to disappear, as did the primate's tail within "our linages of apes"?

Death as sacred

For starters, there's death—its meaning, origin, and purposes that have generally been problematic for Christians who incorporate Darwinism into the Creation account. For Dowd, though, death presents no problem; on the contrary, death is natural, generative, even as sacred as life itself. Dowd writes,

Perhaps there is no more alluring portal for discovering the benefits of evolutionary spirituality than death understood in an inspiring new way. Thanks to the sciences of astronomy, astrophysics, chemistry, geology, paleontology, evolutionary biology, cell biology, embryology, ecology, geography, and even math, we can now not only accept but celebrate that

- Death is natural and generative at every level of reality.
- Death is no less sacred than life.

During the past 500 years, scientists and explorers made important discoveries that revealed how death, more often than not, is a cosmic blessing.[7]

According to Dowd, "if we acknowledge that there is something profoundly right with death, with the fact that we grow old and that we must die, it will be easier to clean up unfinished business before it is too late."[8]

Working logically, even deductively, from his premises, Dowd makes a valid point. If death were part of how God created life on earth, and if God declared the finished creation "very good" (Genesis 1:31), then death must also be good, because it's among the means God used to create life to begin with. And though death-as-the-means-of-life might not be an issue in an atheistic model of origins, for a theistic evolutionary model—especially when the *Theos* is the Lord depicted in Scripture—this view of death becomes difficult to harmonize with the Bible, because the Bible uniformly depicts death as bad, as something opposed to life. Far from death being among the means to generate life, Scripture portrays death as an enemy, an intruder, an unwanted factor to one day be eradicated.

The last enemy that will be destroyed is death. (1 Corinthians 15:26)

He will swallow up death forever. (Isaiah 25:8)

O Death, where is your sting?
O Hades, where is your victory? (1 Corinthians 15:55)

Inasmuch then as the children have partaken of flesh and blood, He Himself likewise shared in the same, that through death He might destroy him who had the power of death, that is, the devil. (Hebrews 2:14)

God will wipe away every tear from their eyes; there shall be no more death, nor sorrow, nor crying. There shall be no more pain, for the former things have passed away. (Revelation 21:4)

For as in Adam all die, even so in Christ all shall be made alive. (1 Corinthians 15:22)

Death is the opposite of life, which helps explain why nothing in the Genesis Creation account even hints at death as part of the life-creating process. Instead, every step of Creation is depicted as "good" until the finished work is declared "very good" (Genesis 1:31)—and nowhere in Scripture is death ever depicted as "good." Nothing evil, nothing portrayed as an "enemy," nothing like death is involved in the Creation story, and to import death into the biblical account of Creation and to make it a fundamental part of that account is like arguing that chastity is part of and fundamental to snuff porn.

Death, or rather just the *potential* of death, doesn't arise until after the creation had already been completed (perhaps with the exception of Eve). And even then, in Genesis 2:17, death was presented only as a possibility, a potential future state, but only conditionally, only if the prohibition against eating from the tree were violated. The fact that plants and fruit were eaten in Eden hardly counts as death, at least in the biblical sense of death. And their existence as "food" (Genesis 1:29) is expressed in the context of what happened *after* life had already been created, and not as part of the creating process itself.

This point cannot be overemphasized: nothing in the Creation account gives any indication that life on earth somehow flowed out of death, like the birth of Minerva out of the brains of Jupiter. Death is not even implied in the texts, and to read death into the Genesis account of Creation—especially the pandemic and universal death that underpins the Darwinian model—is to crassly surrender a basic biblical teaching to culture.

"The biblical view of death," wrote Jacques Doukhan, "is essentially different from the one proposed by evolution. While belief in evolution implies that death is inextricably intertwined with life and, therefore has to be accepted and eventually managed, the biblical teaching of creation implies that death is an absurdity to be feared and rejected. Evolution teaches an intellectual submission to death."[9]

Besides death never being mentioned until after the creation was all but complete, death itself arises only in the context of sin, the undoing of creation. Adam was warned that if he ate from the tree, he would "surely die" (Genesis 2:17). Yet even then death was still only a potentiality, something that could—but not necessarily would—occur. According to the biblical texts, only after the creation had been completed did death become a reality, first seen in God's announcement to Adam that he would return to the dust (Genesis 3:19), and then in the death of whatever animal was used to make clothes for Adam and Eve (Genesis 3:21).

If God used death to create life, why did He caution Adam about death, saying that to eat the fruit of the tree would bring death (Genesis 2:17)? All this powerfully implies that death was not yet a reality. The first mention of death, in the text, is equated with disobedience to the Creator; it is never linked to the act of Creation itself.

"Such disobedience," wrote Norman Gulley, "would bring a curse on nature as well as on Adam and Eve (Gen 3:17–19). When Christ re-creates the earth there will be no more curse (Rev 22:3). Clearly curses and death are linked to disobedience and have nothing to do with Christ's method of creation. If the new earth will have no curse, and the curses came through the fall, and the first creation was 'very good' (Gen 1:31), it is logical that the first creation had no curses or death. That's why Scripture speaks of death as the wages for sin (Rom 6:23) and an enemy (1 Cor 15:26), and never as God's chosen method to create."[10]

What, too, does a theistic evolutionist do with the following texts?

For the wages of sin is death. (Romans 6:23)

To be carnally minded is death. (Romans 8:6)

When desire has conceived, it gives birth to sin; and sin, when it is full-grown, brings forth death. (James 1:15)

Therefore, just as through one man sin entered the world, and death through sin. (Romans 5:12)

By the one man's offense death reigned through the one. (Romans 5:17)

Seeing a problem here, some theistic evolutionists argue that only animal death, not human death, existed before the Fall. That is, sin brought death just to humans, but that animals had been dying for millions of years, all part of the process by which God created life on earth.

This move hardly solves the problem.

First, although sinful, corrupted humans can show great compassion for suffering and dying animals, we must attribute to an infinitely compassionate God billions of years of degradation, violence, starvation, suffering, and death for animals, including advanced mammals and primates resulting in a finished creation He called "very good"?

Second, where and how did the sharp transition occur between two highly advanced hominids (there would have to be a male and female to pass on their advantageous genetic material) who, though themselves subject to death, nevertheless produced the first two *Homo sapiens* (Adam and Eve) "in the image of God" (Genesis 1:27)? Theistic evolution, if it wants to keep some semblance of adhering to the Scriptures, requires us to believe that these two sinless and immortal images of God grew from infancy into moral adults whose wrong choices finally caused them to face the same suffering and death plaguing all other life on earth for billions of years.

And what does this tell us about Jesus and the Cross? It tells us that the Lord incarnated Himself into an evolved ape, first created through the vicious and painfully murderous cycle of natural selection, and He did so to abolish death, "the last enemy" (1 Corinthians 15:26). But how can death be the "enemy" if it was one of God's chosen means for creating humans? The Lord must have expended plenty of dead *Homo erectus*, *Homo heidelbergensis*, and *Homo neanderthalensis* to finally get one into His own image (*Homo sapiens*). *So Jesus comes to save humanity from the very process God used to create it in the first place?*

Such a scenario might be required for Dowd's "evolutionary form of Christianity," but how does one harmonize it with Scripture? According to Dowd, you don't have to. And that's because the biblical teaching about death is, apparently, one of those teachings that have to be changed "almost beyond recognition," and the above texts about death in Romans and James are, apparently, among the texts with "so little utility that they will disappear."

It's unfortunate, but this wide acceptance of theistic evolution among Christians is religious history repeating itself—another sad, painful, and unnecessary capitulation of the church to culture, this time a culture packaged in the seductive and bewitching adornment of scientism. Which is even more painful, because scientism presupposes a purely materialistic, purely naturalistic reality, in stark conflict with the biblical one, which is unambiguous about the origins of life on earth. Plants, animals, humans—all boast a supernatural, not natural, genesis, and the conflation of the two opposing worldviews leads to, frankly, what Dowd admitted: that teachings are changed "almost beyond recognition" and texts are deemed of "so little utility" that they will vanish "just as the primate tail was lost within our lineage of apes."

The premise and the process
Earlier in *Baptizing the Devil,* we used an analogy. A scientist wants to understand the origins of chess (the rules, the board, the pieces) but seeks to do so on the assumption that its origins can be found only from within the game itself (the rules, the board, the pieces). That is, the scientist a priori rejects the possibility of chess originating from something above, outside of, or transcendent to the game itself—particularly from something like human beings. Instead, the only legitimate place to look for its origins is within the pieces, the board, and the rules.

Suppose, though, that the one thing the scientist rules out (human beings) actually is the origin of the game. Suppose the inadmissible was the essential, the requisite they refused. Instead of chess arising out of a primitive form of itself, suppose it was created, from scratch, by humans. And suppose these humans used a radically different process to create the game than the one (based on the false assumption of naturalism) dogmatically theorized by those studying its origins. In such a scenario, two different theories about the origins of chess would exist—one derived solely from within the game of chess itself, and one derived from a source outside the game itself (in this case, human beings).

But suppose, too, that for years the naturalist theory about chess holds sway, becoming the dominant intellectual paradigm, the one believed by the best and the brightest, the feted, the wined and the dined, the world's smartest individuals. However, some people reject the naturalist underpinning of the paradigm, yet accept the paradigm itself. They believe that, yes, human beings did create chess, but because the reigning scientific paradigm is buttressed (they are assured) by so much scientific evidence, they accept it, even though the paradigm is premised on, and cannot be separated from, concepts antithetical to the idea of humans having created chess.

Yes, theistic evolutionists reject the premise (blind unconscious forces created the world), oblivious it seems to the fact that the process flows from the premise like germs from a cough.

Of course, wrong premises don't guarantee an erroneous process, but they certainly increase the odds. Sometimes one gets lucky, but those trying to harmonize evolution with the biblical Creation account have drawn the worst possible hand. They have accepted as truth a process that is antithetical in every way to the biblical account of Creation, and have done so only because the process comes with the epistemological gravitas of the name "science." And, because they can't give up the Bible as the Word of God, and because they believe that the Bible and nature must be in harmony, they are forced to interpret biblical Creation through the reigning scientific paradigm, which (unluckily for them) happens, at for least now, to be evolution.

Even worse, as seen with Dowd and as we will see with other theistic evolutionists, the evolutionary "hermeneutic" for Genesis does not exist in isolation. Creation as presented in the Bible is foundational; biblical truth arises directly from it, as plants arise out of seeds. After all, what biblical teaching has validity apart from Creation? The Fall? Salvation? The Atonement? The Cross? The Resurrection? The Second Coming? These teachings arise directly from the doctrine of Creation, and if that's distorted, what's the likelihood of these escaping unscathed?

Suppose that we get our understanding of origins wrong, *really* wrong. How could such a false start not negatively affect all its derivatives? For many Christians, Creation is now understood, interpreted, and explicated by the heavy, obtuse, and cumbersome baggage of the evolutionary model. And this baggage is, as Dowd admits, carried into other teachings as well, which is why they become distorted "almost beyond recognition."

Even if the universe itself were created billions of years ago, suppose that God—working from whatever material He had already created—had, indeed, fashioned the world, and life on it, in six literal twenty-four-hour periods in the *recent* past, as the Genesis account describes it (at least in any fair reading of it). If so, then how utterly wrong, at the most basic level, the entire evolutionary paradigm would be. And if we get something so foundational as Creation so wrong, how could any theology that would logically and rationally flow from it not be steered in wrong directions right from the start? Whatever one thinks, for instance, about Dowd's theology of death, it's the logical outgrowth of his premises.

But Dowd is hardly alone. This, the penultimate chapter of *Baptizing the Devil*, looks at other Christians writers who, like Dowd, have attempted to incorporate the evolutionary paradigm into biblical Creation texts. The point here is not to judge anyone's heart, motives, honesty, sincerity, or relationship with God. At present, we all "see through a glass, darkly" (1 Corinthians 13:12, KJV), and only when "[we] know even as [we are] known" (ibid.) will we learn that much of what we now "know" was wrong. The point, instead, is to look at what positions these authors take as they try to make the current scientific paradigm regarding origins fit Scripture, and what the theological implications of these positions would be *if taken to their logical conclusions*. As we do, every attempt will be made to quote the authors in context, and to be as fair and as honest with their work as we hope critics will be this one.

Nevertheless, the questions remain: What needs to be done to biblical texts to fit the current scientific paradigm into them, and what happens to crucial biblical teachings when interpreted in the light of a model of Genesis dominated by the reigning scientific paradigm?

The naked presence of infinite reality?

In 1998, Yale University Press published John Polkinghorne's *Belief in God in an Age of Science*.[11] The title itself carries the age's inherent cultural bias that science makes belief in God problematic, even superfluous—a philosophical assertion that Polkinghorne attempts to disarm. A distinguished theoretical physicist/theologian, he dedicated the book to the Society for Promoting Christian Knowledge.

In the context of how people in previous generations saw purpose and design in the creation, he wrote, "Charles Darwin, by the publication of *The Origin of Species*, presented us with natural selection as a patient process by which such marvels of 'design' could come about, without the intervening purpose of a Designer being at work to bring them into being. At a stroke, one of the most powerful and seemingly convincing arguments for belief in God had been found to be fatally flawed. Darwin had done what Hume and Kant with their philosophical arguments had failed to achieve, abolishing the time-honoured form of the argument from design by exhibiting an apparently adequate alternative explanation."[12]

From a Christian perspective, not one line in this paragraph is true. According to Scripture, the created world does, indeed, reveal God's creative power. And from a scientific perspective, not one line of the paragraph has come close to being "proven." Polkinghorne is expressing the mantra—shouted,

proclaimed, etched in stone, repeated on mothers' knees, and presented with
the imposing language of chemistry and physics and biology in prestigious
peer-reviewed journals—that natural selection alone can account for all the
marvels, beauty, function, and complexity suffusing the natural world. Yet,
whether talking about a paramecium, or the human frontal lobe, or everything
in between, these naturalistic explanations are constructed on vast speculative
webs of assumptions, leaps of faith, and bold if not at times reckless forays of
imagination.

Natural selection, even with its cohort, random mutation, has never fully
accounted for a butterfly eye, much less a butterfly itself. Without layers of
speculation built on rows of assumptions, it can't explain a cell wall, much less
a single cell, and even then, with all the grand assumptions, vast gaps remain in
our understanding. Though living in an information Pleistocene age compared
to today, Darwin nevertheless (according to Polkinghorne) showed that "one
of the most powerful and seemingly convincing arguments for belief in God
had been found to be fatally flawed." Did Darwin really accomplish all that, or
is this idea just an intellectual icon of our culture, one that Polkinghorne, saturated like everyone else with that culture, believes just as many smart, educated
people once believed in the Ptolemaic cosmos?

After making these bold blanket statements about how Darwin dismantled
the argument from design, Polkinghorne said that Darwin accomplished this
with his "*apparently* adequate alternative explanation" (italics added). That's a
strange equivocation. Suddenly the word *apparently* qualifies the explanation
that, he claimed, voided what for thousands of years had been perhaps the
most compelling argument for the existence of God? If not contradicting himself, he's muddying things a bit.

Now, one needs to be careful and fair. Polkinghorne did not say that this
process alone created life on earth. He's a *theistic* evolutionist. He's saying, instead, that Darwin's theory *could* explain the living things of the natural world
"without the intervening purpose of a Designer being at work to bring them
into being." Again, that statement is questionable from a Christian perspective
and absurdly speculative from a scientific one regardless of how pandemic the
belief currently is. His words show that, though rejecting the premise of naturalism, he has accepted the process that arises from it.[13]

And with what results? In the context of answering Richard Dawkins' "un-
belief," Polkinghorne, working on the assumption that God does exist, sought
to understand how life arose as it did by looking at the reality of the natural
world. That is, working from the assumption of the process (evolution), what
could he "discover" from the natural world about how it developed? He wrote:

It has been an important emphasis in much recent theological thought about creation to acknowledge that by bringing the world into existence God has self-limited divine power by allowing the other truly to be itself. The gift of Love must be the gift of freedom, the gift of a degree of letting-be, and this can be expected to be true of all creatures to the extent that is appropriate to their proper character. It is in the nature of dense snow fields that they will sometimes slip with the destructive force of an avalanche. It is the nature of lions that they will seek their prey. It is the nature of cells that they will mutate, sometimes producing new forms of life, sometimes grievous disabilities, sometimes cancers. It is the nature of humankind that sometimes people will act with selfless generosity but sometimes with murderous selfishness. That these things are so is not gratuitous or due to divine oversight or indifference. They are the necessary cost of a creation given by its Creator the freedom to be itself. Not all that happens is in accordance with God's will because God has stood back, making metaphysical room for creaturely action. The apparently ambivalent tale of evolutionary advance and extinction, which Dawkins sees as the sign of a meaningless world of genetic competition, is understood by the Christian as being the inescapably mixed consequence of a world allowed by its Creator to explore and realise, in its own way, its own inherent fruitfulness—to 'make itself,' to use a phrase as old as the Anglican clergyman Charles Kingsley's response to Darwin's *Origin of Species*.[14]

In another work, in the context of trying to understand why we face death and decay in this life but won't in the next, Polkinghorne wrote,

First must come the old creation, existing at some distance from the veiled presence of its Creator so that creatures have the freedom to be themselves and to make themselves, without being overwhelmed by the naked presence of infinite Reality. That world is an evolving world in which the death of one generation is the necessary cost of the new life of the next. Yet, the eventual divine purpose is to draw all creatures into a more intimate and freely embraced relationship with their Creator. The realisation of that purpose will be the coming to be of the new creation in which the divine presence is no longer veiled from view but progressively revealed. This present world contains sacraments, covenanted occasions in which the veil is somewhat thinned. The new creation will be wholly sacramental, totally suffused with the divine presence and so released from bondage to mortality by the presence of the divine eternal life.[15]

The freedom of snow

Remember the chess analogy? The process was derived from the premise that no humans created chess. Rejecting that premise, someone nevertheless attributed to humans that very process for creating chess. That is, the process formulated on the assumption that no humans created chess is, now, deemed the process that humans did use to create chess. Without a massive hunk of sheer luck, this attempt at harmony is not likely to work any better than did Polkinghorne's painful attempt above to harmonize biblical Creation with evolution.

Polkinghorne does mention a crucial point in biblical theology, and that is love and the freedom inherent in love. Love, by its very nature as love, has to be freely given or it's not love. God can force all intelligent creatures in the universe to fear Him. He can force all intelligent creatures in the universe to worship Him. He can even force them all to obey Him. But He can't force one intelligent creature to love Him. Love can no more exist without freedom than thought can exist without mind, or than width and length can exist without two-dimensional space. Love—and the freedom it entails—is the key to understanding how sin and evil could arise even in a world originally created perfect. In heaven, Lucifer misused the freedom given him; Adam and Eve, in Eden, misused the freedom given them.[16] In that respect, Polkinghorne was on the right track.

Unfortunately, he took this truth to an extreme realm, extending the freedom inherent in love to—what? Snow, lions, and cells (and, one assumes, everything else, animate and inanimate: rocks, trees, flowers, apes), as part of allowing each "truly to be itself" to "the extent that is appropriate to their proper character." Thus, a cell, given this freedom, will sometimes become cancer and kill an infant, just as snow, also given this freedom, will sometimes become an avalanche that crushes snowboarders. Far from being aberrations or the result of the Fall, this suffering is the "necessary cost" of how God created our world. Snow and cells and lions, being spared the "naked presence of infinite Reality," are given the freedom to "make themselves," even if it means killing and maiming and crushing other parts of a creation that, in the Bible, God deemed "very good" (Genesis 1:31). Also, just how a cell or a lion might be "overwhelmed by the naked presence of infinite Reality," Polkinghorne doesn't say, nor does he explain just how this "naked presence" might manifest itself, especially to cells and lions.

Something's radically off-kilter here, perhaps similar to what we would expect when someone seeks to explain, through a process formulated on the assumption that humans did not create chess, how humans did, in fact, create chess. And that's because Polkinghorne is working from two foundational errors, both contrary to Scripture, but both logically derived from a false process assumed to be true.

First, based on the assumptions of evolution, in which the natural processes of random mutation and natural selection explain creation, he promotes the idea that God somehow stepped back in the creation process "of a world allowed by its Creator to explore and realise, in its own way, its own inherent fruitfulness—to 'make itself.'" This notion is a logical conclusion if one accepts evolution as the process of creation of life on earth. Hence, this idea is repeated, in various ways, by others (see below) trying to meld evolutionary theory with biblical Creation.

Yes, Adam and Eve, as moral beings, were created morally free. Otherwise they could no more be moral than a computer software program that filters out porn can be moral. But Polkinghorne extends the freedom inherent in morality along a continuum all the way down to snow, cells, and lions. Animals, or inanimate matter, through the freedom inhering in love, are also given "the gift of a degree of letting-be," he affirms.

Freedom, a moral trait for moral beings, is applied "to the extent that is appropriate to their proper character" to amoral and even inanimate entities, giving each one the freedom "truly to be itself," or "the freedom to be itself," or to "make itself," or to "have the freedom to be themselves and to make themselves." He wrote in another work that "God accords to the processes of the world that same respect that he accords to the actions of humanity,"[17] which implies a kind of "moral" freedom to amoral reality, hardly a biblical concept.

With the notable exception of Adam and Eve—who were created as moral and, therefore, free beings—nothing in the Word of God implies that during the process of creating the earth and life on it the Lord had "self-limited divine power by allowing the other truly to be itself." Where in the Genesis account is there even a hint of any kind of divine "letting-be" or some kind of autonomous freedom, not only allowing things "to be themselves and to make themselves" but allowing for all the evil, corruption, and death that, apparently, according to Polkinghorne, was "the necessary cost of a creation given by its Creator the freedom to be itself"? (What is a thing "itself," apart from every attribute that God Himself endowed it with from the start?) Polkinghorne's scenario falls apart, because it imposes a process contrary to the Scriptures onto the Scriptures, almost like arguing that (-) p = (+) p.

Everything in the Genesis Creation account points to the immediate and direct supernatural intervention of the Creator. From separating the land from the water (Genesis 1:9, 10), to breathing into Adam "the breath of life" and causing him to become "a living being" (Genesis 2:7), the Lord is portrayed as intimately involved in every aspect of Creation, with no hint of a "self-limited divine power by allowing the other truly to be itself," especially when it leads to, as Polkinghorne has admitted, "the death of one generation" as "the necessary cost of the new life of the next," a process alien to texts about the creation of Adam.

What about the creation of Eve? "And the LORD God caused a deep sleep to fall on Adam, and he slept; and He took one of his ribs, and closed up the flesh in its place. Then the rib which the LORD God had taken from man He made into a woman, and He brought her to the man" (Genesis 2:21, 22). Only after a fully formed Adam does Eve come into existence, and then only from the immediate intervention of the Lord, who—in an act about as intimate and direct as was the creation of Adam—supernaturally fashions Eve from the flesh of Adam. "For Adam was formed first, then Eve" (1 Timothy 2:13) is another text that, together with the Genesis account, doesn't fit well with theistic evolution. If Polkinghorne is correct, the biblical Creation narrative becomes another ancient Near Eastern myth, no closer to the truth than is the *Enuma Elish*, in which the earth is depicted as half the corpse of a murdered god, and the heavens as the other half. In Polkinghorne's scenario, the biblical narrative of Creation is among those teachings changed not "almost beyond recognition" but, truly, beyond it.

His second major error is the assumption that the natural world today is what it has been in the ancient past. Because death, violence, and predation are intricately interwoven into life now, it is assumed—based on unproven metaphysical and philosophical presuppositions—that's how it must have always been and, thus, that's how life (with violence, death, and predation) must have been formed. *Violence, predation, and death are the means of creating life?* That concept itself seems absurd, but, well, *It's science!*

Christians, though, have another source of knowledge, divine revelation, the Bible, which posits a supernatural creative process that, in the beginning, resulted in a natural world quite different from what it is now. Polkinghorne has imposed a speculative, naturalistic, long-age scenario of violence, survival of the fittest, and "the death of one generation" as "the necessary cost of the new life of the next" upon texts that teach nothing about a long-age scenario of violence, survival of the fittest, or the death of one generation as the cost of the new life of the next. This imposition of the present scientific theory of origins on a text that contradicts the present scientific theory is exactly why Polkinghorne's scenario appears so strained, ad hoc, and spurious—a powerful example of what happens when philosophy (science), ideally the handmaiden of theology, becomes its master instead.

An autonomous world

Another attempt to baptize the devil came from Robin Collins, of Messiah College. Writing a chapter for *The Oxford Handbook of Philosophical Theology*,[18] Collins, in a work titled "Divine Action and Evolution," early on revealed his premises and assumptions: "This issue is particularly important given that the broadly evolutionary picture—namely that the universe, life, and human culture have gone through a long developmental process—is now beyond reasonable doubt and yet at the same time constitutes a drastic shift in our understanding of the universe."[19] The claim that evolution is "beyond reasonable doubt" is a philosophical expression built upon layer after layer of shaky scaffolding, but representative of just how influential the Aristotle of our era remains.

Collins then announced his assumptions: "Throughout this chapter, I take it as a well-established theory that life on earth arose through the process of biological evolution, by which I mean the process of descent with modification from the first cell. I will leave open, however, the question of whether this process was guided by God."[20]

The question is left open whether this process was guided by God? Wasn't that the whole point of theistic evolution to begin with? Why would a Christian, with the Genesis Creation account before him, even question whether God had guided the process, unless, in his mind, as apparently in Polkinghorne's, the Genesis Creation account is among the texts with "so little utility that they will disappear"?

On the other hand, given Collins's premise, that life was created through "the process of descent with modification from the first cell," his questioning God's guidance is judicious. Who would want to involve God in the overtly nasty fight to the death over billions of years until some lucky entity's descent-with-modification left it standing on the composted remains of its less fit competitors? Considering the time, the waste, the suffering, *couldn't the good Lord have done a better job?* Some bumbling engineer working so clumsily would have been fired, and yet this is how the powerful and loving Creator, revealed in Christ, created the world? Not the most winsome of ways for a compassionate God to create beings who themselves are called to "love your enemies" (Matthew 5:44) and who are told that "greater love has no one than this, than to lay down one's life for his friends" (John 15:13). Though not a logical fallacy—that is, God could have used selfishness, viciousness, and violence as the means of creating beings He intended to be selfless, kind, and nonviolent—it certainly jumbles metaphors.

Hardcore atheist evolutionists have questioned, understandably so, Christian attempts to meld these two torturously antonymous concepts. "Does evolution pose further problems for theology?" wrote Jerry Coyne. "Yes, and big ones. There is no obvious explanation, for instance, why an omnipotent and loving God who directed evolution would lead it into so many dead ends. After all, over 99 percent of the species that ever lived went extinct without leaving descendants. The cruelty of natural selection, which involves endless wastage and pain, also demands explanation. Wouldn't a loving and all-powerful God simply have produced all existing species de novo, as described in Genesis?"[21]

If God created the world by letting it "make itself," and it made itself through the violent process of evolution, the long war of attrition known as Darwinism, what does that say about God and His character?

Theistic evolutionists, by arguing that evolution is the process through which God chose to create our world—either guiding the process Himself, or letting it go to "make itself"—ultimately posit God Himself as responsible for the billions of years of suffering, death, and violence, the brick-and-mortar of every evolutionary scenario. It's one thing to believe that violence, suffering, and death are aberrations that arose from the perversion of angelic and of human free will; it is a radically different thing to claim that suffering, death, and violence were built into the creation by God from the start—particularly when the biblical account of Creation gives an entirely different scenario, one without any mention of violence, suffering, and death as part of the creation process. These are, instead, core components of an unbiblical ideology imposed upon biblical texts.

And it is an ideology that, obviously, Robin Collins has accepted, for he wrote that God (whether or not He guided it) created the world through "the process of descent with modification from the first cell"—another example of the bewitching influence that the prevailing culture and its intellectual pretensions exert on Christians, especially when packaged as "science." Again, nothing's new here. This is what medieval theologians did with Aristotle, the Darwin of their era, and what many theologians do today with Darwin, the Aristotle of ours.

Actually, this infusion of contemporary "science" into theology goes back even further than the medievals. "In the course of this work of his mature years," wrote historian of science David Lindberg,

Augustine made copious use of the natural sciences contained in the classical tradition to explicate the creation story. Here we encounter Greco-Roman ideas about lightning, thunder, clouds, wind, rain, dew, snow, frost, storms, tides, plants and animals, matter and form, the four elements, the doctrine of natural place, seasons, time, the calendar, the planets, planetary motion, the phases of the moon, astrological influence, the soul, sensation, sound, light and shade, and number theory. For all of his worry about overvaluing the Greek scientific/philosophical tradition, Augustine and others like him applied Greco-Roman natural science with a vengeance to biblical interpretation.[22]

That's fine, assuming that whatever the science of the time happens to be reflects the creation process itself, which—given contemporary science's materialist presuppositions—can't now be the case (remember the chess analogy). The assertion "Well, we have finally got it right" is a philosophical trope. As quoted before but worth a rerun, "Fifty-seven years ago," said Alfred North Whitehead in 1939, "it was when I was a young man in the University of Cambridge. I was taught science and mathematics by brilliant men and I did well in them; since the turn of the century I have lived to see every one of the basic assumptions of both set aside. . . . And yet, in the face of that, the discoverers of the new hypotheses in science are declaring, 'Now at last, we have certitude.' "[23]

Considering all the bogus scientific theories once deemed certain, why do so many Christians bow in obeisance to something as subjective, contingent, and malleable as science, especially when the science is not even about present nature, but nature as it supposedly was eons beyond any direct empirical reach—a science built upon layers of unproven assumptions and imaginative retrodictions (think, for instance, about those studying slime mold to learn about the evolutionary origins of altruism)?

Nevertheless, Collins has embraced the evolutionary model, and he attempts "to offer a plausible speculation as to why God might have created the world through an evolutionary process."[24]

First, he looks at other attempts, including Polkinghorne's and theologian John Haught's. (In an attempt to explain why a loving God would create through evolution, Haught, in a passage Collins quoted, argued that an instantaneous creation could not truly be "independent" of God and thus not be "the recipient of divine love."[25]) Collins quotes Haught again: "A world given a lease to become more and more autonomous, even to help create itself and eventually attain the status of human consciousness, has much more integrity and value than any conceivable world determined in every respect by a 'divine designer.' "[26] Collins then writes, "Under this interpretation, Haught could be seen as extending both the free will theodicy and the soul-making theodicy to the universe itself (as Polkinghorne also seems to do)."[27]

Of course, the ideas of the world becoming "more and more autonomous" (from God, presumably) and being able to "create itself" and eventually attaining "the status of human consciousness"—though interesting cosmological speculations—are contrary to biblical thought, which depicts a physical world dependent upon God not just for its creation but for its continued existence. From a purely scientific perspective (subjective as that inevitably is)—either at the macro level, which can be seen as positing a "clockwork" universe, to the quantum level, where everything appears statistical—nothing like the kind of "free will" with which Haught (and Polkinghorne) want to endow creation is believed to be extant. Collins sees the problem, writing:

> In the case of human freedom, we have a strong intuition that moral re-
> sponsibility requires free will and that moral agency is a great good in and
> of itself. Further, arguably, beings without free will could not authenti-
> cally love God (or even one another) if God determined all their choices.
> Presumably, however, non-human creation neither has moral agency nor
> does it love God (except, perhaps, some higher non-human animals), or
> at least not unless one adopts a radically different view of nature than
> delivered by modern science: namely, a view in which non-human, non-
> higher-animal creation does have a will and can make choices. Neither
> Haught nor Polkinghorne, however, advocates such a view.[28]

Maybe they don't, but their own words betray that they come dangerously close, not because Scripture warrants it (on the contrary), but because their cultural assumptions do.

Interconnections
Collins then takes his best shot. "My own highly speculative proposal begins with the claim that the evolutionary process allows for certain types of inter-connection between humans and non-human creation that are potentially of significant value."[29] His chapter sets out three types of these "interconnec-tions"—emergent, ancestral, and redemptive—that, he argues, an evolution-ary model of creation allows for. He says that, instead of a divine fiat creation of different types of life, each independently crafted de novo "according to its kind" (see Genesis 1:11, 12, 21, 24, 25), an evolutionary model allows for an interconnection between humans and the rest of the creation that a traditional or literal reading of the Genesis account wouldn't allow for.

Now one could easily, even if unintentionally, caricature his position. Thus, those interested should read for themselves the chapter in order to grasp his idea about interconnections within the created world that can occur only through the evolutionary process. His point is that by creating the world through the long process of evolution, the Lord made opportunities "for richer and deeper sorts of interconnections between humans and non-human creation than would otherwise be possible,"[30] especially when the process of universal redemption is completed.

Speculating about how this universal redemption might manifest itself, he wrote, "Finally, I propose that these interconnections gain their full value by being taken up into conscious experience, specifically our conscious experience, God's conscious experience, and if non-human creation becomes conscious, its conscious experience. . . . If, moreover, the higher animals, or even possibly the creation itself, become conscious, they will also share in this richness, and moreover, there will be a bond of appreciation for being redeemed, something I assume is of intrinsic value."[31]

Collins then ended his essay with a quote from an ancient Chinese neo-Confucianist named Chang Tsai (1020–1077): "Heaven is my father and Earth is my mother, and even such a small creature as I finds an intimate place in their midst. Therefore that which fills the universe I regard as my body and that which directs the universe I consider as my nature. All people are my brothers and sisters, and all things are my companions."[32]

He closes, not with Scripture, especially Scripture about Creation, *but with the words of an ancient Chinese philosopher?* With no disrespect intended, he had to—because no Bible text supports his "highly speculative proposal" that God used billions of years of evolution to create the world in order that, when redemption is over and the "universe itself gains a 'soul' of some sort,"[33] humans could commune with it. Maybe Chang Tsai teaches this, but Moses, Jesus, Paul, and other Bible writers sure don't.

Aside from the external conflict with Scripture, something inherent in the theory itself is flawed. Even if these interconnections between human and non-human animals or even inanimate reality were as important as he speculates they are, wouldn't their common source of origins, the Lord, be enough to create an interconnection between them?

Have we not all one Father?
Has not one God created us? (Malachi 2:10)

All things were made through Him, and without Him nothing was made that was made. (John 1:3)

Every house is built by someone, but He who built all things is God. (Hebrews 3:4)

You are worthy, O Lord,
To receive glory and honor and power;
For You created all things,
And by Your will they exist and were created. (Revelation 4:11)

Men, why are you doing these things? We also are men with the same nature as you, and preach to you that you should turn from these useless things to the living God, who made the heaven, the earth, the sea, and all things that are in them. (Acts 14:15)

One could argue that these texts are mostly dealing with human relationships, which is true, but Collins extends this idea of relationships to nonhuman reality as well, and so by using these texts, we are simply following his lead.

If he and Polkinghorne and Dowd want to attribute some kind of "freedom" or potential "soul" or "self-awareness" to nonhuman aspects of the creation, as it seems they do, then shouldn't a common Creator and Sustainer be a greater source for interconnectedness than simply being victors in a four-billion-year struggle dominated by violence, chaos, and chance? Evolution is about competition, dominance, and the survival of the fittest over the weaker. It is, decidedly, not about bonds of connectedness and communion. *Yet, somehow, surviving and beating out everyone else and emerging atop the evolutionary struggle is supposed to cement the foundation for a greater sense of communion between the victors standing over the cold graves of all who came before? And this is how God chose to create and, later, to forge bonds amid the redeemed creation?* From the start Collins merely assumed evolution would lead to more of this interconnectedness; he never proved it.

Built-in evil?
A common motif echoes through most attempts to harmonize Scripture with evolution, all based on a fallacy rooted in science or, rather, in an assumption of science—that the past resembles the present, and that the natural processes now at work (the laws, at least) must have also been at work ages ago. Hence, because "natural evils"—violence, predation, death, extinction—exist now, they also did way back when. Which is why, in theistic evolutionary thinking, violence and death have been "built into the universe"[34] from the start. In other words, "predation, death, and extinction" are "intrinsic to the processes that give rise to life on Earth in all its wonderful diversity."[35]

The notion of the present resembling the past, though reasonable, is no certainty. It's an unproven philosophical assumption, which means that it could be wrong. And according to Scripture, which depicts a creation process with no predation, death, or extinction, it must be wrong, an error that explains the painful contortions theistic evolutionists put themselves through trying to make Scripture fit with what the age and culture have convinced them is true. Or, in some cases, it explains why theistic evolutionists simply dismiss the biblical texts as being of so "little utility that they will disappear"—which is the unstated position of another theistic evolutionary tome, *Physics and Cosmology: Scientific Perspectives on the Problem of Natural Evil.*

This work, edited by Nancey Murphy, Robert John Russell, and William R. Stoeger, starts out with an introduction by Murphy. After talking about the view that natural evil arose as a result of moral evil—i.e., the fall of angels and of original humanity—she writes, "In many respects both biblical criticism and science have called this defense into question. The Genesis story of a first set of parents is no longer considered to be historical. We no longer have the hierarchical cosmos in which such accounts were developed, and natural history shows that there must have been millions if not billions of years of death before humans entered the scene. How can these natural evils now be reconciled with the creator's perfect goodness?"[36]

The book attempts to show just that: the Creator's goodness despite creating the world with millions and billions of years of death as the means of creating human life, even though she states that much of this book will "involve not only responses to but refinements or even rejections of the questions and resources as I have characterized them."[37] That sounds fine, but whatever refinements or rejections occur along the way, the premise of the book is that, for some reason, God—who notices when a sparrow falls (Matthew 10:29)—used billions of years of evolution to create life as it is now. The authors assume that the biblical texts about a literal six-day creation of life on earth, or about a perfect earth without suffering and death, or about the fall of Adam and Eve are "not historical"—theological Newspeak for saying that the texts are of so "little utility that they will disappear." Or, frankly, that they are false.

Thomas Tracy, while questioning the idea that the existence of evil is necessary for the existence of good, wrote, "Rather, natural evils may occur simply as a necessary consequence of establishing a lawful system of nature that provides the required context, or background conditions, for achieving the good that God intends."[38] In other words, God had to create a world with natural evils; they are not unintended consequences that resulted from the perversion of freedom but are, instead, "a necessary consequence" of whatever "good that God intends." God, then, is directly responsible for all natural evil, and His culpability goes back to the creation process that He Himself used.

Following a similar route, Murphy wrote, "The gist of the foregoing argument is the claim that if God is to have living, intelligent, free, loving partners for relationship, then the universe God created had to be almost exactly as it is with respect to the ways in which nature produces human and animal suffering, and in which creatures are limited and subject to imperfections. Natural and metaphysical evil are unavoidable by-products of choices God had to make in order to achieve his purposes in having creatures who could know, love, and serve him."[39]

Again, if God wanted to create beings who could love, then He had to create them with moral freedom. But she is saying that this freedom, *of necessity*, leads to the natural evil of suffering and death, which, according to the argument, was how God chose to create life on earth to begin with. As have others we have looked at so far, she appears to apply this concept of "freedom" to non-rational, even inanimate, nature as well. According to this view, natural evil and human and animal suffering are not aberrations, but were built into the creation by God as much as was the law of gravity. Suffering, she argues, is "an unwanted but unavoidable by-product of conditions in the natural world that have to obtain in order that there be intelligent life at all."[40]

Natural evil and human and animal suffering, then, are not even "collateral damage" but (in this thinking) the "unavoidable by-product" of God's original plan for life on earth. Along with "the herb that yields seed according to its kind" (Genesis 1:12), and "every living thing that moves, with which the waters abounded, according to their kind" (Genesis 1:21), suffering, predation, violence, death, famine, pestilence, extinction, earthquakes, floods, volcanoes were (we are told) written into the creation blueprint itself. Yet for some inexplicable reason, none of these evils were mentioned in the biblical texts! In her explanation, rather than the beautiful, orderly, and idyllic account depicted in Genesis 1 and 2 as the direct result of God's creative power, "human and animal suffering" were the direct result of that power. How could they not be? After all, isn't that what the current scientific model of origins teaches? And if you accept that model, what other choice do you have but to assume that suffering, death, predation, and extinction were requisite from the start, though not even hinted at in the Creation texts?

"Toil and death are," wrote Murphy, "the consequences of the finely tuned laws of physics that allow us to be here."[41] Instead of being the consequences of sin and the Fall (Genesis 3:17–19), toil and death are the consequences of the finely tuned laws of physics that God used to create our world. (Suffering, floods, famine, and death were, then, hardwired into the numbers, letters, and symbols of the formulas themselves.) Suffering, evil, death—aberrations of the creation—have been converted into the means of creation instead. Talk about calling "evil good" (Isaiah 5:20)!

In a powerful book on theodicy,[42] theologian Sigve Tonstad wrote about a pagan opponent of Christianity, Celsus, who, in the second century, penned attacks on the faith. Like theistic evolutionists today, Celsus claimed that evil was simply built into the fabric of the creation itself and not the result of some moral fall. Tonstad quoted Celsus: "I turn now to consider the existence of evil, which is analogous to matter itself in that there can be no decrease or increase of evils in the world—neither in the past nor in the future. From the beginning of time, the beginning of the universe, there has been just so much evil, and in quantity it has remained the same. It is in the nature of the universe that this be the case, and depends on our understanding of the origins of the universe itself."[43] When Celsus wrote that "it is in the nature of the universe that this be the case," he sounded like Polkinghorne, who wrote, "*It is the nature of lions* that they will seek their prey. *It is the nature of cells* that they will mutate, sometimes producing new forms of life, sometimes grievous disabilities, sometimes cancers. *It is the nature of humankind* that sometimes people will act with selfless generosity but sometimes with murderous selfishness" (italics added). Theistic evolutionists, it seems, aren't the intellectual heirs just of Galileo's Inquisitors but also of an early pagan opponent of Christianity as well.

Adam and Eve

No wonder theistic evolutionists struggle to harmonize their view of creation with the character of a loving and perfect God, a God, in their view, who though giving us one story about Creation (the one found consistently throughout the Old and New Testaments) in fact created us in a manner not even remotely close to that account. Then, worse, the Creator made humanity wait for Charles Darwin, in the nineteenth century A.D., to finally reveal the truth that God had camouflaged in His Word for millennia, hiding it with bogus stories about an orderly, wonderful, and "very good" (Genesis 1:31) Creation that was corrupted through the fall of two beings, Adam and Eve—who, it turns out, couldn't have possibly existed, at least as they are depicted in Scripture.

Murphy is clear about what she thinks of the biblical account of Adam and Eve. "I would go much further here," she writes, "and say that human nature created *de novo* [from new] with good moral character is an incoherent idea."[44] A good moral character, she argues, must be acquired from something that had not been there in the past. So humanity could not have started out morally upright but, instead, needed "dangers, hardships, pain, and other kinds of suffering"[45] to obtain that character. The biblical account of Adam and Eve, in which they were made in the "image of God" (Genesis 1:27)—and thus were created from the start with a good moral character, a starting point from which they could even grow further morally—is, she says, "incoherent."

This move (which, by the way, puts Genesis 1–3 into the "myth" category and makes at least part of it "incoherent") is another example of taking reality as it is now—i.e., flawed human beings who can grow through "dangers, hardships, pain, and other kinds of suffering"—and retrodicting it to the beginning of humanity itself. It's another manifestation of the fundamental error of theistic evolution: conflating results with the cause, akin to studying prostitution to discover the origins of sex.

As a result, the Fall, too, becomes "not historical," which means not only that the early texts in Genesis are relegated to the level of myth, but also that Paul's discourse in Romans 5:12–19, about Christ coming to undo what Adam did, becomes—*what?*

> Therefore, just as through *one man* sin entered the world, and death through sin, and thus death spread to all men, because all sinned— (. . . For if by the *one man's* offense many died, much more the grace of God and the gift by the grace of the *one Man, Jesus Christ,* abounded to many. . . . For if by the *one man's* offense death reigned through the one, much more those who receive abundance of grace and of the gift of righteousness will reign in life through *the One, Jesus Christ.*) Therefore, as through *one man's* offense judgment came to all men, resulting in condemnation, even so through *one Man's* righteous act the free gift came to all men, resulting in justification of life. For as by *one man's* disobedience many were made sinners, so also by *one Man's* obedience many will be made righteous. (Romans 5:12–19; italics added)

If, as Murphy claims, the idea of Adam being created with a good moral character is "incoherent," then Paul's discourse here must be "incoherent," too, because his point is that Jesus came to remedy Adam's offense, which is nonsense if Adam didn't exist or were created de novo flawed. Paul's words would have to be interpreted to mean something radically different from what he's saying, just as the words in Genesis 1–3 have to be turned upside down and inside out to make them fit billions of years of evolution. Paul makes an unambiguous one-to-one correspondence between Adam and Jesus; each one is portrayed as a real flesh-and-blood human being. How, then, can Murphy mythologize Adam, but not Christ? She can't, which means that her speculation falls apart unless she does to Jesus what she does to Adam, a move that she probably (one hopes) wouldn't make.

Many Christians see the problem inherent in attempting to harmonize an evolutionary model with Genesis. The attempts, writes William VanDoodewaard, "that deny the existence of a real Adam or Eve face even more significant theological difficulties in relation to passages like Romans 5 and 1 Corinthians 15, where Paul grounds his understanding of the reality of the covenant of grace and the person and work of Jesus Christ in the historical reality of the first man. Negation of the reality of Adam as the first human, specially created by God in His image, undermines redemptive history and the reality of the person and work of Christ. Here the quest for the historical Adam begins to erode the historical, and present, Jesus."[46]

A noninterventionist God?

Murphy then expresses another idea that permeates most attempts to harmonize evolution with a loving God who created life through the violent and difficult process that scientists posit as the means of human origins and existence.

"It is the general consensus among liberal theologians," she writes, "as well as among scholars working in the area of theology and science, that God's action must be understood in a noninterventionist manner. I have argued that God has apparently decided not to violate the 'natural rights' of created entities to be what they are. This means in part that God voluntarily withholds divine power out of respect for the freedom and integrity of creatures."[47]

Unfortunately, she then takes this crucial truth (though the issue is not "natural rights," but the freedom inherent in love) and pushes it to absurdity. "This relation between God and creatures," she continues, "is one of God's highest purposes in creating. *This mode of divine activity extends all the way through the hierarchy of complexity within the created world.* Hence God cooperates with, but does not overrule, natural entities."[48] In other words, in respecting the "natural rights" of "natural entities"—rocks, fish, bugs, snow, lions, cells, "all levels of reality"[49]—God does not intervene, but just lets them "be what they are," even if, unfortunately, "what they are" leads to great suffering. Besides—what "they are" is precisely what God made them to be, so it's hard to see how this theology leads to any successful theodicy.

It gets even worse. In the context of final redemption and how it relates to creation via the process of evolution, Denis Edwards (in the same volume) wrote, "What does it [final redemption] have to say in the light of the natural evil that is built into the universe from its origin? What it offers is an account of a God whose nature is to love and respect the natural world in its emergence and in its integrity, who does not overrule the natural world, but works in and through its processes bringing all things finally to healing and fulfillment in God's self."[50]

God will use (Edwards argues) the same natural processes "built into the universe from its origin"—the processes that have caused suffering, pain, death, extinction, and disease—to bring ultimate healing and fulfillment. Bad enough that these processes were what God used to create us. But now we're being told that these same processes will be what God works with to bring all things "finally to healing and fulfillment in God's self"?

This is quite a different scenario than the one depicted all through Scripture, which teaches a supernatural, as opposed to a natural, denouement of this present world and its ills.

But the day of the Lord will come as a thief in the night, in which the heavens will pass away with a great noise, and the elements will melt with fervent heat; both the earth and the works that are in it will be burned up. Therefore, since all these things will be dissolved, what manner of persons ought you to be in holy conduct and godliness, looking for and hastening the coming of the day of God, because of which the heavens will be dissolved, being on fire, and the elements will melt with fervent heat? Nevertheless we, according to His promise, look for new heavens and a new earth in which righteousness dwells. (2 Peter 3:10–13)

Edwards takes what exists now and not only retrodicts it into the past but projects it far into the future, too, even toward ultimate redemption (see below). *The natural process that God used in creating us and that brought so much suffering will be the same means used toward redeeming us as well?* If this scenario were true, one could justly retort, "Thanks, Lord, but no thanks."

Rather than accepting the clear biblical account of a world created perfect but that became perverted because of the fall of rational beings (first angels, then humans) who abused the free will inherent in love and fell into sin, leading to natural evils—these theistic evolutionists have a completely different scenario. The natural evils of suffering, death, sickness, and extinction were necessary, they declare, built in by God, who could not intervene without violating the "natural rights" or the "integrity" of "created entities to be what they are"—even if some of those entities happen to be nonrational, even non-living, and even if these entities, being "what they are," cause terrible human and animal suffering.

This concept expresses a motif in many theistic evolutionary apologetics, the idea of a noninterventionist God, or what has been called the "argument from neglect."[51] The gist, as we have seen, is that God respects the "integrity," or the "natural rights" or the "freedom," of the created world to be whatever it will naturally be. Again, this may be fine for rational beings in their moral choices, but when applied—as it appears to be by these people—to all of creation, animate and inanimate, it borders on animism. (Again, what, pray tell, are the "natural rights" of nonliving entities—the kind of things that, for instance, cause floods, earthquakes, famines, and other natural evils?)

This move, rooted, logically enough, in an evolutionary paradigm, does lead to some interesting tweaks in order to make the entire dismal scheme internally consistent. For instance, Philip Clayton and Steven Knapp wrote that "a benevolent God could not intervene *even once* without incurring the responsibility to intervene in every case where doing so would prevent an instance of innocent suffering."[52]

Really? What about all of Christ's miraculous healings, in which a benevolent God frequently intervened directly to prevent innocent suffering? Jesus' healing miracles, it seems—along with any other miraculous healings, Old and New Testament—have to be interpreted "almost beyond recognition" because science as now practiced teaches a model of creation that demands a noninterventionist God. Because science has now provided the hermeneutical framework for these Christians, what other choice do they have?

The notion of a noninterventionist God arises not from the biblical texts themselves, but from the unfortunate submission of Christians to the claims of science. What about all the direct, divine supernatural interventions of God, when He completely "violated" the "natural rights" of the material world—from the Flood, to Sodom and Gomorrah, to the fire from heaven on Mount Carmel, to the dead people Jesus raised, to Moses' lifting the bronze serpent and healing those bitten by snakes, to the supernatural affliction and then healing of Nebuchadnezzar, to the resurrection of Jesus from the tomb? From the beginning of Scripture to its end, God intervenes in numerous ways that "violate" the natural order of the physical world, at least as that order is understood now. Scripture reveals God repeatedly intervening in the natural world, imposing His will on everything He created—except (it seems) human and angelic free will.

Nevertheless, theistic evolution, in order to justify natural evil, argues that God doesn't do that, because it would be a violation of the "integrity" of nature. This theology subordinates the power of God to the natural order, which would be bad enough—except that it subordinates God's power to a natural order that itself has been corrupted.

In short, in this theology, the Lord didn't speak the world into a perfect existence; rather, He spit, gagged, and coughed out random natural processes that, of necessity, include natural evil, suffering, and death. And, apparently, it's through these same processes that this noninterventionist God is going to redeem us as well. *And all this is supposed to show His love and goodness despite the natural evil that was necessary, and not contingent, to the very process of creation itself?*

This attempted theodicy does not work because it cannot work. It's about as close to being a deductive fallacy as an inductive one could be. As in the chess analogy, it's assuming a process that, at the most basic level, contradicts the biblical account and any reasonable concept of God's goodness.

Two Adams, two Eves?

However painful these arguments, the agony increases when Christians try to harmonize science's theories about origins with the most crucial doctrine of biblical theology—the atonement of Jesus. The scope of the problem was already seen with Murphy's assertion that the idea of a newly minted and morally perfect Adam was "incoherent." Her position is highly problematic, because—according to Scripture—Christ's death was predicated on a sinless Adam in paradise, whose fall Christ came to redeem. In contrast, evolution is predicated on an environment of death, violence, and predation in which no Adam in paradise could have ever existed, as Murphy has logically asserted (from her evolutionary premises).

"In terms of the gospel of Jesus Christ," wrote R. Albert Mohler Jr., "the most urgent question related to beginnings has to do with the existence of Adam and Eve as the first parents to all humanity and to the reality of the fall as the explanation for human sinfulness and all that comes with sin. This question has become especially urgent since the Bible's account of beginnings is being increasingly repudiated. We are not talking about arguments over the interpretation of a few verses or even chapters of the Bible. We are now dealing with the straightforward rejection not only of the existence of Adam and Eve but of both Eden and the fall."[53]

Mohler's right. In any conceivable evolutionary paradigm, a sinless Adam and Eve in paradise becomes "incoherent," as Murphy declares. Even in the most generalized evolutionary model, how could two sinless beings who don't know death have evolved into existence? Who were their parents, and what happened to them? How could the evolutionary transition from hominid to *Homo sapiens* occur in one generation—from parents who weren't humans capable of sin, to their offspring, Adam and Eve, who were? And at what age did Adam and Eve become morally culpable?

Paul assumed that Adam and Eve were real people; he had to, because their literal existence was central to his theology of atonement and the Fall.[54] Meanwhile, Jesus Himself said, "From the beginning of the creation, God 'made them male and female.' 'For this reason a man shall leave his father and mother and be joined to his wife, and the two shall become one flesh'; so then they are no longer two, but one flesh. Therefore what God has joined together, let not man separate" (Mark 10:6–9). Christ's wording puts a fully formed male and female at "the beginning of the creation," as opposed to two beings who—after billions of years of suffering, extinction, and death—arrived very late on the evolutionary timescale. Jesus says that humans came at the "beginning of the creation"; current science says that they came at the far end. It's obvious, unfortunately, whom these Christians believe.

However, science has proclaimed that the evolutionary process is true, and, given its intellectual prestige, what self-respecting Christian intellectual can go against science? What this capitulation means, however, is that for these

Christians the Genesis Creation account becomes relegated to the level of myth, much like the story of the boy who cried wolf. What matters is the point of the story, not whether the boy or the wolf are fictitious. If evolution were true, then the six days of Creation, the seventh-day Sabbath, and Adam and Eve would be no different from the fictitious boy and the fictitious wolf. Which means just about all we can take from Genesis 1–3 is that God created the world.

"Biological death," wrote Arthur Peacocke, "was present on the earth long before human beings arrived. It was the prerequisite of our coming into existence through the creative process of biology which God himself has installed in this world. . . . God had already made biological death the means of his creating new forms of life. This has to be accepted, difficult though it may be for some theologies."[55]

Difficult for "some theologies"? For any theology, actually, that assumes that the written text of Genesis bears at least some resemblance to what actually happened at the Creation. Peacocke assumes that death, violence, and suffering were "prerequisite" for human existence, an assumption—contrary to what the texts themselves say, even in their broadest reading, and based solely on philosophical predilections—that comes heavy-laden with challenges to other teachings that arise directly from the Creation story, such as the atoning sacrifice of Jesus.

Realizing the problem, Desmond Ford has made a fascinating proposal that reveals to what lengths Christians will go to try to fit an evolutionary model into the biblical account. Ford, a Protestant theologian from Australia, has always placed a strong emphasis on Christ's substitutionary death on behalf of fallen humanity. Biblically, however, this theology is predicated on a literal Christ who came to undo what a literal Adam did. "For since by man came death, by Man also came the resurrection of the dead. For as in Adam all die, even so in Christ all shall be made alive" (1 Corinthians 15:21, 22). Ford is unambiguous about how requisite a sinless Adam and the Fall are to Christianity, especially to the Cross. "There is a sense," he wrote, "in which the whole Bible rests on the historicity of the Fall recorded in Genesis 3. If there was no Fall there is no need of redemption and, therefore, no need of Christ and his Cross."[56] However, it's hard, if not impossible, to conceive of a literal Adam—an originally sinless being whose eventual fall brought death to all humanity—having been created through evolution.

Ford, though rejecting Darwin's naturalism, has opted for a form of theistic evolution called "progressive creationism,"[57] a more nuanced and sophisticated incarnation of the same idea. However tagged, the premise of billions of years of evolution, guided by God or not, does not solve the dilemma of how a sinless Adam, whose transgression Christ came to remedy, can be jerry-rigged into the paradigm.

Determined, nevertheless, to get a sinless Adam and the Fall into his "progressive creationism," Ford argues that the Adam of Genesis 1–3 is a different Adam—separated by a vast gap in time—from the Adam brought to view beginning in Genesis 4:1.

"Adam and Eve in Genesis 1," he claims, "were not the parents of Cain and Abel. . . . The idea that there are two Adams, separated by vast ages, may confound those who think literally. . . . The Adam of Genesis 1-3 is different from the Adam of chapter 4. . . . The Adam of chapters 1-3 is prehistory whereas the Adam of chapter 4 onwards lives in a world of about ten thousand years ago. The Adam of chapter 4 is a different man."[58]

To buttress this thesis, Ford says that the word *ha-adam*, translated either as "Adam" or as "the man," in Genesis 1–3 points to the first Adam. The word *adam*, without the initial *ha* (the definite article "the"), is the other Adam, who first appears in Genesis 4. *Ha-adam* is the sinless, pristine Adam, the man of Genesis 1–3, who fell into sin; but *adam* is the next Adam, the one of Genesis 4 onward, who is separated from the first Adam by tens of thousands of years of violence, death, and suffering.

However, Genesis 3:24 and 4:1, the two verses where the transition between the two Adams supposedly takes place, demolish Ford's argument. The word *ha-adam* (the man), supposedly referring (in Ford's view) only to the Adam of Genesis 1–3, also appears in Genesis 4:1, in reference to Ford's other Adam. Hence, the linguistic distinction between his two Adams falls apart in the first instance at where it is supposed to be revealed.

"So He [God] drove out the man [*ha-adam*]; and He placed cherubim at the east of the garden of Eden, and a flaming sword which turned every way, to guard the way to the tree of life. Now Adam [*ha-adam*] knew Eve his wife, and she conceived and bore Cain, and said, 'I have acquired a man from the LORD'" (Genesis 3:24–4:1).

Not only is the same word, *ha-adam*, used in both verses; the Adam of Genesis 4:1, like the Adam of Genesis 1–3, had a wife named Eve! And yet we are supposed to believe that these texts are referring to two completely different Adams and two completely different Eves, with one Adam and Eve separated by tens of thousands of years from the other Adam and Eve?

Ford presents this view in his latest book, *Genesis Versus Darwin*. Despite the title, however, Ford rejects a literal six-day creation and the universality of Noah's flood, arguing that both are parables meant to teach not history, but spiritual truth. "Genesis does concern a week," he writes, "but it's a parabolic not a literal week."[59]

According to Ford's "progressive creationism," which he claims harmonizes the Bible and current science, God started simple life billions of years ago, during which the Lord progressively created "ascending life forms" until He made the first Adam, *ha-adam* of Genesis 1–3, who, unfortunately, sinned (hence, the gospel is "preserved").

Ford doesn't say what happened after this first Adam sinned, except that between "Genesis 3 and 4 lie many thousands of years of human existence, and include people such as Neanderthals and Cro-Magnons who sprang from Adam the first."[60] (We are to believe that these supposed human precursors, Neanderthals and the like, were the offspring of Adam and Eve?) According to Ford, the "Neanderthals mysteriously become extinct and their more gifted successors"—meaning us—"dominated earth."[61]

Ford's position remains problematic even besides his painful exegesis of Genesis. How did a sinless Adam and Eve, the Adam and Eve of Genesis 1–3:24, come to exist in the first place? "God by creative fiat," Ford wrote, "brought life into existence, and then at appropriate times his touch or mere will brought the required changes for the abrupt appearances of new species. Finally, Genesis 1:26-28 was fulfilled in God's creation of Adam and Eve."[62] In other words, amid billions of years of violence, predation, and death, every now and then, "at appropriate times," God just popped out a new species, including, eventually, a fully formed and fully functioning and wholly holy Adam and Eve, who then fell into sin. (Notice how this view hardly jibes with Murphy or with a "noninterventionist" God.) According to Ford, this process is how humans came into existence, even though Genesis 1–3 teaches nothing about billions of years of death, randomness, and violence but, actually, teaches the contrary.

With no disrespect intended, one can kindly ask: How does a man who (in his own words) has "studied the Bible for over seventy-five years and thousands of books concerning it"[63] come up with something so obviously strained? The answer is that Ford's "progressive creationism" is another example of what happens when well-meaning people subordinate the Word of God to whatever the latest science happens to be. Referring to the great gap that he posits existed between the first Adam and Eve and the second ones, he explained God's thinking in allowing it. "It was God's intention," he wrote, "that the meaning of this gap should become apparent only when it was needed—in the era dominated by modern science."[64]

Dominated is right, even to the point where some of the most crucial biblical teachings must be reinterpreted "almost beyond recognition" or deemed of "so little utility" that they will vanish "just as the primate tail was lost within our lineage of apes." Instead of Scripture being interpreted by Scripture, it's now interpreted by the latest published findings in such journals as *Nature*, *Science*, and *Cell*. Some have argued for a hermeneutic that applies the "scientific method" (whatever that is) to Scripture. But what's going on here isn't applying the *methods* of science to Scripture but the *claims* of science. Ford's words are a striking admission of the intellectual abdication of even the plainest teachings of God's Word to whatever the latest and greatest science happens to be, which now is evolution, a model that denudes not just the Creation story, but whatever biblical theology that arises directly from it, including Christ's death on the cross.

God's errors?

One of the most prestigious scientists today is Francis Collins, director of the National Institutes of Health (NIH), in Bethesda, Maryland, and the leader of the Human Genome Project. He is also known for his "unshakable faith in God and scripture."[65] In 2006 he came out with the highly acclaimed (and *New York Times* bestseller) *The Language of God*, in which he makes a case for the compatibility of faith and science, even if science happens to promote billions of years of Darwinian evolution. Collins found no contradiction between his Christian faith, which, one assumes, is shaped by his "unshakable faith in God and scripture," and the theory of evolution or, more precisely, the neo-Darwinian synthesis.

Talking about Darwin's claim that natural selection accounts for evolution, Collins wrote, "In the mid-nineteenth century, Darwin had no way of knowing what the mechanism of evolution by natural selection might be. We can now see that the variation he postulated is supported by naturally occurring mutations in DNA. These are estimated to occur at a rate of about one error every 100 million base pairs per generation."[66] Collins argues that Darwinian natural selection, "the elegant mechanism of evolution,"[67] is how God created life on earth.

But this "elegant mechanism" is based on genetic mutation, "one *error* every 100 million base pairs per generation" (italics added).

Error? God created life on earth through the use of errors? Never mind that everything in the Genesis Creation account points to the entire creation process being carefully and precisely made by God. What, anywhere, in any biblical depiction of Creation, Old Testament or New, but especially in the Genesis account, gives the slightest indication that error, of any kind, anywhere was involved in the creation of life? Worse, these errors weren't sideshows, peripheral events that just happened along the way; they were not like superfluous words that an author edits out before finishing the final product. On the contrary, according to Collins, these errors constituted the precise means and methods God used for the creation of life in all its wonderfully adapted and various forms.

With no disrespect intended, only the most seditious reinterpretation of the texts could allow for what Collins suggests. If he's correct, it would be as if the point of the story about the boy who cried wolf is that it's just fine to keep sounding false alarms. Even if the Genesis story were meant allegorically, what's the point if the allegory itself conveys a message that completely conflicts with the reality it's supposed to be allegorizing?

Collins is making the same epistemological mistake as others who attempt to reconcile evolutionary theory with the biblical account of Creation—because errors (mutations in DNA) exist now, he's assuming that they must have existed in the beginning as well and thus were the direct means God used to create the different kinds of life on earth. However, that is not a necessary conclusion from a logical or a scientific perspective; and from a biblical standpoint it's flat out wrong.

But it's science! So what? The commonly promoted idea of cold, hard, rationalistic scientists objectively following the evidence wherever it leads has long been known to be a myth, even before Kuhn made that knowledge fashionable. Science does not originate in some transcendental, objective realm that delivers unalloyed truth to humanity. Science is the work of scientists, subjective human beings, and as such it comes burdened with all the prejudices, foibles, fears, and presuppositions of everything human. And this subjectivity includes the eminent Collins, whose only chance to escape the übersubjectivity of empirical epistemology is in the scriptural account of Genesis (the closest thing we have to a transcendental, objective realm that delivers unalloyed truth to humanity). Yet despite his "unshakable faith in God and scripture," he has, unfortunately, as have many others, rejected Scripture for a model that contradicts it in every conceivable way on the question of human origins.

A better job?

Cannot one, reasonably and fairly, ask Francis Collins, Nancey Murphy, Desmond Ford, and all the other scientists, theologians, or scientist/theologians who accept some form of theistic evolution or progressive creationism this question: *Why does the scriptural account of Creation vary so greatly from what they claim happened?* When Jesus told the parable of the sower (Matthew 13) or the parable of the landowner who built a vineyard and leased it (Matthew 21) or the parable of the man who planted a fig tree (Luke 13) or when Nathan the prophet told King David the story of the rich man who had many flocks and herds (2 Samuel 12), was there not, in each case, a clear *parallel* between the specifics of the story itself and the larger, broader message each parable was to convey?

Why, then, in the Genesis Creation account, from the first day to the expulsion of Adam and Eve from Eden, is this "parabolic" account, this allegory, at odds with—even contradictory to—the truths that it was meant to teach? If any of the various theistic evolutionary models are even close to being correct, it would make the Lord an extremely incompetent storyteller in regard to the most foundational of all Christian teaching: human origins, the doctrine upon which all Christian belief rests. Jesus is the "Word" (John 1:1), the one who made "man's mouth" (Exodus 4:11), so if, in fact, evolution were true, certainly He could have done a better job of giving us *the only account we have of our origins* than the one told in Genesis. None of us were there to see the earth's creation (Job 38); so we, as believers, need to accept what the Lord says, even if what He says (according to theistic evolutionists) wasn't even close to what happened.

If Darwin got it right, God might as well have told us that the stork brings babies as to inspire Genesis 1–3. If creation took four billion years, as opposed to six days; if creation happened only through a process of violence, death, extinction, and error, as opposed to the orderly and intricately planned account given in Genesis; and, if natural evil were built in instead of the result of the Fall—one could reasonably ask: *Why should we believe anything depicted in Scripture?* What other crucial truths does Scripture mask by an account that contradicts actual events? If Genesis 1 and 2 are metaphorical, allegorical, shouldn't the metaphors or allegories at least parallel, to some degree, whatever truths that they are supposed to be revealing? Even if Genesis 1 and 2 are not to be taken as a literal account (six twenty-four-hour days, God creating man out of the dust, breathing life into his nostrils, etc.), one is still very hard pressed to find any reasonable way to fit an evolutionary model into a creation account that contradicts it at every level. If evolution is true, then Christians have to believe that Darwin got it better than did Moses, or even than did the Lord Himself.

The breath of life

Take, as one example, a foundational text about the origins and the nature of humanity. In any evolutionary model, this text has to be interpreted in an insanely broad manner that renders it of "so little utility" that, in practicality, it needs to be discarded, because it teaches nothing about how humanity came into existence other than that, contra atheism, God was somehow involved. Beyond that, in any evolutionary model, it's all but useless.

The text?

And the LORD God formed man of the dust of the ground, and breathed into his nostrils the breath of life; and man became a living being. (Genesis 2:7)

The Hebrew reads that God formed "the man," as in one person (the NIV translates it "the man"). The words "his nostrils" reflects the singular again, as does the phrase "and the man became a living being." The relevant verbs and nouns and possessive pronouns in Genesis 2:7 show that one man, the man, was created.

In contrast, Genesis 1:26 reads, "Then God said, 'Let Us make man in Our image, according to Our likeness; let them have dominion over the fish of the sea, over the birds of the air.'" In this verse "man" comes without the definite article "the." The word "man" here, specifically in this context, is referring to humanity, plural, as revealed in the clause that immediately follows: "let them [plural] have dominion over the fish of the sea."

In Genesis 2:7, "the man," this one man, is created first—then, afterward, God breathed into "his nostrils the breath of life" and that man became "a living being." Thus, even before the man was alive, before he had breath, he had nostrils, a nose. This single detail alone debunks every scenario presented above. In any evolutionary model how could nostrils possibly have formed on a being who was not yet living?

Let's be logical. If the man already had a nose, then he must have had lungs, for what good is a nose without lungs? And what good are lungs without blood? And human blood demands a heart, and a heart needs (among many things) a sophisticated nervous system, which in a human means a brain. If the man had nostrils, then he had a face, and if he had a face then he had a head, which means a skull, and so forth. If we accept the verse for what it says and reject this mantra about taking the text "seriously but not literally" (no evolutionary model can take this text, and most others in Genesis 1–3, "seriously"), then this verse posits a model of creation impossible to harmonize with evolution.

That's precisely why many Christians, accepting, as does Ford, the "dominance" of modern science even over Scripture, have implicitly, if not openly, rejected the text for what it says. After all, in an evolutionary paradigm, what possible message could it have been meant to convey? And, whatever message it was, couldn't God have done a better job of conveying it other than by employing imagery that conflicts with what happened? Couldn't the God who told us the story of the prodigal son have used imagery that at least somewhat paralleled what happened? If evolution were true, and this is a metaphor God used to explain it, then the story of the prodigal son (Luke 15) could be interpreted to mean that even if someone repents from their sinful ways and returns to God, the Lord will reject the person. This interpretation is no more ludicrous than applying an evolutionary model to Genesis 2:7, or even to Genesis 1–3 as a whole.

Everything about Genesis 2:7 implies that the man was *first* created as a whole entity—but a lifeless one, a complete contradiction to any evolutionary model. Only after having a complete human body did he become a "living being," and then only through a direct, unique, supernatural act of God that was completely different from how any of the other creatures were created. What a harsh contrast to evolution, in any form, theistic or atheistic, which rejects the radical break between human and animals, positing instead that humans are not *like* apes, but that "we *are* apes,"[68] just a more evolved rendition.

Thus, if one takes, at face value, many theistic evolutionists' claim to revere the Scriptures, cannot one ask: *How can evolution be harmonized with this text?* Can't they see an irreconcilable contradiction between it and even the broadest evolutionary scheme? Why would the Lord have inspired the writing of this creation model if, in fact, He used an entirely different one? What good is the text if the opposite of what it teaches is true?

And there was evening and there was morning

Other than the whimsies of evolutionary scientists, what criteria determine what's allegorical or what's literal in the Genesis account? One assumes that because God Himself is supposedly beyond the purview of science (at least according to the philosophical presuppositions of some scientists; others argue that science has all but disproved the existence of God[69]), theistic evolutionists can still accept God's role in the Creation account. But it's a role excruciatingly different from what the texts themselves teach, even in the most imaginative and labored readings. If as honest as Dowd, theistic evolutionists would have to admit that, in terms of depicting the process of life's origins, Genesis 1–3 is useless.

According to Genesis, God was immediately involved in every aspect of the Creation account. The common refrain "And God said, let there be . . . and it was so" makes the creation of life on earth a direct result of God's spoken word. No hint of fits, starts, stops, violence, extinctions, or of divine non-interventionism, or of a "letting-be," or any of the accoutrements that theistic evolutionists rivet onto the texts to make them fit the scientific paradigm.

The idea of God's spoken word, so central to the account itself, becomes allegory—another myth with no historical validity—one that teaches almost nothing about our origins, while the little it does teach has deceived believers for millennia about those origins and would continue to do so today but for Charles Darwin. That is, unless for billions of years God "spoke" the various mutations into existence needed for life to evolve on earth. ("And God said, Let the HspB5 gene mutate, and it was so." "And God said, Let the ABO gene mutate, and it was so.") If indeed so, then it would certainly not be "*random* mutation," which, according to the neo-Darwinian synthesis, is the driving force behind the creation. Mutation, yes, *but random?* What's left of the integrity of language itself, much less Scripture, if the texts about God's spoken word at the Creation, "And God said, let there be . . . and it was so," are a parable for eons of genetic mutations, random or otherwise?

Numerous biblical scholars, meanwhile, who *don't* believe that the Genesis Creation account is literal, or who might even be theistic evolutionists or progressive creationists, will nevertheless argue that the author *meant* it as a literal account of creation. If they are correct, and what was written is not even close to being what really happened, then—*what?*

If the author, inspired by the Holy Spirit (2 Timothy 3:16), meant it literally, but creation actually took billions of years instead of six days, it would mean that for the millennia of recorded history—from the whole Israelite period up through the New Testament era, up to the Protestant Reformation and beyond—the Lord's church wallowed in myths regarding human origins until God, in His infinite wisdom, raised up His divinely appointed one, Charles Darwin, at best an agnostic, to free believers from centuries of belief in a creation story that was no closer to truth than were the ancient pagan creation accounts. Not just humanity in general, but the church itself, lived in darkness on a crucial, foundational teaching until, as Ford argued, the "era dominated by modern science" revealed that God's Word, in regard to origins, was wrong on every particular. This position is fine for someone who doesn't accept the Bible as inspired. But how does a Christian, who takes the Word of God as God's word, accept such a view, especially when the Genesis texts are so contrary to the evolutionary model?

And nothing in the Genesis account so in-your-face contradicts every evolutionary model more than does the time frame that the Word of God explicitly, and without equivocation, gives for the creation of the basic features of the earth and the origin of all life on it. "Then God saw everything that He had made, and indeed it was very good. So the evening and the morning were the sixth day. Thus the heavens and the earth, and all the host of them, were finished. And on the seventh day God ended His work which He had done, and He rested on the seventh day from all His work which He had done" (Genesis 1:31–2:2).

Thousands of years later, the Lord, at Sinai, reiterated the same teachings in the Ten Commandments themselves. "Remember the Sabbath day, to keep it holy. Six days you shall labor and do all your work, but the seventh day is the Sabbath of the LORD your God. In it you shall do no work: you, nor your son, nor your daughter, nor your male servant, nor your female servant, nor your cattle, nor your stranger who is within your gates. For in six days the LORD made the heavens and the earth, the sea, and all that is in them, and rested the seventh day. Therefore the LORD blessed the Sabbath day and hallowed it" (Exodus 20:8–11). It's one thing for nonbelievers to reject the validity of these verses, but for Christians to do so as well—even though these words were written by the finger of God Himself (Deuteronomy 9:10; Exodus 31:17, 18)—reveals the degree to which believers have been seduced by culture.

In the Genesis account, each day is depicted not only by *yom*, the Hebrew word for a twenty-four-hour day, but also with the refrain, repeated six times, "and there was evening and there was morning, day one," day two, day three, etc. (see Genesis 1:5, 8, 13, 19, 23, 31). This phrase depicts each day with the two overt, physical phenomena—an evening and a morning—that compose a single twenty-four-hour day as humans have experienced from antiquity. And though other cultures didn't always divide their days into twenty-four periods of an hour each, as we do, all understood the reality of an evening and a morning as the two major components of a single day (for the Jews, a new day began at sunset). An "evening and a morning," then, is a rather strange modifier to include if a text really meant billions of years instead of a twenty-four-hour day.

"The phrase 'evening and morning,'" wrote Richard Davidson, "appearing at the conclusion of each of the six days of creation, is used by the author to clearly define the nature of the days of creation as literal 24-hour days."[70] Outside of the Genesis 1 account of Creation, every reference to "evening and morning," either with the word for "day," *yom* (nineteen times), or without it (thirty-eight times), refers to a literal twenty-four-hour day, no exceptions. The inclusion of the phrase "and there was evening and there was morning" points to the reality of a single day, an evening and a morning as we experience them ourselves. Arguing that we need to try to determine what the author and the audience would have understood from the text, John Walton wrote that "it is extremely difficult to conclude that anything other than a twenty-four-hour day was intended. It is not the text that causes people to think otherwise, only the demands of trying to harmonize with modern science."[71]

And yet evolutionary science (like so much science) is at best—what? Twenty percent hardcore empirical evidence stretched and extrapolated into 80 percent speculation shaped by metaphysical assumptions constructed around culture, peer pressure, psychology, philosophy, and other variables that have nothing to do with the immediate science. Why pit such subjectivity against explicit biblical texts?

Another indication that the text means a literal six-day creation is the seventh-day Sabbath, which was intricately linked to the preceding six days and flows directly from them. "Then God saw everything that He had made, and indeed it was very good. So the evening and the morning were the sixth day. Thus the heavens and the earth, and all the host of them, were finished. And on the seventh day God ended His work which He had done, and He rested on the seventh day from all His work which He had done" (Genesis 1:31–2:2).

Any attempt to convert those six days into an allegory for eons is refuted by the fourth commandment itself: "Remember the Sabbath day, to keep it holy. Six days you shall labor and do all your work, but the seventh day is the Sabbath of the Lord your God. In it you shall do no work: you, nor your son, nor your daughter, nor your male servant, nor your female servant, nor your cattle, nor your stranger who is within your gates. For in six days the Lord made the heavens and the earth, the sea, and all that is in them, and rested the seventh day. Therefore the Lord blessed the Sabbath day and hallowed it" (Exodus 20:8–11).

Nothing in the text, nor its context, hints at anything other than a literal twenty-four-hour day. Many theistic evolutionists acknowledge that the author meant a literal seventh-day Sabbath that refers to the literal six-day creation preceding it. The only reason to believe that it's referring to anything else, billions of years, in fact, is the imposition of the present scientific paradigm. Otherwise, how much clearer or explicit could the text be?

Wherever one stands on the seventh-day Sabbath-Sunday question, the point remains: the seventh-day Sabbath, a literal twenty-four-hour period, has existed since antiquity as a weekly memorial of a six-day creation. To accept the evolutionary paradigm, a Christian would have to believe that God used every seventh day as a memorial of billions of years, as opposed to six literal days. Which would be problematic enough itself, even if He had not explicitly told us otherwise.

There is another problem if the six days of Creation, as expressed in Genesis 1–3 and in the Ten Commandments, are not an accurate depiction of what happened. "The irony of this conclusion," wrote John T. Baldwin, "is that in the original presentation of the Ten Commandments as recorded in Exodus 20, the ninth prohibits the bearing of false witness. But the progressive creationism theory causes God Himself to tell a lie in the fourth commandment, thereby transgressing His own law."[72]

What else could it be depicted as if not as outright deception?

Look at these verses from Genesis 1:

Then God said, "Let there be light"; and there was light. (v. 3)

Then God said, "Let the waters under the heavens be gathered together into one place, and let the dry land appear"; and it was so. (v. 9)

Then God said, "Let the earth bring forth grass, the herb that yields seed, and the fruit tree that yields fruit according to its kind, whose seed is in itself, on the earth"; and it was so. (v. 11)

Then God said, "Let Us make man in Our image, according to Our likeness. . . ." So God created man in His own image. (vv. 26, 27)

Everything was planned, precise, calculated; nothing random, arbitrary, or chancy. It would take a very strange interpretation to derive randomness out of Genesis 1. Nothing is left to chance, nothing. Everything is very precisely created in its time and in its place. Nothing even hints at randomness.

Second are these texts:

So God created great sea creatures and every living thing that moves, with which the waters abounded, according to their kind, and every winged bird according to its kind. . . . Then God said, "Let the earth bring forth the living creature according to its kind: cattle and creeping thing and beast of the earth, each according to its kind"; and it was so. And God made the beast of the earth according to its kind, cattle according to its kind, and everything that creeps on the earth according to its kind. (Genesis 1:21–25)

The texts reveal, unambiguously, that each creature was made after its own kind; that is, each one was made separately and distinctly from the others.

Even from a nonliteralist interpretation of Genesis, two points are obvious: nothing was random in the act of Creation, and there was no common ancestry for the species.

Now, along comes Darwinian evolution, which in its various incarnations teaches two things: (1) randomness and (2) common ancestry for all species. How, then, does one interpret Genesis through a theory that, at its most basic level, contradicts Genesis at its most basic level? As we have seen in the previous examples, the only way to do so is to interpret the text in a way that all but destroys various biblical teachings—the Cross, the reliability of Scripture, the origin of sin and death, the character of God, and the unique nature of humanity.

Beginnings and endings

Attempts to meld evolution with Scripture don't come without cost; whatever is gained in one hand is lost in another, except that the gain is grossly outweighed by the loss. Each step closer to the word of humanity takes people a greater step away from the Word of God; every inch toward Darwin is five away from Moses, Paul, even Jesus. Worse, evolution does its greatest damage at the biggest moments of biblical history.

If evolution is true, the Genesis account of origins teaches us almost nothing correct about how God created the world. Instead, it has for thousands of years led people astray with a fairy tale regarding what's arguably the most important question humans can ask: *Who are we?* It's hard to imagine more divergent worldviews than those of Genesis and evolution, even when theistic evolutionists clumsily shove a Creator into the mix.

Further down the timeline, evolution makes suspect, if not irrational, the atoning death of Jesus, which the Bible connects with the consequences of the actions of a literal Adam—"For if by the one man's offense many died, much more the grace of God and the gift by the grace of the one Man, Jesus Christ, abounded to many" (Romans 5:15). How does Christ undo what Adam did if the biblical depiction of a sinless and pristine Adam is "an incoherent idea"?

Otherwise, what? God used processes of violence, selfishness, and dominance of the strong against the weak in order to create a morally flawless and selfless being who then "falls" into a state of violence, selfishness, and dominance of the strong over the weak—a state from which he has to be redeemed or face final punishment? How ironic: the principles that God used to create people are the opposite of the principles those people are supposed to live by. Then are we not following God and the dictates of nature as He ordained it, when we advance our own interests at the expense of the less "naturally selected"? In an evolutionary paradigm, we should eliminate the weak, making way for those already closer to the "image of God"—the process in which all this pain and suffering and death was to culminate. *Homo erectus* didn't become *Homo sapiens* by following the golden rule, so why should we? Unless, that is, the Lord used a process of creation whose principles He condemns when they are expressed and manifested in those whom He created.

The premise of human sinfulness—derived from a sinless Adam who fell into sin by using his freedom—is the key doctrine upon which rests Christ's incarnation, ministry, death, and resurrection. The fall of a sinless Adam, whose fall Christ came to redeem, is a foundational doctrine of the Christian faith. No matter how unambiguous Paul was in Romans 5, linking a literal Christ to a literal Adam, theistic evolutionists have no choice but to discard everything in Scripture depicting Adam as a literal being—unless they want to embrace Ford's precarious move. Adam and Eve become symbols, like Romulus and Remus, the mythical founders of Rome.

When Paul writes, "For as in Adam all die, so in Christ all will be made alive" (1 Corinthians 15:22, NIV), to be consistent, shouldn't those who make a myth of the man in the first clause do the same for the man in the second? Or what about this text? "For as by one man's disobedience many were made sinners, so also by one Man's obedience many will be made righteous" (Romans

5:19). How does one spiritualize or allegorize away the first man without doing the same for the second, and what serious Christian is willing to do that to the second one, Jesus? But, to be consistent, what other choice do they have?

However, theistic evolution demolishes not just biblical teachings about protology (the study of first things and origins) and soteriology (the study of salvation). Eschatology (the study of last things) takes a big, if not fatal, hit too.

It's strange how many Christians will kowtow to every scientific pronouncement about Creation. Ready and willing, they will chip away at the most obvious meaning of the biblical texts in order to make room for Darwin, or they will allegorize verses into a hazy spiritual vapor easily configured to fit science's latest proclamation about origins. Yet these same Christians balk at science's claims about the *end* of all things. On protology, they surrender; on eschatology, they fight back.

Though scientists don't agree on the *how* of the end, they are all but unanimous on the *what*, which is that, in the long term, the universe and all life in it is doomed.

British physicist and astrobiologist Paul Davies wrote,

> The Milky Way blazes with the light of a hundred billion stars, and every one of them is doomed. In ten billion years, most that we see now will have faded from sight, snuffed out from lack of fuel. . . .
> . . . The universe, currently aglow with the prolific energy of nuclear power, will eventually exhaust this valuable resource. The era of light will be over forever.[73]

Whether the cosmos faces this thermodynamic equilibrium (a benign way of talking about the "cosmic heat death") or whether it's sucked into a black hole or compressed into a clump of dense matter the size of a fist or ripped apart (a few various scenarios scientists project for our very-long-term future)—the universe, scientists claim, cannot last forever. This position comes, of course, in stark contrast to biblical texts that refer to an eternal existence.

> And in the days of these kings the God of heaven will set up a kingdom which shall never be destroyed; and the kingdom shall not be left to other people; it shall break in pieces and consume all these kingdoms, and it shall stand forever. (Daniel 2:44)

> Those great beasts, which are four, are four kings which arise out of the earth. But the saints of the Most High shall receive the kingdom, and possess the kingdom forever, even forever and ever. (Daniel 7:17, 18)

There shall be no night there: They need no lamp nor light of the sun, for the Lord God gives them light. And they shall reign forever and ever. (Revelation 22:5)

What, too, about the texts regarding eternal life? "For the wages of sin is death, but the gift of God is eternal life in Christ Jesus our Lord" (Romans 6:23). Christ says of a believer, "I will raise him up at the last day" (John 6:54). Wonderful, but where is this redeemed one supposed to live in a destroyed universe?

Whatever reasons these Christians use to justify their acceptance of science's claims about origins but not about endings, evolutionary theory creates insuperable problems for biblical eschatology as well.

For starters, should the following texts about the re-creation of the heavens and earth be as radically reinterpreted as are the texts about the original Creation?

For behold, I create new heavens and a new earth;
And the former shall not be remembered or come to mind. (Isaiah 65:17)

"For as the new heavens and the new earth
Which I will make shall remain before Me," says the LORD,
"So shall your descendants and your name remain." (Isaiah 66:22)

Nevertheless we, according to His promise, look for new heavens and a new earth in which righteousness dwells. (2 Peter 3:13)

Will this new heaven and new earth be created by divine fiat—God speaks, and it is—something similar to what was unambiguously depicted in Genesis 1 and 2? Or will life have to endure, again, the rigor and joy of natural selection and survival of the fittest for billions of years until a new world, one "in which righteousness dwells" (2 Peter 3:13), finally appears? If God used billions of years to create the world the first time—with the vicious and violent process of evolution as the means—is that how He is going to do it the second time too?

If not, why not? If God restrained Himself in the first Creation, bestowing the "gift of a degree of letting-be" on the rocks, trees, and lions; or if "predation, death, and extinction" were "intrinsic to the processes that give rise to life on Earth in all its wonderful diversity" in the first Creation—shouldn't these same processes be intrinsic in the second? And if He does do it that way, what a radically different understanding of what Christians believe in regard to eschatology. What Christian, whose hope rests in a future creation of a new heaven and a new earth, thinks that it's going to happen through billions of years of evolution? But if God doesn't do it that way the second time, why did He do it that way the first, as we are assured He did by theistic evolutionists—leaning on the unchallenged authority of science shaped and limited by materialism?

The resurrection of the dead

Then, too, what about the resurrection of the dead—a central teaching of eschatology? Regardless of various postulations about the nature of the soul and/or the immediate fate that awaits the Christian at death, most serious Bible-believing Christians understand that their ultimate hope is found in the resurrection of the physical body at the end of time, as Scripture teaches.

"If there is no resurrection of the dead, then Christ is not risen. And if Christ is not risen, then our preaching is empty and your faith is also empty. Yes, and we are found false witnesses of God, because we have testified of God that He raised up Christ, whom He did not raise up—if in fact the dead do not rise. For if the dead do not rise, then Christ is not risen. And if Christ is not risen, your faith is futile; you are still in your sins!" (1 Corinthians 15:13–17).

How much clearer could the apostle Paul be when he linked our resurrection directly to Christ's? Instead of going forward from Christ's resurrection to the believer's, he's working backward (at least from a Western perspective), from effect to cause. If we are not resurrected (effect), then Christ wasn't, either (the cause). And though saying little about specific events in Christ's life, Paul said a lot about Christ's resurrection, because in His resurrection (the cause) exists the surety of our resurrection (the effect). Unless one takes these texts, too, "seriously but not literally," then without the physical resurrection of the faithful at the end of time, the Christian hope is futile and meaningless.

Paul continues: "But now Christ is risen from the dead, and has become the firstfruits of those who have fallen asleep. For since by man came death, by Man also came the resurrection of the dead. For as in Adam all die, even so in Christ all shall be made alive. But each one in his own order: Christ the firstfruits, afterward those who are Christ's at His coming" (1 Corinthians 15:20–23).

Adam falls; Christ redeems the fall. And through Christ's resurrection (the redemption of that fall), we have the promise of our resurrection as well. But what happens to Paul's argument if a literal sinless Adam is, as Murphy argues, a nonstarter? The theology—from a literal Adam to a literal Jesus to a literal resurrection of the dead at the end—so central to the Christian's faith, has its foundation kicked out even before it begins once a literal Adam is spiritualized away, precisely what theistic evolutionists must do.

And what about the physical resurrection of the redeemed? Though purely a supernatural act, how long is it supposed to take? In the following texts, Paul depicts the resurrection of the saints at the end of time; and, if his words are taken at face value—that is, literally *and* seriously (as opposed to just seriously but not literally)—he sure makes the resurrection sound instantaneous.

> But I do not want you to be ignorant, brethren, concerning those who have fallen asleep, lest you sorrow as others who have no hope. For if we believe that Jesus died and rose again, even so God will bring with Him those who sleep in Jesus. For this we say to you by the word of the Lord, that we who are alive and remain until the coming of the Lord will by no means precede those who are asleep. For the Lord Himself will descend from heaven with a shout, with the voice of an archangel, and with the trumpet of God. And the dead in Christ will rise first. (1 Thessalonians 4:13–16)

> Behold, I tell you a mystery: We shall not all sleep, but we shall all be changed—in a moment, in the twinkling of an eye, at the last trumpet. For the trumpet will sound, and the dead will be raised incorruptible, and we shall be changed. For this corruptible must put on incorruption, and this mortal must put on immortality. (1 Corinthians 15:51–53)

The dead rise—and do so, incorruptible. And this transformation from death to eternal (immortal) life happens in a moment, in the twinkling of an eye—a creation process that sounds as contrary to evolution as does the Creation in Genesis.

What, then, are we supposed to believe, according to a theistic evolutionary model, about the resurrection? God uses a long, protracted process taking billions of years to, finally, create out of the earth itself *Homo sapiens*—beings originally made in His image? These all die and then disintegrate into constituent parts that, over the ages, become scattered atoms only. What about those who became corpses in 2500 B.C. or those burned at the stake 500 years ago or those whose bodies, after weeks in the water, have been devoured by sharks, crabs, whatever? By the time of their resurrection, how much is left for God to work with? Nevertheless, "in a moment, in the twinkling of an eye," they are re-created, resurrected, and given immortality. God will take a corpse eaten by crabs in the Aegean Sea 2,400 years ago and, instantaneously, restore it not just to life but to eternal life!

How does this happen? Even the staunchest theistic evolutionist can't possibly believe (though Edwards might accept something like this) that this second creation of humanity will be done through the same processes as the first one. Considering that those resurrected will be resurrected as humans, immortal ones at that, from precursors much more primitive than whatever the immediate precursors to image-of-God-humanity were supposed to be, why would the Lord do it instantly the second time while the first creation took billions of years?

And where is the speculation here in this second creation about the "gift of a degree of letting-be" or about God giving life "the freedom to be themselves and to make themselves, without being overwhelmed by the naked presence of infinite Reality"? The acceptance of current scientific theories about origins (which readers should know by now aren't anywhere near as solid as popularly portrayed) has forced theistic evolutionists to ram this alien ideology into Scripture regarding the original Creation. Yet, regarding our second one, it all falls by the way.

Why?

Besides the obvious fact that they don't believe God will use billions of years of evolution as the means of resurrecting the dead, they could argue that the resurrection at the end of time is a supernatural event, outside the purview of science, which would therefore mean that science has nothing to say about it. Of course, the claim that the supernatural is outside of science is a philosophical assumption, not a direct scientific conclusion.

But according to Scripture, the first Creation was also a purely supernatural act. God speaks and it becomes real. God creates man out of the dust of the ground, and breathes into him the breath of life. God puts Adam to sleep and creates Eve out of his rib. What can science possibly teach us about these acts of Creation, other than that, based on its presuppositions, they did not happen? What else could science teach us about a supernatural creation when, a priori, it dismisses the supernatural as the means of creation? (Think, again, of a detective investigating a murder who, a priori, assumes the guilty person innocent; whomever else the detective arrests for the crime will, of necessity, be the wrong one.) Instead, given its own philosophical presuppositions, science has assumed a naturalistic scenario that automatically rules out the supernatural picture depicted in Scripture. Hence, because of its philosophical assumption of naturalism, science has become as useless in depicting what God has done in the past, at the first Creation, as it is about what He will do in the future, at the second one.

And so, what happens when Christians, adopting a scenario formulated upon naturalism, impose the supernatural on it? This chapter has shown what happens: the biblical Creation, "in the beginning," is allegorized into a fairy tale; the biblical atonement of Christ's death on the cross becomes grounded upon a lie (because no sinless Adam existed); and the biblical depiction of the new creation, the resurrection of the dead at the end of time, lapses into absurdity.

None of this would be necessary but for what has dogged faith from the start—the overwhelming power of culture, of myth (though at the time it's believed, it is not deemed "myth"). And, in this case, the cultural myth is the dogmatic certainty of science, especially when speculating, through numerous philosophical assumptions, about a reality forever out of its immediate reach—and that is, life's origins.

---

1. *The Complete Poems: Anne Sexton* (New York: Mariner Books, 1999), 349.

2. Michael Dowd, *Thank God for Evolution: How the Marriage of Science and Religion Will Transform Your Life and Our World* (New York: Viking, 2008).

3. Quoted in ibid., Kindle edition, front matter.

4. Quoted in ibid.

5. Ibid., under "Author's Promises."

6. Ibid., chap. 4 (italics added).

7. Ibid., chap. 5.

8. Ibid.

9. Jacques B. Doukhan, " 'When Death Was Not Yet': The Testimony of Biblical Creation," in Klingbeil, *Genesis Creation Account,* 340.

10. Norman R. Gulley, "What Happens to Biblical Truth if the SDA Church Accepts Theistic Evolution?" *Journal of the Adventist Theological Society* 15, no. 2 (Autumn 2004): 48.

11. John Polkinghorne, *Belief in God in an Age of Science* (New Haven, CT: Yale University Press, 1998).

12. Ibid., 5.

13. Meanwhile, Polkinghorne does show a healthy understanding of the limits of science, writing in another work: "The intertwining of theory and experiment, inextricably linked by the need to interpret experimental data, does indeed imply that there is an unavoidable degree of circularity involved in scientific reasoning. This means that the nature of science is something more subtle and rationally delicate than simply ineluctable deduction from unquestionable fact. A degree of intellectual daring is required, which means that ultimately the aspiration to write about the *logic* of scientific discovery proves to be a misplaced ambition." Polkinghorne, *Quantum Physics and Theology,* 5 (italics in the original).

14. Polkinghorne, *Belief in God,* 13, 14.

15. John Polkinghorne, *Science and Religion in Quest of Truth* (New Haven, CT: Yale University Press, 2011), 106, 107.

16. The concept of moral freedom is seen, first, in Eden, with Adam and Eve. Here they were, in the midst of a wonderful garden filled with many other trees, all of them freely available for the pair to eat from, except from the tree of the "knowledge of good and evil." The existence of the tree of the knowledge of good and evil was, it seems, a test of loyalty. Would these morally free beings, given so much, obey this one command? The stark reality of that freedom became apparent in their blatant abuse of it. "When the woman saw that the tree was good for food, that it was pleasant to the eyes, and a tree desirable to make one wise, she took of its fruit and ate. She also gave to her husband with her, and he ate" (Genesis 3:6). Perfect beings, created by a perfect God, in a perfect world, nevertheless were capable of disobedience. And God did not stop them, either. He respected their moral freedom. He had to; if He wanted them to love Him, they had to be truly free. Thus here, at the foundation of the world, and of humanity itself, the

principles of freedom inherent in God's government, a moral government based on love, are made manifest.

This moral freedom can be seen, in fact, even further back than in Eden. Talking about Lucifer, an angel in heaven, the Bible records God saying to him:

> You were the seal of perfection,
> Full of wisdom and perfect in beauty.
> . . . .
> You were the anointed cherub who covers;
> I established you;
> You were on the holy mountain of God;
> You walked back and forth in the midst of fiery stones.
> You were perfect in your ways from the day you were created,
> Till iniquity was found in you. Ezekiel 28:12–15.

First, Lucifer was a perfect being created by a perfect God, just as Adam and Eve were. Only Lucifer was in a perfect heaven, while Adam and Eve were on a perfect earth. Also, the Hebrew word for "created" in the texts about Lucifer (from the root *bara*) is the same root used in Genesis 1:1 ("In the beginning God *created* the heavens and the earth" [italics added]). The verb exists in the Old Testament only in the context of God's creative activity. Only God can *bara*. Nevertheless, what happened to Lucifer, a being created (*bara*) by God? "Iniquity was found" in him. But how could this be, unless, as with Adam and Eve in Eden, Lucifer in heaven had moral freedom? This iniquity could not have arisen were not the potential for it already there. And how could that potential have not been there if moral freedom existed in the perfect environment of heaven, similar to the way it existed on earth in Eden?

Thus, as far back as the Word of God takes us, the freedom inherent in love is revealed. God created Lucifer, as well as Adam and Eve, with the ability to obey or disobey. Otherwise, they wouldn't really be free, and without freedom they couldn't love. Here is the origin of evil, pain, and suffering.

17. John C. Polkinghorne, *Science and Providence: God's Interaction With the World* (Philadelphia: Templeton Foundation Press, 2005), 78.

18. Robin Collins, "Divine Action and Evolution," in Flint and Rea, *Oxford Handbook of Philosophical Theology.*

19. Ibid., 241.

20. Ibid., 243.

21. Coyne, *Faith Versus Fact*, 147.

22. David C. Lindberg, "That the Rise of Christianity Was Responsible for the Demise of Ancient Science," in *Galileo Goes to Jail, and Other Myths About Science and Religion*, ed. Ronald L. Numbers (Cambridge, MA: Harvard University Press, 2009), 18.

23. Quoted in Ricard and Trinh, *Quantum and the Lotus*, 238 (italics in the original).

24. Collins, "Divine Action and Evolution," in Flint and Rea, *Oxford Handbook of Philosophical Theology*, 243.

25. Quoted in ibid., 244.

26. Quoted in ibid.

27. Ibid., 244, 245.

28. Ibid., 245.

29. Ibid., 247. He stresses, too, that these "interconnections" are not the sole reason that God created in an evolutionary manner, but "only that they provide one reason."

30. Ibid., 258.

31. Ibid., 256.
32. Quoted in ibid., 259.
33. Ibid., 252.
34. Denis Edwards, "Why Is God Doing This? Suffering, the Universe, and Christian Eschatology," in *Physics and Cosmology: Scientific Perspectives on the Problem of Natural Evil, Volume 1*, ed. Nancey Murphy, Robert John Russell, and William R. Stoeger (Vatican City State: Vatican Observatory Publications; Berkeley, CA: Center for Theology and the Natural Sciences, 2007), 248.
35. Ibid.
36. Nancey Murphy, "Introduction," in Murphy, Russell, and Stoeger, *Physics and Cosmology*, xii.
37. Ibid.
38. Thomas F. Tracy, "The Lawfulness of Nature and the Problem of Evil," in Murphy, Russell, and Stoeger, *Physics and Cosmology*, 171.
39. Nancey Murphy, "Science and the Problem of Evil: Suffering as a By-Product of a Finely Tuned Cosmos," in Murphy, Russell, and Stoeger, *Physics and Cosmology*, 140.
40. Ibid., 131.
41. Ibid., 151.
42. Sigve K. Tonstad, *God of Sense and Traditions of Non-Sense* (Eugene, OR: Wipf and Stock, 2016).
43. Quoted in ibid., 47.
44. Murphy, "Suffering as a By-Product," in Murphy, Russell, and Stoeger, *Physics and Cosmology*, 140 (italics in the original).
45. Ibid.
46. VanDoodewaard, *Quest for the Historical Adam*, Kindle edition.
47. Murphy, "Suffering as a By-Product," in Murphy, Russell, and Stoeger, *Physics and Cosmology*, 135.
48. Ibid. (italics added).
49. Ibid.
50. Edwards, "Why Is God Doing This?" in Murphy, Russell, and Stoeger, *Physics and Cosmology*, 264.
51. Philip Clayton and Steven Knapp, "Divine Action and the 'Argument From Neglect,'" in Murphy, Russell, and Stoeger, *Physics and Cosmology*, 183.
52. Ibid. (italics in the original).
53. Quoted in VanDoodewaard, *Quest for the Historical Adam*, Kindle edition.
54. See Romans 5:12–19; 1 Corinthians 15:21, 22, 45; 1 Timothy 2:13, 14; 1 Corinthians 11:8, 9.
55. Arthur Peacocke, "The Challenge of Science to Theology and the Church," in *The New Faith-Science Debate: Probing Cosmology, Technology, and Theology*, ed. John M. Mangum (Minneapolis: Fortress Press, 1989), 16.
56. Desmond Ford, *Genesis Versus Darwinism: The Demise of Darwin's Theory of Evolution* (Desmond Ford, 2015), 165.
57. Ibid., 158.
58. Ibid., 156, 157.
59. Ibid., 65.
60. Ibid., 154.
61. Ibid., 164.
62. Ibid., 154.
63. Ibid., xi.

64. Ibid., 155.

65. Collins, *The Language of God*, back cover.

66. Ibid., 131.

67. Ibid., 201.

68. Richard Dawkins, *A Devil's Chaplain* (Boston: Houghton Mifflin, 2003), 22 (italics in the original).

69. See Victor J. Stenger, *God: The Failed Hypothesis* (Amherst, NY: Prometheus Books, 2007). The front cover claims, "How Science Shows That God Does Not Exist."

70. Davidson, "The Genesis Account of Origins," in Klingbeil, *Genesis Creation Account*, 78.

71. John H. Walton, *The NIV Application Commentary: Genesis* (Grand Rapids, MI: Zondervan, 2001), 81.

72. John T. Baldwin, "Progressive Creationism and Biblical Revelation: Some Theological Implications," *Journal of the Adventist Theological Society* 3, no. 1 (Spring 1992): 112.

73. Paul Davies, *The Last Three Minutes* (New York: BasicBooks, 1994), 49, 50.

CHAPTER 11

THE WISDOM OF THE WORLD

osmologist Stephen Hawking began his famous *A Brief History of Time* with a story, often retold but losing none of its point for all its retelling. In one version, Bertrand Russell—having just lectured on the orbit of the earth around the sun—was confronted by a little old lady in tennis shoes who said, "Everyone knows that the earth sits on the back of a giant turtle." Russell, jesting, responded, "What does that turtle sit on, ma'am?" Without missing a beat, she answered, "Another turtle." When he began to ask what that turtle sat on, she cut him short, saying, "Save your breath, sonny; it's turtles all the way down."

Wrote Hawking, "Most people would find the picture of our universe as an infinite tower of tortoises rather ridiculous, but why do we think we know better? What do we know about the universe, and how do we know it?"[1]

Hawking had a point, as did the little old lady, too, even if hers went beyond the ontology of the universe to something more fundamental, and that is the nature of knowledge itself, especially about the natural world.

"Nature," wrote Heraclitus, "loves to hide."[2]

It did then, 2,500 years ago, when Heraclitus wrote; and it does today, especially when the nature that one is investigating is, supposedly, hundreds of millions or even billions of years old. If aspects of life today—scanned, dissected, X-rayed, MRI-ed, proton-beamed, assayed, catalogued, etc.—remain elusive, what other than bluster can explain the dogmatism with which we are assured that millions of years ago whale ancestors were originally warm-blooded land creatures who then migrated to the seas before evolving into the spouting and splashing leviathans we see today?[3]

Despite all the propaganda about objectivity, science, like most knowledge, exists only within a system, the framework through which it interprets the world. Science does so maybe even more so than most disciplines, because the scientific-industrial complex has sharply dogmatized the boundaries of its system. The system, the paradigm, functions as the lens, the filter, and template through which reality is interpreted. The paradigm itself isn't questioned; on the contrary, it provides grist for the questions. The paradigm is to the questions what grammar, logic, and language are to this sentence.

Every now and then someone steps back and questions the system, whether in science or something else—which is fine. But upon what premises are the new questions established? New questions presuppose new assumptions, a new starting point beyond, and outside, the old. Fine, but upon what is that new foundation based? How can you test the system other than by going outside of it, which requires a new foundation, a new system? Again, no problem, assuming that the new foundation is valid. But that can be questioned only by going outside of it, and on and on . . . *It's turtles all the way down!* We have to stop with something, because sooner or later we have to base our beliefs on something.[4]

And this goes especially for the theory of evolution, which by nature must work with speculations and assumptions about things that don't even exist. It's one thing to study the moon or the endocrine system of the bullfrog; it's radically another to study objects or events that, according to your paradigm, were supposed to have existed or happened millions or billions of years ago. Despite the indefatigable agitprop that assures the world that only ignorant buffoons don't believe in the macroevolutionary paradigm, the paradigm itself is an edifice built upon assumptions and speculations built upon assumptions and speculations, most if not all of which can be (or already have been) challenged.

It's like the question "Have you stopped beating your wife?" Assuming that you were beating your wife, that's a logical question. But if you never did, the question presupposes a false reality—and that's what this book postulates that the evolutionary paradigm does. It presupposes a false reality, one that by constant repetition and constant promotion has ensnared millions, even those who ideally should know better, because they have an outside source, one inspired by the Creator[5] as opposed to the creatures themselves.

Groundless

But doesn't Christianity do something similar? Doesn't Christianity, too, reach a point where justification stops, a point where our arguments hit an end point, and then we just have to base our beliefs on something?

Of course. But Christianity comes with the realization of our epistemological limits built in. It's called "faith," and far from being a weakness (as faith is in science), faith is an integral part of that system. It's as if God knew beforehand our human limits and thus built that realization into the system of truth itself, even made it a fundamental component.

In a sense, both science and Christianity are groundless, in that both work within frameworks built upon unproven assumptions, things that have to be taken on, well, faith. The big difference is that for Christianity faith isn't an admission of weakness or failure. On the contrary, faith is an essential part of the package, an a priori acknowledgement that the foundations of knowledge can take us only so far, and then we have to step out beyond the seen or the proven. "Faith is being sure of what we hope for. It is being sure of what we do not see" (Hebrews 11:1, NIrV).

However different their approaches, Christianity and science are both faith ventures—systems of belief that, in and of themselves, can't get us to that bottom turtle even though we know it's there. Whether we're seeking it as tiny superstring loops in ten-dimensional space or as quantum fields or as God Himself, sooner or later faith (another word, perhaps, for assumptions and presuppositions?) fills in where our inquiry inevitably ends.

Years ago, a Christian creationist was confronted by a theistic evolutionist. "Scientists have discovered fossil remains of fish more than fifty million years old," he declared with the certainty that only evolutionists (theistic or atheistic) can exude.

The creationist responded, "So your claim that fossil remains of fish more than fifty million years old have been found is an apodictic statement deduced from universal, necessary, and certain principles, right?"

Of course not. It was a rhetorical question designed to show the evolutionist that, regardless of whether the claim was true, his statement was based on assumptions that were hardly universal, necessary, and certain.

Now, that evolutionist might have had what he believed were good reasons for that belief, based on those assumptions. He might even have had reasons that anyone, confronted with the evidence, could find compelling for that belief, again based on those assumptions. He might even have had what many would see as good reasons for holding those assumptions.

But none of this guarantees that his belief is true. It's a statement built upon other beliefs, all of which sooner or later bottom out. In short, it is still a "faith" statement, in the sense that somewhere along the line unproven things have to be assumed.

"In the end," continued the creationist, "we all have to put our faith in something, don't we?"

The question is: *In what?*

"The only game in town"

Despite the constant flackery that evolution—the inorganic-material-to-*Homo-sapiens*-undirected-over-billions-of-years version—has been "proven" by none other than science itself, the evolutionary scenario remains a cultural phenomenon, one buttressed by the epistemology gravitas of the scientific-industrial complex, which has assumed an authority that none dare challenge without the certitude of ridicule.

But remember how this began. Darwin didn't start from an überobjective neutral zone when he proposed his theory. Working from an erroneous view of what evil in the creation revealed about God (or even if God existed), Darwin proposed an alternative explanation for that creation and for the evil in it. Even before noticing the variations in finch beaks[6]—from which he later surmised that all life on earth (plants, animals, trees, bugs, fish, human beings) in its amazing complexity evolved over billions of years from a simple chemical organic compound—Darwin already believed in evolution. He just theorized natural selection as the mechanism.

However—and this is crucial—long before much of the touted "evidence" for evolution (readers of this book should know by now how subjective evidence can be, especially for events occurring supposedly millions or even billions of years out of our immediate reach), an effective amen corner in England and the United States, including prominent Christians, had put the theory on the map, long before all the "overwhelming," "absolute," "unassailable," "uncontestable," "undeniable," and "certain" evidence had been found for it.

Talking about biologist Thomas Huxley, "Darwin's bulldog," author Tom Wolfe wrote,

> In June of 1860, he starred in a much-written-about British Association for the Advancement of Science debate over Evolution against the Church of England's most renowned public speaker, Bishop Samuel Wilberforce. He went on to create the X Club, a group of nine prominent naturalists, including Hooker, who met every month at some restaurant or a club and set about—very successfully—stacking influential university science faculties with Darwinists. The X Clubbers had a big hand in creating the pro-Darwinist journal *Nature* (which thrives to this day). They attacked every Darwin doubter the moment he dared raise his voice. That mode of intimidation only intensified over time, leading to what is still known today as "the Neo-Darwinist Inquisition."[7]

From the start (this was 1860!), Darwinian marketing and public relations apparatchiks (today "the Neo-Darwinist Inquisition") have always been much more successful in promoting the culture of Darwinism than scientists have been in "proving" it. The PR has worked phenomenally, which explains why millions unquestionably accept the theory, despite unsolved problems in most every nook and cranny. The evolutionary model is just assumed, part of the cultural landscape, like Sunday football in America, Bastille Day in France, and the royals in Great Britain.

"Despite its obvious failure," wrote Michael Denton, "Darwinism has retained its hypnotic hold on the biological mind primarily because cumulative selection has been 'the only game in town.'"[8]

And no wonder. With the help of "Darwin's bulldog" and his X Club, "the only game in town" became the only game, period. Generations of young scientists were taught not to question the evolution paradigm, but to interpret all that they saw through it. Everything—from the function of the Golgi apparatus[9] to how humans can do math[10]—is seen through the lens of evolution.

How not? Because they already assume that it's true, it's no surprise that they always find evidence for it, no matter where they look. "Facts," wrote Mary Midgley, "are not gathered in a vacuum, but to fill gaps in a world-picture which already exists."[11]

A whale spout? No problem. Evolution explains it. The human love of music? A no-brainer. Natural selection and random mutation. The color of a peacock feather? Survival of the fittest. Human consciousness? What else, but the amazing process of biological evolution? Human cruelty? Evolution has got it covered. Human altruism? Evolution explains that too.

"Such assumptions," wrote Whitehead, "appear so obvious that people do not know what they are assuming because no other way of putting things has ever occurred to them."[12]

It's like the Aristotelian/Ptolemaic geocentric cosmos, tweaked, modified, revamped, and reinterpreted to make recalcitrant data fit. The same is true of Darwinism, the Aristotelianism of today, and just as erroneous. With enough tweaking, revamping, revising, retrodicting, expanding, speculating, whatever (or with what has been called by Imre Lakatos a "protective belt"[13] of auxiliary hypotheses)—every anomaly can be made to fit. Those, meanwhile, who don't get with the program face, to one degree or another, a modern version of what Galileo faced when he challenged the Darwinism of his day.

The wisdom of the world

For now, even with the edifice cracking, the cultural dominance of Darwinism is complete, at least among the intellectual elites and the high priests of those elites, the scientists. Unfortunately, this cultural hegemony has seeped into the church, which helps explain the tortured apologia in chapter 10.

"What is a little more difficult to understand, at least at first," wrote Phillip E. Johnson,

is the strong support Darwinism continues to receive in the Christian academic world. Attempts to investigate the credibility of the Darwinist evolution story are regarded with little enthusiasm by many leading Christian professors of science and philosophy, even at institutions which are generally regarded as conservative in theology. Given that Darwinism is inherently naturalistic and therefore antagonistic to the idea that God had anything to do with the history of life, and that it plays the central role in ensuring agnostic domination of the intellectual culture, one might have supposed that Christian intellectuals (along with religious Jews) would be eager to find its weak spots.[14]

Most don't; those who do are, unfortunately, the exceptions. How sad, too, that some of the most vigorous attacks against biblical creationism come from within Christianity itself. Ron Osborn's *Death Before the Fall* is a full-frontal assault by a Christian myrmidon against a "fundamentalist" (i.e., a literal six-day creation) reading of Scripture. This book speaks against the ignorance, shallowness, fear, intellectual vacuity, rigidness, lack of self-criticism, "spirit of censure,"[15] intolerance, irrationality, "foreclosed identities,"[16] and so forth of conservative creationists. Osborn wrote an imaginative chapter conjuring up parallels ("Anxiety," "Alienation and Suspicion," "Nostalgia," "Elitism," "Salvation by Knowledge," "Surrealism," "Authoritarianism and Absolutism"[17]) between biblical creationists of today and the gnostic heretics of New Testament antiquity.

Why such calumny against Christians who believe what God said in one of the Ten Commandments ("For in six days the LORD made the heavens and the earth, the sea, and all that is in them, and rested the seventh day" [Exodus 20:11]) over, for instance, the texts in the latest findings in the journal *Nature,* with such articles as "The Seahorse Genome and the Evolution of Its Specialized Morphology"[18] or "Evolution: How Snakes Lost Their Legs"?[19]

Yet one wonders: Have Christians like Ron Osborn really thought through the implications of their beliefs? If these people are correct, even if only in their assumption that theistic evolution is how God created life on earth, it means *what?*

It means that even though Scripture teaches that God created the present world in six days ("and there was evening and there was morning, day . . ."), He didn't.

It means that though Scripture says that God "rested on the seventh day from all His work which He had done" (Genesis 2:2), He didn't.

It means that though Scripture teaches that God made each kind[20] separate one from another, "each according to its kind" (Genesis 1:24), He didn't.

It means that though Scripture says that "the LORD God formed man of the dust of the ground, and breathed into his nostrils the breath of life; and man became a living being" (Genesis 2:7), He didn't.

It means that though Scripture teaches that "the rib which the Lord God had taken from man He made into a woman, and He brought her to the man" (Genesis 2:22), He didn't.

It means that though God said "Behold, I Myself am bringing floodwaters on the earth, to destroy from under heaven all flesh in which is the breath of life; everything that is on the earth shall die" (Genesis 6:17), He didn't.

It means that though Scripture teaches that "just as through one man sin entered the world, and death through sin" (Romans 5:12), that's not what happened, because death was built in from the start.

It means that when Scripture teaches that "as in Adam all die, even so in Christ all shall be made alive" (1 Corinthians 15:22), it's false because a pristine, sinless Adam could not have existed.

What all these together mean is that though Scripture says God "cannot lie" (Titus 1:2), He can, and has, even about Creation and the most important theological truths. And worse, it means that God spread those lies through the Holy Scriptures, the one foundational and authoritative record He left to humanity about Creation and the origin of life on earth.

All this, despite Christians having millennia of historical examples of believers compromising truth with the "wisdom of this world" (1 Corinthians 3:19), including when this wisdom came packaged, as in the Galileo trial, as "science." The text says, too, that this worldly wisdom is "foolishness with God" (ibid.). If, only, people could transcend the worldview wired into their DNA from their culture (supposedly Scripture should help people transcend their culture, but how can it when it, too, is subsumed by the culture it is supposed to transcend?) they would see how implausible the paradigm is. Ancient creation myths seem less foolish than what modern science declares to be the means of human origins. Nevertheless, in our culture today, common sense, reason, and the plain testimony of Scripture are squelched before science's ex cathedra claims.

And what does science claim, at least at present, regarding the world's origins?

The scientific theory du jour (these theories tend to come and go) is that our universe arose out of nothing.[21] Even most creation myths have enough common sense to start with something but, according to what some scientists tell us, the cancellation of two nothings created the universe and everything in it, and who dare argue with scientists?

Then, out of this nascent universe created from two nothings canceling each other out, gravity caused massive clumps of burning material to form. One eventually cooled down to become the early earth. Over billions of years,

primitive chemicals and natural processes became complicated organic molecules. These molecules somehow (and, as Robert Hazen has said, no one knows
how) became living cells. However, this spontaneous generation from nonlife
to life didn't occur through random mutation or natural selection, because
genes weren't yet formed, so they couldn't randomly mutate—and how could
inorganic material be naturally selected?

However they arose, these spontaneously generated cells managed to replicate themselves and, over billions of years of random mutation and natural
selection, evolve into everything from fruit flies to brontosauruses to human
beings. (Also, one wonders what forces of natural selection and random mutation would turn these early cells into seventy-ton dinosaurs so long ago? What
a process of natural selection and random mutation that must have been!)

Besides mutating into everything else alive on earth, these cells eventually
morphed into human brains endowed with rational self-awareness and self-
consciousness. Beginning with nonthinking, nonconscious material—"air,
water, and rock"[22]—and through the natural process of chemistry and physics,
our conscious minds arose. In this paradigm, enforced by the hegemons of
the scientific-industrial complex, our abilities to love, to create, to think about
ourselves are merely the lawful actions of material entities and the mechanical
forces operating on them, because whether in molten rocks well above 1000°C,
a thermal vent, or a shallow pool, that's all they ever were to begin with.

One doesn't have to be a biblical creationist to be skeptical. In his article
titled "Against Materialism," Laurence BonJour wrote that "there is no good
reason for any strong presumption in favor of materialism; and the main materialist view fails to offer any real explanation of a central aspect of mental
states, namely their conscious character, meaning that there is no good reason
to think that it is correct as an account of such states."[23]

Again, this current model, based on the philosophical assumptions of the
prevailing culture, insists that our consciousness—just like placentas, strawber-
ries, and whale spouts—arose only by random mutation and natural selection
in a universe that came out of two nothings canceling each other out and
creating all that exists.

Now, one could probably create a small library of detailed, scholarly, peer-
reviewed scientific papers about all these amazing evolutionary happenings.
But so many unanswered questions about human consciousness (it remains
one of the greatest mysteries of our existence) remain unsolved, even though
our minds can be X-rayed, dissected, and studied in minute detail every day
in labs all over the world. And yet even when answers to questions about our
minds today are far beyond us, we are to take seriously speculations and assumptions about how our brains, and the self-awareness and self-consciousness

associated with them, supposedly evolved millions of years ago? When all these detailed, scholarly, peer-reviewed scientific papers by renowned scientists in well-established journals, with tons of endnotes referencing other detailed, scholarly, peer-reviewed scientific papers by other renowned scientists in other well-established journals, assure us that millions of years ago human consciousness evolved through random mutation and natural selection, one thing is certain. Whatever profound new ideas are propounded from this research, whatever new breakthroughs are discovered, or even whatever great new technology might arise—it's all built upon assumptions and presuppositions and speculations built on assumptions and speculations whose justifications ran out long before the theories reached whatever conclusions they expect us to believe.

Of course, here is where theistic evolutionists would chime in, saying, *No, it wasn't by those processes alone; Jesus Himself started and guided it.* After all, according to the Bible Jesus was the Creator. "Without Him nothing was made that was made" (John 1:3). From a biblical perspective, therefore, Christ was the one who, according to the theologians in chapter 10, created life through the long, drawn-out process of evolution, with evil built in from the start, despite the inconvenient fact that the biblical texts teach nothing about a long, drawn-out process of evolution with evil built in from the start.

At this point, the argument will of necessity turn to interpretation, to hermeneutics, to how one reads the text. Fair enough. But even if one rejects a literal reading of Genesis, what reasonable way exists to read the evolutionary model into Scripture? When you have to argue that the Adam and Eve of Genesis 1–3 are different beings, separated by one hundred thousand years, from the Adam and Eve in the next verse, Genesis 4:1—you are no longer doing serious exegesis. You are turning the texts into wax in order to fit them into whatever form the predominant ethos of the culture takes (in this case, the form of science). Ford, Murphy, Collins, and the others are simply making the Bible jibe with the latest in science, because they believe the science over any reasonable reading of the texts.

And what happens if the science is wrong? We get everything from two Adams and two Eves, to no Adam and no Eve, to God creating via evolution in order to protect creatures from "being overwhelmed by the naked presence of infinite Reality."[24] Atheists such as Jerry Coyne see how strained and ad hoc it all is. "Of course," he wrote, "more liberal theologians have rushed into the breach with some solutions. But in the end they're worse than the problem, for the solutions are so clearly contrived that they can hardly be taken seriously."[25]

He's right. The argument for evolution as a means of creation that spares creatures from "being overwhelmed by the naked presence of infinite Reality" shows the absurd lengths needed in order to make the Word fit culture. If your hermeneutics allow you to read billions of years of suffering, extinction, and death into texts that teach only six days of creation with no suffering, extinction, or death, then you can read any ideology from any source into the Bible and make it say anything you want, which means the Word of God becomes null and void.

As we saw, philosopher of science Karl Popper (see chapter 5) argued, metaphorically, that science was like a structure built over a swamp. "Science does not rest upon solid bedrock," wrote Popper. "The bold structure of its theories rises, as it were, above a swamp. It is like a building erected on piles. The piles are driven down from above into the swamp, but not down to any natural or 'given' base; and if we stop driving the piles deeper, it is not because we have reached firm ground. We simply stop when we are satisfied that the piles are firm enough to carry the structure, at least for the time being."[26]

If true for the sciences that theorize about the present, about things now—turtles, quasars, human consciousness—how much deeper and murkier must the swamp get when composed of hypothetical events out of the reach of the structure above it and that have never been observed and never will be, because they are forever buried in the mire of the past? Those in the structure can function, make predictions, create technology, get peer-reviewed papers published by others sharing their paradigm, and even create an entire intellectual and technological complex right there on the surface of the swamp, or down just far enough to be certain that "the piles are firm enough to carry the structure." It's especially easy to maintain the structure when whatever is pulled from below is, by default, interpreted through the only allowed paradigm—and even easier when what doesn't fit is ignored, rejected, or assumed to be something that the paradigm will eventually explain, rather than something that threatens it. The stability is assured even more when by common consent anything outside the paradigm is derided, demeaned, and dumped into the same category as Holocaust denial. No question, in this context the structure functions; it works; it's sustainable; it propagates itself; it creates its own narratives; and it grows—no matter the muck that underpins it.

And what that muck has done to Christians who have allowed it to underpin their theology is a modern manifestation of what happens when the faithful incorporate culture into faith, no matter how contrary to faith. The only difference between theistic evolutionists and atheists such as Richard Dawkins is that Dawkins doesn't believe God started the process or had anything to do with it unfolding. On most everything else—the timing; the means; the eons of death, extinction, suffering; the specific processes themselves (whether God-guided or not)—professed Bible-believing Christians dance in a tango with Richard Dawkins and his atheist ilk. What does it say about the spell of culture when educated, intelligent, and well-meaning Christians have more in common with the author of *The God Delusion* than with the author of Genesis?

Surely, we are better than that. And, surely, Ron Osborn, Nancey Murphy, Des Ford, John Polkinghorne, et al. are too. But, as with so many others, the lure of culture has gotten the better of them, at least for now.

Outdated with embarrassing speed

They're not alone. Alister McGrath is Andreas Idreos Professor of Science and Religion at the University of Oxford. In his book *The Science of God*, he makes this prescient statement: "Any theology which is based on contemporary scientific theories will find itself outdated with embarrassing speed."[27]

At first glance, that sounds like an echo of *Baptizing the Devil*. It's not. After showing how unwise it was for past theologians to have tied their theology so closely to Newton's theories, which were superseded by Einstein's work, McGrath wrote, "The same issue arises in connection with William Paley's celebrated *Natural Theology*, the credibility of which was unassailable in 1830, yet fatally compromised by 1870 through the rise of Charles Darwin's theory of natural selection. Yet this is the inevitable consequence of rapid scientific advance: any theology which is based on contemporary scientific theories will find itself outdated with embarrassing speed."[28]

This is an astonishing capitulation.

First, by 1870, the entire argument for God, from design, was "fatally compromised" by Darwin? Within a mere eleven years after the publication of *On the Origin of Species* the whole idea espoused in Scripture about how God's creative power was revealed in the creation was, McGrath claims, trashed? What a testimony—not to the power of Darwin's theory (which was still decades away from all the arguments that supposedly make the evidence for evolution "at least as strong as the evidence for the Holocaust"[29]), but to the power of Huxley and his X Clubbers. Quite a public relations coup that could, in just over a decade, upend the millennia-old argument for a Creator God from design—all from a book that aficionados readily admit was often flawed.

Second, could not one argue that Paley wasn't even doing science, but biblical theology? "For since the creation of the world His [God's] invisible attributes are clearly seen, being understood by the things that are made, even His eternal power and Godhead, so that they are without excuse" (Romans 1:20). Or "I will praise You, for I am fearfully and wonderfully made; marvelous are Your works, and that my soul knows very well" (Psalm 139:14). These are just a few of many texts pointing to the revelation of God in the creation itself.

Apart from any science, or any scientific theory, could not one look at the created world and see an overwhelming revelation of God's creative power—a revelation that was, we are to believe, "fatally compromised," that is, destroyed by the scientific theory that Darwin proposed in his book *On the Origin of Species*? Paley was doing theology just as much as science, and yet, according to McGrath, Darwin's science disproved Paley's theology.

Third, the irony is painful. McGrath, a theistic evolutionist, who warns against tying any theology to "contemporary scientific theories," does precisely that: he has tied his theology to a "contemporary scientific" theory, evolution, so strongly, in fact, that he disses the foundational theological idea that design in the world reveals evidence of a designer.

McGrath defends his methodology by arguing that it is based, not on any specific theory but on the "working methods and assumptions of the natural sciences"[30] (talk about being subjective!). These broad assumptions are (believe it or not) "a belief in the regularity of the natural world, and the ability of the human mind to uncover and represent this regularity in a mathematical manner."[31]

The regularity of the natural world? No wonder McGrath is a theistic evolutionist as opposed to a biblical creationist. He has no choice. First, this assumption about the natural world is (as we have seen) a philosophical position, not a scientific one. After all, how could anyone, based on the limited amount of nature that humans have studied, know that it must always function with regularity? Worse, this assumption automatically excludes the biblical account, which depicts a process of creation outside "the regularity of the natural world." By default, his first assumption has to lead him astray (again, think of the murder in which, a priori, the detective rules out the murderer as a suspect).

The ability of the human mind to uncover and represent this regularity in a mathematical manner? Readers should know by now just how presumptuous that view is. How could McGrath possibly prove that the human mind is able to uncover and represent this world in an accurate mathematical manner? He can't, so he just assumes it.

How well has this view worked, anyway? It took the human mind only 1,500 years after the death of Christ to work out that the earth moved (it took Rome a few hundred more). And today, we have the smartest and best and brightest human minds teaching us such things as the whale's ancestor once had four feet and walked on earth before entering the water and morphing into a whale. Nor can we forget the universe-from-nothing model (which is filled with mathematical formulas), another example of the human mind's supposed ability to uncover nature.

Though McGrath later hedged his bets, even admitting a "radical possibility"[32] that Darwinism might no longer be accepted as the best explanation for life, for now he does what he warns others about: he ties his theology to a "contemporary scientific" theory, in this case a theory that mocks biblical faith, including Christ's death on the cross, at the most fundamental level possible, the level of Creation itself.

Why have good people like McGrath and others so readily placed their faith on something so speculative, so contingent and contrary to Scripture as evolutionary events that supposedly occurred millions, even billions of years out of our reach, all based on a theory derived from a theological misunderstanding about the nature of the creation to begin with? The answer is easy. Despite the absurdities, flaws, and billion-year leaps of inductive faith that underpin evolutionary theory—*It's science!*

And science today has become culture, which, from the golden calf to the Jim Crow south, continues to challenge and often defeat the faithful, a defeat exemplified by these attempts, done with the evangelistic fervor of a Billy Graham, to baptize the devil. But, as seen, the devil doesn't get baptized, or even wet, no matter how hard the faithful try to immerse him.

1. Hawking, *Brief History of Time*, 1.

2. Quoted in Gottlieb, *Dream of Reason*, 41.

3. "Evolution of Whales Animation," Ocean Portal, Smithsonian Institution, https://ocean.si.edu/ocean-videos/evolution-whales-animation.

4. What all this shows is that "science is a human activity. It is created by finite, flawed human beings attempting to search for the ultimate truth. The data sets that we examine are limited, the theories that we come up with are tentative, and the equations that we find are incomplete. We are not promoting some type of silly postmodernist belief that science is not real. Rather, what we are saying is that the ways human beings find and describe these laws of nature are simply human." Yanofsky, *Outer Limits of Reason*, 251, 252.

5. "All Scripture is given by inspiration of God, and is profitable for doctrine, for reproof, for correction, for instruction in righteousness" (2 Timothy 3:16).

6. "If Darwin had gone no further than providing an explanation for the evolution of finch beaks and other cases of microevolution, he might have gone down as a notable Victorian naturalist. But Darwin (as I pointed out in Chapters Two and Three of *Evolution: A Theory in Crisis*) went much further. He became one of the most influential thinkers in Western intellectual history by making the radical claim that the origin of all the novelties in the history of life, all the taxa-defining traits, all complexity, all order, could be explained by extending or extrapolating, over great periods of time, the same simple, undirected, and 100-percent-blind mechanism of cumulative selection that fashioned the different finch beaks on Galápagos." Michael Denton, *Evolution: Still a Theory in Crisis* (Seattle: Discovery Institute, 2016), 40, 41.

7. Tom Wolfe, *The Kingdom of Speech* (New York: Little, Brown, 2016), 47, 48.

8. Denton, *Evolution*, 277.

9. M. J. Klute, P. Melançon, and J. B. Dacks, "Evolution and Diversity of the Golgi.," *Cold Spring Harbor Perspectives in Biology* 3, no. 8 (August 2011), https://www.ncbi.nlm.nih.gov/pubmed/21646379.

10. "How Does Evolution Explain Human's Innate Capacity for Mathematics?" Quora, https://www.quora.com/How-does-evolution-explain-humans-innate-capacity-for-mathematics.

11. Mary Midgley, *Evolution as a Religion*, rev. ed. (London: Routledge, 2002), 2.

12. Whitehead, *Science and the Modern World*, 61.

13. Imre Lakatos, and Alan Musgrave, eds., *Criticism and the Growth of Knowledge* (Cambridge, UK: Cambridge University Press, 1970), 135.

14. Johnson, "What Is Darwinism?" in Bauman, *Man and Creation*, 187.

15. Ronald E. Osborn, *Death Before the Fall: Biblical Literalism and the Problem of Animal Suffering* (Downers Grove, IL: IVP Academic, 2014), 79.

16. Ibid., 82.

17. Ibid., 86–94.

18. Qiang Lin et al., "The Seahorse Genome and the Evolution of Its Specialized Morphology," *Nature* 540 (December 15, 2016): 395–399, http://www.nature.com/nature/journal/v540/n7633/full/nature20595.html.

19. "Evolution: How Snakes Lost Their Legs," *Nature* 538 (October 27, 2016): 430, 431, http://www.nature.com/nature/journal/v538/n7626/full/538430e.html.

20. The term *species* has a different meaning now than the biblical "kind." No one should believe that God created separately every living species that exists today, but that in the beginning God created many different kinds of living organisms ("of various kinds" in some paraphrases). He clearly did not create a single ancestral species from which everything else evolved.

21. Lawrence M. Krauss, *A Universe From Nothing: Why There Is Something Rather Than Nothing* (New York: Free Press, 2012).

22. Hazen, "Origins of Life," part 1, p. 14.

23. BonJour, "Against Materialism," in Koons and Bealer, *The Waning of Materialism*, 10.

24. Polkinghorne, *Science and Religion in Quest of Truth*, 106.

25. Coyne, *Faith Versus Fact*, 129.

26. Popper, *Logic of Scientific Discovery*, 94.

27. Alister E. McGrath, *The Science of God* (Grand Rapids, MI: William B. Eerdmans, 2004), 29.

28. Ibid.

29. Dawkins, *The Greatest Show on Earth*, 8.

30. McGrath, *The Science of God*, 29.

31. Ibid.

32. Ibid., 30.

79 Wet picnicic table - Solid bed Rock - swamp
81 Quantum   nothing + nothing = universe ?